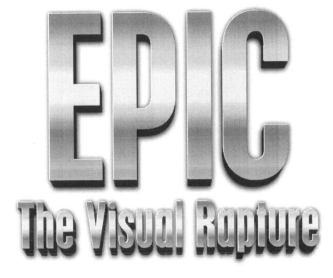

EPIC
The Visual Rapture

Rick A. Blomgren, A.I.A.

Published by Revere Today, LLC

EPIC The Visual Rapture

To contact the publisher or author,
please send written correspondence to:

Revere Today, LLC, Publishing
2973 Harbor Blvd., PMB # 527
Costa Mesa, CA 92626

www.epicthevisualrapture.com

Editor: Shirl Thomas
Text Editor: Larry Urish
Formatting and Layout: Lee Pound
Cover Design: Jeffrey D. Brown (jeffreydbrown.com)

ISBN: 978-0-9906486-0-4

Contents

Hebrews 4:12-13

[12] For the word of God is living and active and sharper than any two-edged sword, and piercing as far as the division of soul and spirit, of both joints and marrow, and able to judge the thoughts and intentions of the heart. [13] And there is no creature hidden from His sight, but all things are open and laid bare to the eyes of Him with whom we have to do.

Dedications

I dedicate this book to

Jesus the Christ my Lord and Savior

I love you Jesus, and I thank you for loving me.
You are the King of kings and Lord of lords.
All praise and glory be given to you!

My Bible Teacher

Thank you for your wisdom, love, and understanding of both
Jesus and His Bible. I love you, and I thank God for placing me
within your life's path. The knowledge of the Bible I have
learned from you has created the desire to
share this exciting story with others.

Matthew 13:16-17

[16] *But blessed are your eyes, because they see; and your ears, because they hear.* [17] *For truly I say to you that many prophets and righteous men desired to see what you see, and did not see it, and to hear what you hear, and did not hear it.*

Preface

In this book I share a magnificent story about our world today and what is happening all around us . . . an amazing story containing both intrigue and mystery. It is a story about the loving God of Abraham, Isaac, and Jacob, our One Triune God — God the Father, God the Son Jesus, and God the Holy Spirit the Comforter. God is preparing the world for some amazing things. In His Bible, He shares with us a precise series of events, His **Road Map**, explaining what has taken place and what will soon take place. God explicitly explains how He will personally protect and save the people who love Jesus from some severe events coming in the near future. God's Word details His final Divine plans for our world, and how this will all play out . . . all incredibly amazing.

When we read the Bible and then take a look at all the current distress and unrest in the world — almost totally centered around Israel — it seems quite clear to see we live in the Biblical last days prior to the Rapture and Tribulation. By placing Christians in this specific time in history, God has truly blessed us. For centuries mankind has said the Lord would return. Upon deeper study, the Bible shows us, without a doubt, it will occur within the **generation** that began with the rebirth of the State of Israel. We need no more guessing or speculation. The Bible also shows us that God wants to finish a few more things for us all to **witness** before He takes us home with Him in what I believe the Bible tells us will be a grand **visual Rapture**, not in secret.

After reading the New Testament, many think Jesus came only to teach us how to live a Godly life. This is, in part, true but much more fills the pages. He taught for the long term and, during His ministry, foretold of what the future would hold. In conversations with His disciples, Jesus made reference to the destruction of the temple, later followed by a rebuilding. He uses the temple to represent Himself, and the rebuilding to refer to

His resurrection: rising after three days, going away for a long time, and then returning at some point in the distant future — which is now.

Jesus also uses parables in the Scriptures; they intertwine with parallels related to the time He lived on earth and what would happen far into the future. He chose parables because, had He spoken directly, the disciples would not have understood the entire plan. They **did not need** to know certain things for their time; however, **we need** this information today — specifically.

This is also why God gave us **prophecies** (predictions in advance) **to witness** in the last days. Recognizing prophecies that have already reached fulfillment and why they occurred might wake up some people. This book explains end time prophecies that have **already happened** and **others soon to come**, so when some readers begin to **see** additional events actually starting to happen, they need not be shocked, and can feel less fearful.

My book is meant to share insights related to what God has told us to look for. This book is in His hands and if it helps even a few people, I will have succeeded.

Additionally, what will soon occur within three world religions — Christianity, Judaism, and Islam — will play a critical role in foretelling and learning when the visual Rapture is about to happen. Exploring detailed issues related to their histories, backgrounds, and futures holds the key to understanding what will soon happen and why. Incredibly, God's literal next prophecy in the Bible will resolve the entire emerging radical Islam situation. God will do this on His own, without mankind's help, in the not-too-distant future. God is going to do so in one grand, spectacular event.

If thoughts of the end times have troubled you in the past or you have found this topic generally uncomfortable, this exciting new explanation of events might start to put you at ease regarding the whole subject. I will explore how God has provided wonderful news, especially for Christians in His Bible. The good news: Christians will be taken home, by Jesus, to be with Him just before some serious travail begins in this world. The process of Jesus taking Christians at the Rapture may actually be completely different than what we have possibly assumed.

Unfortunately, so many people prefer to ignore altogether this whole topic of end times prophecy. But ignoring Scripture doesn't eliminate what it says. Sometimes the truth can be a bit disconcerting, but the good news: God gave us the Bible and His prophecies so Christians can understand what is happening and feel at peace. We can then wisely prepare for the inevitable. God does not want us to experience fear of the end times.

In the Bible, God tells us how He hates sin of any kind and that He will come soon to remove it from the world. God plans to do this in the seven-year Tribulation talked about in the Bible in the last book of the New Testament: the book of Revelation. The word **revelation** means **revealing**. In the Bible, God explains how He will soon bring all things back into harmony. Revelation should **not be feared** but, rather, **revered**.

The Tribulation period of soon-to-come wrath, addressed in Revelation, is not and never was intended, in any way, for those who have accepted Jesus as their personal Savior **prior** to the Rapture. By studying God's detailed plans, we can gain comfort through the full understanding of what He has provided for us in His Word. He wants us to **literally prepare** to welcome Him back upon His return in a visual Rapture just prior to the start of His great Tribulation.

I hope to provide a beautiful picture of our loving Lord Jesus. I want to show you His clear and precise plans for our future. Jesus has provided us with the light to know how He desires for us to navigate in these final days. May you find new levels of peace and joy, as I have found, from what God is sharing with us for our current time.

Prologue

Biblical end time prophecies and Eschatology (the art and science used for the interpretation of Biblical Scripture) have intrigued me most of my life. Current events in our world today strongly correlate with accounts of events predicted in the Bible. The words in the Bible clearly show a prophetic **Road Map** provided by God. He shows us, without a doubt, that Jesus will indeed soon return to take Christians home with Him in the Rapture. But will this Rapture happen mysteriously in *"the twinkling of an eye"* or *"like a thief in the night"* as many churches still teach? If the answer is yes, then why does Jesus tell us, in such great detail, in His Bible, to literally and diligently watch for His return? Why give us so many clear instructions, to both **look** and **watch** for Him, if we will simply secretly disappear, instantly, without any warning? He instructed us thusly because the Rapture **will not** take place in secret. On the contrary, His words depict a **spectacular visual event.**

The doctrine called **imminence** (Appendix C) tells of our instantaneous secret disappearing and has created a theological quandary within the Christian community. Prior to the twentieth century, the church had not actually seen any of God's end time prophecies taking place as talked about in the Bible. For the last 1,900 years, the idea of our being taken up or Raptured went beyond explanation because no visual Biblical proof of any end time prophecies actually happened. Due to perceived prophetic silence for such a long duration, the church developed the imminence doctrine, as a way to cope with impatience and a possible lack of overall Biblical understanding.

This generally accepted concept has never felt right to me. Has God ever sneaked around about what He does regarding His family? No. So then, what do these *"twinkling of an eye"* and *"thief in the night"* ideas really mean?

The Bible states God's boldness in making Himself known. He always does things in astonishing ways. Think about the Exodus as one example. God could have easily provided a fleet of ships to get His people across the sea, but that would not have shown a grand visual representation of His enormity. God parted the sea, creating a dry path for His people to cross. This also allowed for a dramatic and highly visual way to defeat the enemy . . . a spectacular set of events. What about Noah's flood or the destruction of Sodom? These were not timid events. God's actions created **monumental visual statements.**

Because God is immense, this seemingly weak imminence doctrine became a serious disconnect for me. After some detailed study on this subject, it now seems obvious that He has literally shown us how to know exactly when the Rapture will occur. God's entire plan became recognizable to me by truly paying attention to His explicit instructions in the Bible.

A large number of churches today seem comfortably situated on automatic pilot and do not appear to pay thoughtful attention to God's possible true intentions. The Lord tells us to hold to a higher standard those who teach the Bible, because we expect them to get things right. Could some of our church leaders possibly have missed contemporary Biblical truths? Have old and tired accepted traditions blinded some of our church leaders to the unique and special time in which we currently live? Is it a possibility many present-day members of the ministry and clergy have become, for the most part, actually milquetoast on this whole end times subject? The answer to all three questions is **yes.**

In fact, when some church leaders try to talk about the end times, their congregations get a bit uncomfortable, so it appears they then choose to back off the subject. With the unchecked continued acceptance of this antiquated view of imminence, one should anticipate reasoned discomfort. Due to this weak, flawed thinking about God's plans, no wonder so many people feel unsettled regarding this topic.

But what if the whole story is actually more beautiful than we ever could have imagined? For our comfort, assurance, happiness, joy, and all for His infinite glory, God has actually provided us with precise clarity explaining all about when He will return. He has given us the specific information we need so we can know, without any doubt, when He will come for us in the Rapture. I believe we have absolutely nothing to dread and a great deal to give thanks for. God has everything magnificently designed.

By using His Biblical instructions in conjunction with both past and current historical world events, and by cross-referencing between those multiple sources of knowledge and wisdom, a much brighter and glorious story has come into light . . . a viewpoint that magnifies God's greatness well beyond the current churches' old, tired and outdated doctrine of imminence. So, will God take us away at the Rapture quietly and with no warning? Or will He actually make this event a huge statement allowing the entire world to hear the trumpets and see us all leave during a **visual Rapture**? What the Bible shares with us about this coming event is stunning. Remember, God always does things big for His glory alone. So, which of these two ideas—a secret hidden Rapture or a spectacular visual one—gives you goose bumps? Which one of these two options would represent God's magnificent and true nature more majestically?

Over the years I have collected multiple pieces of what I now believe is God's expressed Biblical **Road Map** for the last days. I now understand the entirety of their importance in my final thought process. As an architect, I basically put highly complicated puzzles together. This particular Bible puzzle, related to the end times and the coming visual Rapture, has turned into a precise and fascinating endeavor. With the final pieces thoughtfully collected and in place, I can now share this wonderful story with you.

The word **Rapture** does not appear in the Bible. The modern usage depicts a collective description of many scriptural references. In numerous verses, God speaks of: being taken up, caught up, redemption, raised imperishable, gathering together, escape—all encompassed in the Greek word *"harpazo"* (harpad'-zo), used in His original text, 1 Thessalonians 4:17. The word **Rapture** comes from the Latin verb *"rapiemur"* which has the same meaning as harpazo.

If you are not a Bible reader and have not read God's word personally, please do not let this stop you from proceeding with this story. I will provide the actual *Bible text* for more than half of the verses referenced in this book, used to support my thinking. I did this so those of you not familiar with God's Scriptures can actually view some of the wonderful things contained in His excellent book. In some instances, I provide only Biblical reference for support without showing the text. *The New American Standard* version provides all the verses unless noted otherwise. I accept the Bible as the singularly true inerrant Word of the Living God and provide compelling evidence to support its accuracy in Appendix A.

Matthew 7: 13-14
13 "Enter through the narrow gate; for the gate is wide and the way is broad that leads to destruction, and there are many who enter through it. 14 For the gate is small and the way is narrow that leads to life, and there are few who find it.

Luke 13:23-24
23 And someone said to Him, "Lord, are there just a few who are being saved?" And He said to them, 24 "Strive to enter through the narrow door; for many, I tell you, will seek to enter and will not be able.

Jesus tells us, specifically, in the Bible, to enter His kingdom by the *"narrow gate"* as *"the gate is wide and the way is broad that leads to destruction."* God tells us about the many people who mistakenly believe they are saved Christians (Appendix B). God allows mankind to live barely enough years to fully understand His expressed requirements for salvation . . . just enough time to figure it out. Our lifespan is like a job interview for eternity. We need to get it right. We have only one chance at this.

Matthew 7:13-14 and Luke 13:23-24 both imply that many people will not accept what the Bible truly says, because it will not fit in with the many false doctrines man has incorrectly espoused about Jesus over the centuries. This explains why God tells us the gate is narrow and few will find Him.

God sent John the Baptist, a humble yet bold man, to announce the arrival of Jesus. John understood the importance of his ministry and took great joy in sharing about Him. He expressed the view of his service for the Lord as follows:

John 3:30
³⁰ *He must increase, but I must decrease.*

John the Baptist is a wonderful role model for all Christians. I desire for the Lord to increase by sharing what I believe to be His soon-to-come prophetic plans. God's **Road Map** for us is incredible.

In the world today, from a purely Christian context, diametrically opposed views are frequently shared. They all require specific faith in one form or the other. People will either accept an all-knowing Jesus and what He tells us in His Bible, or they may choose to place their faith in science and the theories of man's discoveries. I understand that some people, who do not believe in any God, or even other deities or faiths, may actually have disdain for what I share. The analysis provided may even lead to a perception from non-Christian groups that I possess intellectual weakness, or mental bankruptcy, and appear highly uninformed. I predict this will happen, especially from a nonbeliever or members of other non-Christian faith systems. The Bible tells us to expect such a reaction. If you feel this way, please try to check out all the provided information objectively.

I've read many different views of end time Eschatology and studied in some detail a wide variety of pre-, mid-, and post-Tribulation Rapture theories. I firmly believe in a pre-Tribulation Rapture. Within the majority of the older concepts, when one examines their entire sequences, all their precepts lack reasoned completion, leaving **many holes**. One great example of a **hole** is from Luke 17:32 where God tells us to *"Remember Lot's wife."* This relates to the end times and the Rapture. Almost all current prophecy viewpoints seem to have skipped over this verse as irrelevant. It actually has great pertinence.

Did you know the Bible tells us how the world will appear normal and at peace until the very day both the visual Rapture occurs and the Tribulation begins? But how can this be, peaceful and both on the same day? **This is a literal Biblical message.** Very likely, this indicates how the world probably will not experience the effects of anything severely major before Christians are visually Raptured. Issues like EMP attacks (Electromagnetic Pulse) or nuclear wars or even full societal or financial collapse (Road Warrior-type stuff) will happen **after Christians are removed**. This logically means the likelihood of Christians not having to experience much more than the severe emotional and psychological scorn and full marginalization the world will have for any person who has truly accepted Jesus as their personal Savior. Will the world be a safe place? No. Crime, hate, hardened hearts, immorality, cheating, lying, deceptions, and all forms of lawlessness will prevail and worsen daily. Over time Christians will need to constantly be on guard and praying for God's protection, which He will provide.

2 Timothy 3:12-13
¹² Indeed, all who desire to live Godly in Christ Jesus will be persecuted. ¹³ But evil men and impostors will proceed from bad to worse, deceiving and being deceived.

The best example I can think of regarding what Christians will need to do when things get really tough relates to how we react to a coming snowstorm. When we know in advance a harsh storm is coming, and realize we will need to experience it, we put on the appropriate heavy coats, boots, a warm scarf, and hat. We do exactly what is needed for the type of approaching storm. We know of the devastation to come, but have thoughtfully protected ourselves in advance from the effects of the harsh elements. We cannot fight the storm, but can deal with it appropriately. In the last days, we need to spiritually prepare in a similar fashion.

When Jesus taught His disciples, He told them they would have a difficult mission and needed awareness of their battle with the Deceiver, and to be shrewd, and trust in Him alone for direction as our guide. This instruction is also highly valid for us today, as our mission in the last days will be perilous:

Matthew 10:16
¹⁶ Behold, I send you out as sheep in the midst of wolves; so be <u>shrewd</u> as serpents and innocent as doves.

God provides direction in the Bible regarding many situations to diverse groups and people. Everything said and taught can and should be gleaned by us today as examples of how to deal with all life's situations. God expects us to learn by the examples He shared with others in His Bible and use the knowledge for our current time:

2 Timothy 3:16-17
¹⁶ All Scripture is inspired by God and profitable for teaching, for reproof, for correction, for training in

righteousness; [17] *so that the man of God may be adequate, equipped for every good work.*

In John 8:57-59 Jesus preached truthfully to a group of Jews, yet not being politically correct for His day. When asked a question, His answer was not received well by the crowd. They started picking up stones, and note what is said in verse 59: Jesus did the shrewd thing: He *"hid Himself"* for protection:

John 8:57-59

[57] *So the Jews said to Him, "You are not yet fifty years old, and have You seen Abraham?"* [58] *Jesus said to them, "Truly, truly, I say to you, before Abraham was born, I am."* [59] *Therefore they picked up stones to throw at Him, but Jesus <u>hid Himself</u> and went out of the temple.*

Understanding God's expressed plans and warnings for the future have put my mind at peace. I believe, with all my heart that God protects us much more than we give Him credit for. He truly loves us. In these final perilous days we need to remember: our joy and peace must be in Jesus alone, nothing else. I am thankful God has given us sound direction for our time . . . one of His multiple blessings.

We who live in the United States have been blessed, for so long, to live in a wonderful, free, mostly God-loving and Biblically moral country. Until recently, we have lived with a great deal of comfort. Many issues today contradict the Bible's teachings and are accepted as societal norms, causing a major recalibration of morality. What is right is wrong, and what is wrong is right from a Biblical context. So, unfortunately, our country is changing drastically and rapidly accelerating, morally downhill right before our eyes. For God's Biblical plans to come to fruition, this moral decay all needs to happen. As the world gets progressively darker, we need to prepare, in advance, for the inevitable. Knowledge is powerful and the Bible is our knowledge. We can either learn about what will come, accept issues now, and feel joy, or we can suffer as this all unfolds due to a lack of understanding.

Some of my friends say we should fight to bring morality back to our country. I understand their sentiments. Unfortunately, we cannot possibly change societal behavior in these last days. The Bible tells us this. Realistically, we cannot put out a forest fire with a squirt gun. We need to face a hard, yet wonderful truth that **Jesus is on the way**. He will fix all this soon. Try looking forward to the big event in full peace and comfort knowing Jesus will soon come.

In our busy lives, so few Christians open their Bibles regularly anymore. Some people even accept the notion the Bible may be outdated, that it was written for a different time, and that all religions really worship the same God. They think the Bible may no longer have relevancy in our new intellectually enlightened world. Some have even decided the Bible may actually be comprised of fables or myths — a work of fiction. Christians know nothing could be further from the truth. Please pay specific attention to the word *"myth."* God tells us explicitly that this myth concept will become highly accepted and used in great abundance, related to the entire Bible, in the last days.

Mankind secularists, collectively in the world today, have started opening the door for the implementation of a new One World Government and Church. They believe this will lead to final world peace . . . exactly what God tells us they will think in the last days.

1 John 2:15-17
¹⁵ Do not love the world nor the things in the world. If anyone loves the world, the love of the Father is not in him. ¹⁶ For all that is in the world, the lust of the flesh and the lust of the eyes and the boastful pride of life, is not from the Father, but is from the world. ¹⁷ The world is

passing away, and also its lusts; but the one who does the will of God lives forever.

God's visual Rapture will be magnificent to behold for many profound and wonderful reasons. All of mankind will see it. This story will turn upside down much of the fearful thinking about the entire end times subject. The whole concept of a visual Rapture makes the study of the ends times vibrant, exhilarating, and a joyful topic—not a frightening one.

God's prophecies, His **Road Map**—and their expressed sequences, as provided in the Bible—lead us in a clear, unambiguous path directly to the visual Rapture. Do you know the Bible literally tells us the arrival of the Rapture **should not at all be a surprise to Christians?** But how can this be? The Bible tells us even Jesus does not know the day or the hour. However, a small twist regarding this point shows us clearly how Jesus, today, does actually know when the visual Rapture will arrive.

Jesus, in Matthew 13, makes reference to the **Prophet Isaiah.** This Old Testament Prophet explains about events in the future related to the end times. In Matthew 13:16-17 Jesus tells us the generation that will actually see end time prophecies happening, as explained in the book of Isaiah, is blessed. I want to place emphasis on the word *"see"* as this has significant meaning. God wants us to *"see"* His prophecies in these last days.

Matthew 13:16-17

16 But blessed are your eyes, because they see; and your ears, because they hear. 17 For truly I say to you that many prophets and righteous men desired to see what you see, and did not see it, and to hear what you hear, and did not hear it.

Elaborating on the **imminence theory**: not only do many Christians today believe the Rapture will happen without warning, but they also believe that **no prophecies need to occur first.** With the prophesied **rebirth of the State of Israel** on May 14, 1948, everything changed. The world **has witnessed** the first series of specific finite end time prophecies as explained in the Bible, they have become reality. This rebirth no longer gives any reason for doubt. God is showing Himself to the world at this time. But is the world paying attention? Are Christians paying attention?

With end time prophecies actually happening **for us to witness today,** why do so many churches choose not to acknowledge them? A major prophecy related to end times is something seriously negative called **apostasy** . . . the marginalization and watering down of both faith in Jesus and His Bible. The world today is not paying attention to God's literal depiction of this prophecy, so there is a strong case that we are witnessing its fulfillment. It may be for this reason many churches today seem to be doing **feel-good preaching** and not detailed sermons relating to our amazing time in history.

The Bible, both Old and New Testaments, is all about Jesus, His identity, and His love for all humanity and particularly Israel. Scripture tells us about God's hopes and desires for His entire Jewish family—both natural born and adopted members, the Christians (Romans 11:17). Jesus, through His Bible, requires us as Christians to love and care for Israel, to help them find their way home to Him. The book of Revelation discloses how Israel will finally, at the end of the Tribulation, recognize Jesus as their Messiah (Appendix D). The detailed and beautifully designed story shows a loving God.

Psalm 122:6-7
*⁶ Pray for the peace of Jerusalem: "May
They prosper who love you. ⁷ "May peace
be within your walls, and prosperity
within your palaces."*

Prologue

Isaiah 40:1-2
¹ "Comfort, O comfort My people," says your God.
²"Speak kindly to Jerusalem; and call out to her, that her
warfare has ended, that her iniquity has been removed, . . .

I make it a rule to use the Bible as the support for what I present. As we proceed, I would expect nothing less than the Christians reading this book wanting to do the same with the information provided. A person must walk with God in his or her own way and not just that of any organization or some other person's individual points of view. God teaches us all, individually, through our personal time in His Word with Him alone. God then asks us to share what we learn from Him with others. After we share, God will do all the heavy lifting.

Additionally, Scriptures actually show us how Jesus tells us the visual Rapture event holds special importance. God actually has multiple **final blessings, a gift,** and **a reward** for living, informed Christians at the visual Rapture. Specifically for Christians who have a passion for end times prophecy and who ultimately understand the Lord's specific and clear final requests of us just prior to His visual Rapture event.

In short order, the secular world will blame Christians as the ones trying to prevent true global peace from happening. Actually, in the last days, Christians will try to warn the people of the world about difficult times quickly approaching and how we can offer a loving solution. We will try to share the world's happenings with our friends, but the vast majority of people will not listen and will think of us as delusional. The world on the outside will appear to them as getting its act together which, unfortunately to their unexpected surprise, will soon turn out to be incorrect. God will come soon, **as a thief**, to **steal away the secular world's false peace**. He will dramatically announce this to the whole earth by taking Christians home with Him, first, in the **visual Rapture**. What a harsh surprise, **on that day,** for those **watching us leave**.

As the Global Community gets progressively worldlier, the secular masses will almost totally silence Christians. We will need to live within a debased and decadent society for a short time, but God has provided us with His specific end times prophetic **Road Map** for a loving reason. By witnessing all of God's prophecies in sequence, we should be able to see the finish line and know, with some confidence, **approximately** when He will arrive. As faithful Christians we have nothing to fear; **God is in full control.**

This exciting version of end time's prophecy will provide a positive perspective and one that shows the tremendous grandeur of our Lord. Its perception explains how much God loves us; speaks to us; directs us; protects us; and how He will guide us, as believers, in the last days through His total, unconditional love. *"God is love,"* and any view of the end times void of providing comfort for His family would be a theory I do not choose to accept.

1 John 4:16-18
16 We have come to know and have believed the love which God has for us. <u>God is love</u>, and the one who abides in love abides in God, and God abides in him. 17 By this, love is perfected with us, so that we may have confidence in the day of judgment; because as He is, so also are we in this world. 18 There is no fear in love; but perfect love casts out fear, because fear involves punishment, and the one who fears is not perfected in love.

The Bible tells us Jesus will win in the end . . . our glorious hope in our loving Lord.

I am excited about what I have learned and how God has supported me in this entire process. We live in a wonderful and special time in history and are the blessed **final generation**.

Matthew 24:34

34 Truly I say to you, this generation will not pass away until all these things take place.

CHAPTER 1

GOD'S ROAD MAP

TWENTY-FOUR PROPHECIES

God's **Road Map** explains what He expects
Christians to know and to look for leading up to His
visual Rapture and the start of the Tribulation.

God's **Road Map** brings attention to **twenty-four** significant, specific end time prophecies. **Twelve** have already occurred or have started and will remain ongoing. There are an additional set of **twelve** prophecies as explained in the Bible that as of late 2014 should begin to occur at almost any time.

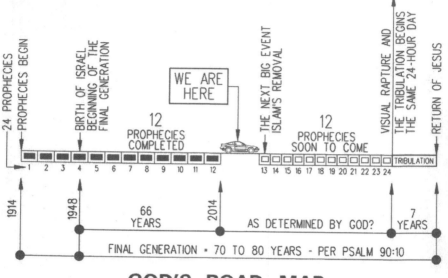

GOD'S ROAD MAP

The **thirteenth** prophecy relates specifically to Israel. This monumental event will change the course of human history. All **twenty-four** specific end time prophecies must occur prior to the visual Rapture. When we start to see the final twelve prophecies begin to happen rapidly, we will gain a precise understanding of God's intentions.

I propose some ideas and interpretations of God's Scriptures that may, at face value, feel a bit discomforting within a certain denomination of our current Christian Church family. I talk about a group that attends church regularly, but may predominantly only follow church-created rituals and doctrines. We must all take care not to easily accept only organizational or individual's interpretations of the Bible without our own personal verification through reading the Scriptures—recorded straight from the original author, God. We should trust but also must verify. I back up my expressed Biblical observations regarding this current Church's doctrines with Scriptures right out of the Bible. I plan on letting God Himself define His own intentions. The Bible alone holds God's pure truth.

Some Christian Church groups today—including the one above—seem to fully discount the whole idea of Biblical end time prophecies obtaining fulfillment. They also may not believe in a literal Rapture of the Church and a literal Tribulation period. They conclude these events are allegorical. Many groups base their beliefs on man-made doctrines including remnants of the old thinking regarding Purgatory, A-Millennialism, Higher Criticism, and also Replacement Theology, where Israel in the New Testament is considered the Christian Church. The Bible completely contradicts all aspects of these false teachings. Anyone who denies the truth of a pending Rapture also denies what God's Word literally tells. God may very likely allow these groups to enter the Tribulation for a false belief that these literally spoken Biblical events will not happen. Take great caution regarding these false beliefs and place your trust in Jesus and His Bible alone.

God knew false and misguided belief systems would become rampant and increase in the end times. For this reason God provided His prophecies, His **Road Map** for us to *"see"* leading up to the visual Rapture and the Tribulation. Once finding awareness of what God specifically has told us in His word, we must not willfully turn a blind eye to His direct and clear warnings. Everyone must personally gain full knowledge of God's prophecies to recognize and understand their full significance.

This book includes concepts that have nothing to do with politics. I will not go into anything other than what the Bible tells us all for our current-days. The Bible is not a Democrat, Independent, or Republican document. It is the Word of the living God. The Bible contains God's guidance and truths for us all, His beloved creations. He has unnegotiable requirements, which mandate thoughtful consideration and specific individual choices during our lifetimes. God tells us, also, that it does not matter who holds political office, as nothing will deter His plans. **The Lord chooses our leaders** so we have no need for concern. Throughout the Bible, God addresses the subject of how to deal with the leaders of our day. This is obviously important to Him. As the world and its coming leaders progressively turn solidly against what the Bible tells us is right, we need to remember that God knows what He is doing. We need only to understand how God wants us to deal with this, and Jesus gives us solid direction.

Romans 13:1-3
¹ Every person is to be in subjection to the governing authorities. <u>For there is no authority except from God, and those which exist are established by God.</u> ² Therefore whoever resists authority has opposed the ordinance of God; and they who have opposed will receive condemnation upon themselves. ³ For rulers are not a cause of fear for good behavior, but for evil. Do you want to have no fear of authority? Do what is good and you will have praise from the same.

1 Timothy 2:1-3
¹ First of all, then, I urge that entreaties and prayers, petitions and thanksgivings, be made on behalf of all men, ² for kings and all who are in authority, so that we may lead a tranquil and quiet life in all Godliness and dignity. ³ This is good and acceptable in the sight of God our Savior, . . .

1 Peter 2:13-17
¹³ Submit yourselves for the Lord's sake to every human institution, whether to a king as the one in authority, ¹⁴ or to governors as sent by him for the punishment of evildoers and

the praise of those who do right. 15 For such is the will of God that by doing right you may silence the ignorance of foolish men. 16 Act as free men, and do not use your freedom as a covering for evil, but use it as bond slaves of God. 17 Honor all people, love the brotherhood, fear God, honor the king.

I make **no predictions**. Rather, I show an interpretation of prophecy using only the Bible as its own clear and precise **Road Map.** God explains His intended chronology and timeline for Himself out of His own word.

Please accept some repetition of verses. Many scriptures contain multiple meanings and instructions for us.

Some people say those of us proposing that the end times are upon us are uninformed and possibly false prophets. Actually, no prophets—in the true sense of the word—live at this time in the world. God needed prophets only until He completed His entire original scribed text. The Bible tells the whole and complete story as God initially intended. It already includes all pertinent knowledge and instructions, with no need for revisions, or modifications by anyone, at any time in history, either past or present. Those of us talking about the end times simply use as our guide what God's original prophets have already provided for us. Interpretation is not a prophetic event.

The long period of waiting for the Lord's return described in Isaiah 61:2 *"the favorable year of the Lord"* has lasted 2,000 years, and will lead us to *"the day of vengeance of our God."* The Bible indicates our wait is almost over.

Isaiah 61:1-2
1 The Spirit of the Lord God is upon me, because the Lord has anointed me to bring good news to the afflicted; He has sent me to bind up the brokenhearted, to proclaim liberty to captives and freedom to prisoners; 2 to proclaim the favorable year of the Lord and the day of vengeance of our God; to comfort all who mourn.

The *"favorable year of the Lord"* refers to the time from the ascension of Jesus up until the time of His visual Rapture event. The *"day of vengeance of our God"* denotes the coming Tribulation. This *"favorable year"* is a relational time frame, meant to indicate a long period of time. How do we know this? We know, per the Bible: *"the day of vengeance of our God,"* the Tribulation, will last for a defined seven-year period. This seven-year period can then be proportionally likened to a day. Using these two time frames, in the verses above, both a *"year"* and *"day"* we can then conclude God established a general time relationship in these verses. A day is likened to seven years by referring to the *"day of vengeance"* — the Tribulation period. Then a year by comparison becomes a long period of time, a couple thousand years proportionally.

God indicates that we will know this long period of time, *"the favorable year of the Lord,"* will come to an end when we start to *"see"* God's end time prophecies happening. Therefore, God intended for us to *"see"* His prophecies. He explicitly tells us to *"look"* for them in His Bible. We must look for His signs showing us this long period of time is coming to an end. We have arrived.

The wonder in God's Word will magnify when we see the **final twelve** prophetical events starting to happen as illuminated in the Bible and chronicled below. Their fulfillment will validate the proposed interpretations.

Here is God's **Road Map, twenty-four** significant prophecies — some, simple things to watch for, others highly detailed and intricate. All twenty-four must take place before both the visual Rapture and Tribulation. We have and will witness them. I list them all for you now, and then follow up on each in various levels of additional detail. Note: **twelve** have either reached completion or are ongoing. The final **twelve** will soon start to occur.

GOD'S ROAD MAP

PROPHECIES COMPLETED OR ONGOING

1.   TWO MAJOR BIRTH PAINS, WWI AND WWII
2.   PREPARING THE LAND OF ISRAEL FOR THE JEWS
3.   UNITED NATIONS FORMS
4.   REBIRTH OF THE *NEW* STATE OF ISRAEL
     Prophecies 1-4 are covered with more specificity in Chapter 2.
5.   RETURN OF THE JEWS TO THE HOLY LAND
6.   CAPTURE OF JERUSALEM
7.   GAZA ABANDONED
8.   THE FALLING AWAY (APOSTASY)
9.   INCREASE IN TRAVEL AND KNOWLEDGE
10. RISE OF ANTI-SEMITISM
11. MARK OF THE BEAST (TECHNOLOGY)
12. ISRAEL DWELLING SECURELY

PROPHECIES THAT WILL HAPPEN IN SHORT ORDER

13. THE EZEKIEL 38 AND 39 ATTACK ON ISRAEL
     This will likely occur between the fall of 2014 and the spring of
     2017. This attack will remove radical Islam from the world by
     God's hand alone, as detailed in Chapter 3.

Prophecies 14 through 23 happen after Ezekiel 38 and 39. The
visual Rapture will take place shortly after prophecy 24 begins.

14. FIRST STAGE OF CONVERSION OF THE JEW
15. REBUILDING OF BABYLON (Iraq not Rome)
16. ONE WORLD GOVERNMENT AND ECONOMY
17. ONE WORLD CHURCH AND FALSE PROPHET
18. BUILDING OF THE THIRD TEMPLE IN JERUSALEM
19. WORLD GOVERNMENT BREAKS INTO 10 KINGDOMS
20. RISE OF THE ANTICHRIST (after the 10 kingdoms)
21. TIME OF PEACE & SAFETY IN THE UNBELIEVING WORLD
22. THE APPEARANCE OF ELIJAH
23. FEAR, SCOURGE, THE ANTICHRIST, AND HIS COVENANT
     Just **prior to the signing** of the covenant between the Antichrist
     and Israel, the visual Rapture will dramatically occur. The cov-
     enant signing with Israel (just after prophecy # 24 below) starts
     the seven-year Tribulation.

24. **SIGNS ON THE DAY OF THE VISUAL RAPTURE**
The visual Rapture will happen for the whole world to witness. It occurs **only hours before Israel's covenant is signed** with the Antichrist starting the Biblical Tribulation period. The visual Rapture and the start of the Tribulation must happen within the very same 24-hour day.

1. TWO MAJOR BIRTH PAINS, WW1 AND WW2

Matthew 24:4-8

4 And Jesus answered and said to them, "See to it that no one misleads you. 5 For many will come in My name, saying, 'I am the Christ,' and will mislead many. 6 You will be hearing of wars and rumors of wars. See that you are not frightened, for those things must take place, but that is not yet the end. 7 For nations will rise against nations, and kingdoms against kingdoms, and in various places there will be famines and earthquakes. 8 But all these things are merely the beginning of birth pangs.

These verses tell us that after a long period of time, *"the favorable year of the Lord"* established in Isaiah 61:2, we will view major signs of His return. When we see *"wars and rumors of wars," "famines and earthquakes," "all these things"* will designate the *"beginning of birth pangs"* (birth pains). Birth pangs must then logically lead to a birth.

Two significant major prophetical *"birth pangs"* have happened: World War I (1914-1918) and World War II (1939-1945). They had incredible importance related **specifically** to the formation and rebirth of the prophesied new State of Israel on May 14, 1948. This rebirth officially started the calendar for the **final generation** of the last days. I will elaborate on this in more detail in Chapter 2. WWI, specifically, set in motion the availability of the land for the establishment of a new Jewish State, and WWII provided a strong reason for the Jews to return to Israel from all over the world.

2. PREPARING THE LAND OF ISRAEL FOR THE JEWS

Zephaniah 2:1-2
¹ Gather yourselves together, yes, gather, O nation without shame, ² before the decree takes effect, the day passes like the chaff, before the burning anger of the Lord comes upon you, before the day of the Lord's anger comes upon you.

After WWI, Great Britain had control of the land we know today as Israel. Arthur Balfour of the British Government declared this land as a national homeland for the Jewish people. Britain created an official document called the *Balfour Declaration* officially preparing the land for the upcoming rebirth of the State of Israel.

3. UNITED NATIONS FORMS

Luke 21:29-32
²⁹ Then He told them a parable: Behold the fig tree and all the trees; ³⁰ as soon as they put forth leaves, you see it and know for yourselves that summer is now near. ³¹ So you also, when you see these things happening, recognize that the kingdom of God is near. ³² Truly I say to you, this generation will not pass away until all things take place. ³³ Heaven and earth will pass away, but My words will not pass away.

Please notice the word *"see"* in the verses above. God uses this word quite often.

After WWII, the parable above foretold the formation of the United Nations. The *"fig tree"* represents Israel, and *"all the trees"* refers to the **United Nations**. The United Nations formed in 1945 right after WWII ended. It holds great significance related to both the formation of the State of Israel, which occurred in 1948, and to the ultimate formation of the One World Government, which will soon come. The term *"this generation"* will, as mentioned, have great importance.

4. REBIRTH OF THE *NEW STATE OF ISRAEL*

Matthew 24:32-34

[32] *Now learn the parable from the fig tree: when its branch has already become tender and puts forth its leaves, you know that summer is near;* [33] *so, you too, when you see all these things, recognize that He is near, right at the door.* [34] *Truly I say to you, this generation will not pass away until all these things take place.*

Israel had been scattered for 1,900 years, since the destruction of the second Temple in Israel at 70 AD. In this Scripture, God says to look for something *"when its branch has already become tender and put forth its leaves."* This is symbolic of new life sprouting or rebirth. Israel is reborn on May 14, 1948 . . . chronologically the starting point of the literal **final generation**. Note, the word *"see"* is used again.

5. RETURN OF THE JEWS TO THE HOLY LAND

Ezekiel 37:11-14

[11] *Then He said to me, Son of man, these bones are the whole house of Israel; behold, they say, 'Our bones are dried up and our hope has perished. We are completely cut off.'* [12] *Therefore prophecy and say to them, 'Thus says the Lord God, Behold, I will open your graves and cause you to come up out of your graves, My people; and I will bring you into the land of Israel.* [13] *Then you will know that I am the Lord, when I have opened your graves and caused you to come up out of your graves, My people.* [14] *I will put My Spirit within you and you will come to life, and I will place you on your own land. Then you will know that I, the Lord, have spoken and done it, declares the Lord.'*

Zephaniah 2:1-2
¹ Gather yourselves together, yes, gather, O nation without shame, ² before the decree takes effect, the day passes like the chaff, <u>before the burning anger of the Lord comes upon you.</u>

Jeremiah 31:8
⁸ Behold, I am bringing them from the north country, and I will gather them from the remote parts of the earth, among them the blind and the lame, the woman with child and she who is in labor with child, together; A great company, they will return here.

The return of the Jews to the Holy Land (the second Exodus) actually began slowly in the late 1800's and moved at a slow pace, until the end of WWII. Hitler killed almost one half of all the Jews alive during his satanic reign of terror in WWII. After WWII, the Jews no longer felt safe outside of Israel. With anti-Semitism growing rampant, the migration of the Jews back to Israel has happened at an accelerated pace and continues to this day — another key sign indicating the end times have arrived. In Zephaniah 2:2, God says *"before the burning anger of the Lord comes upon you."* . . . prior to the beginning of the Tribulation.

6. CAPTURE OF JERUSALEM

Luke 21:24
²⁴ and they will fall by the edge of the sword, and will be led captive into all the nations; and Jerusalem will be trampled underfoot by the Gentiles <u>until the times of the Gentiles are fulfilled.</u>

The Gentiles trampled Jerusalem underfoot until the Israeli 1967 six-day war. In that short war, the Jewish people took back control of Jerusalem for the first time in over 1,900 years, fulfilling the *"time of the Gentiles."*

7. GAZA ABANDONED

Zephaniah 2:3-4
³ Seek the Lord, all you humble of the earth who have carried out His ordinances; seek righteousness, seek humility. Perhaps you will be hidden in the day of the Lord's anger. ⁴ For Gaza will be abandoned and Ashkelon a desolation; Ashdod will be driven out at noon and Ekron will be uprooted.

Gaza is a portion of land that existed within the current State of Israel. This is a simple prophecy, but important. God tells us only to watch, in the last days, for a time when Israel will give land away — specifically Gaza. In 2005, searching for peace, Israelites abandoned control of Gaza (out of Jewish control) as prophesied. Note the Jews will abandon Gaza close to the day of the Lord's anger. The *"day of the Lord's anger"* is one of many commonly accepted Biblical terms for the Tribulation. Also, today we are watching the enemies of Israel, who now live in Gaza, shooting thousands of missiles at them. Had Israel not abandoned Gaza — something God did not want — they would not have this problem today.

8. THE FALLING AWAY (APOSTASY)

2 Thessalonians 2:1-3
¹ Now we request you, brethren, with regard to the coming of our Lord Jesus Christ and our gathering together to Him, ² that you not be quickly shaken from your composure or be disturbed either by a spirit or a message or a letter as if from us, to the effect that the day of the Lord has come. ³ Let no one in any way deceive you, for it will not come unless the apostasy comes first, and the man of lawlessness is revealed, the son of destruction,

1 Timothy 4:1
¹ But the Spirit explicitly says <u>that in later times some will fall away from the faith, paying attention to deceitful spirits and doctrines . . .</u>

2 Timothy 4:3-4
³ For the time will come when they will not endure sound doctrine; but wanting to have their ears tickled, they will accumulate for themselves teachers in accordance to their own desires, ⁴ <u>and will turn away their ears from the truth and will turn aside to myths.</u>

Apostasy, the falling away from faith in Jesus, is happening. Soon, one current significant Christian denomination will as an organization *"fall away from the faith."* Deceitful *"doctrines"* is a key concept in these verses. This current denomination will follow man-made *"doctrines"* that do not, in fact, line up with what God teaches in His Bible as truth. A great deal of evidence supports this thinking. **Road Map** prophecy #17 will address this in additional detail.

I will likely be attacked and belittled for the empirical information I will share regarding the future of this one specific, current Christian Church. However, I offer this information with compassion, not disdain. If you start to feel some irritation, or find what I'm going to share offensive, I ask only for one kindness. Please read through it all, trying to maintain objectivity. What the course of future history holds is yet undetermined. What you choose to do with this information, individually, in the near future is then between you alone and Jesus. Be aware and watch what might happen very soon.

Hundreds of worldwide organizations have come into existence over the last two-hundred years, preparing for the coming prophesied One World Church. Their main goals: to discredit the Bible and its **fundamentals** as the sole source of truth. The man of lawlessness, the Antichrist, will be revealed (**Road Map** prophecy #20) as apostasy reaches a peak. The One World Church and the Antichrist both come into existence before the *"day of the Lord"* arrives. The Tribulation.

Hebrews 5:11-14
11 Concerning him we have much to say, and it is hard to explain, since you have become dull of hearing. 12 For though by this time you ought to be teachers, you have need again for someone to teach you the elementary principles of the oracles of God, and you have come to need milk and not solid food. 13 For everyone who partakes only of milk is not accustomed to the word of righteousness, for he is an infant. 14 But solid food is for the mature, who because of practice have their senses trained to discern good and evil.

The Deceiver continues to water down sin so, some Christians have no problem accepting and justifying any action they choose to pursue—all issues that do not follow Biblical instruction: premarital cohabitation, abortion, cheating, lying, pornography, listening to lustful or hateful music, and basically all unscriptural practices that make people more susceptible to fall away from God's real truth. Through Jesus, Christians, upon asking, receive grace and forgiveness for all these weaknesses—even after salvation. What a wonderful and gracious Lord we have. If the Lord can forgive, we need to follow His lead and do the same for our friends.

9. INCREASE IN TRAVEL AND KNOWLEDGE

Daniel 12:4
4 But as for you, Daniel, conceal these words and seal up the book until the <u>end of time; many will go back and forth</u>, and <u>knowledge will increase</u>.

God showed Daniel the events that would occur in the far distant future during the *"end of time,"* which is our current-day. He told him *"many will go back and forth"* (travel will be easy.) A mere one hundred and eleven years ago, man traveled by air for the first time. Jets today can take us anywhere on earth within one day. As for knowledge increasing, look at a smartphone. The entire knowledge of the world is available now, if desired, in the palm of your hands.

10.   RISE OF ANTI-SEMITISM

Psalm 83:1-4
[1] O God, do not remain quiet; Do not be silent and, O God, do not be still. [2] For behold, Your enemies make an uproar, and those who hate You have exalted themselves. [3] They make shrewd plans against Your people, and conspire together against Your treasured ones. [4] They have said, Come, and let us wipe them out as a nation, that the name of Israel be remembered no more.

The majority of the countries currently surrounding Israel have a strong hatred for the Jewish State and its people. This hate is called **anti-Semitism**. Many Islamic people hate Israel and have stated their desire to rid the world of the Jews.

11.   MARK OF THE BEAST (TECHNOLOGY)

Revelation 13:15-18
[16] And he causes all, the small and the great, and the rich and the poor, and the free men and the slaves, to be given a mark on their right hand or on their forehead, [17] and he provides that no one will be able to buy or to sell, except the one who has the mark, either the name of the beast or the number of his name. [18] Here is wisdom. Let him who has understanding calculate the number of the beast, for the number is that of a man; and his number is six hundred and sixty-six.

During the entire seven-year Tribulation, mankind will have to endure difficult times—even in the first half of God's punishment period. I speculate that during the entire Tribulation, building things and creating new technologies will be the last thing on people's minds. In the early days they will want only to survive. The technology actually exists today to keep track of everything we do. National sovereignty restricts world leaders from abusing this power. After **Road Map** prophecy #13, with the completion of the Ezekiel attack, all countries will likely forfeit their sovereignty safety nets.

The Bible tells us that during the Tribulation at the midpoint, Satan will indwell the Antichrist. He will require all people to take his mark on their bodies or be killed. Anyone who takes the mark can never be with Jesus, Revelation 14:9-11. This mark guarantees eternal damnation and is applied to the right hand or forehead. After the midpoint of the Tribulation, no person should ever take this mark. Nobody can buy or sell without having it during the last half of the Tribulation. I choose to leave with Jesus prior to the Tribulation at the visual Rapture. I do not plan on finding out personally how the mark will work.

12.   ISRAEL DWELLING SECURELY

Ezekiel 38:8
[8] *After many days you will be summoned; in the latter years you will come into the land that is restored from the sword, whose inhabitants have been gathered from many nations to the mountains of Israel which had been a continual waste; but its people were brought out from the nations, and they are living securely, all of them.*

Ezekiel 38:11
[11] *and you will say, 'I will go up against the land of un-walled villages. I will go against those who are at rest, that live securely, all of them living without walls and having no bars or gates,*

Ezekiel 38:14

14 Therefore prophesy, son of man, and say to Gog, 'Thus says the Lord God, On that day when My people Israel are living securely, will you not know it?

Israel has lived securely and safely in **un-walled villages** for sixty-six years. The Hebrew word in the original text for this is *"batach,"* which means a **place of refuge** and **safety**. Currently no walls **inside** Israel separate internal *"villages."* Israel is *"living securely"* because of their confidence that they can easily defend themselves from any one of the neighboring countries surrounding them. God did not use *"shalom"* in these verses, which is the word for **peace.** Note that He specifically uses the word for **refuge** and **safety** in the verses above, not **peace,** a significant distinction.

The impending problem: many of the Islamic countries currently surrounding Israel now think (scheme) collectively they could rid the world of them . . . exactly what God wants them to believe. This is good news for both, Christians and Jews even though the thought of an impending battle may seem frightening. God tells us, He will prevail.

To this point, all of the 12 prophecies discussed have either been fulfilled as singular events, or are ongoing and shall remain continuous for God's purposes.

Road Map prophecy #13 is **THE NEXT BIG EVENT.** This will change the current course of mankind. **Road Map** prophecies 13-24 are the 12 final events that will soon occur in God's Divine story.

13.   THE EZEKIEL 38 AND 39 ATTACK ON ISRAEL

Ezekiel 39

1 And you, son of man, prophecy against Gog and say, 'Thus says the Lord GOD, Behold, I am against you, O Gog, prince of Rosh, Meshech and Tubal; 2 and I will turn you around, drive you on, take you up from the remotest parts of the north and bring you against the mountains of Israel. ³ I will strike your bow from your left hand and dash down your arrows from your right hand. ⁴ You will fall on the mountains of Israel, you and all your troops and the peoples who are with you;

(Chapter 3, provides additional scriptures, and analysis.)

This interesting, precise, and complicated prophecy explains, in great detail, about a major attack coming at any moment now against Israel by its surrounding neighbors, who hate Israel. Ezekiel 38 and 39 tells us how God will deal with and completely resolve today's radical Islam situation and how He will protect and provide a major victory for Israel—a pivotal event in world history. **Road Map** prophecies 14-24 will happen after Ezekiel 38 and 39, relatively quickly—possibly within three and a half years. Here are some foundational historical issues critical to understanding the reasoning for this prophecy to occur soon.

Today people belong to many different religions that have a variety of names and definitions professing their particular versions of God such as: Judaism/Christianity, Islam, Buddhism, and Hinduism. Many different internal factions exist within all these major groups. Also, people believe in a multitude of other smaller religions regionally and around the world as well.

I place special emphasis on three groups that will play major roles in how the end days play out per God's **Road Map**: **Judaism, Christianity, and Islam**. Jews and Christians have an intimate connection, because Christianity is actually a splinter group of Judaism. Christians accept Jesus as our Jewish Messiah. These three religions all claim Abraham as their patriarch, but the similarity ends there. Imperatively, we must understand the distinctions that define and clearly separate these groups. We also need to comprehend how these belief systems will soon play significant roles in world events. I provide substantial evidence that one of these three groups does not believe in the same God, even though they claim, along with the other two, full relationship to the same patriarch Abraham. But how is this possible?

1 Timothy 2:5

[5] *For there is <u>one God</u> and <u>one mediator</u> between God and mankind, the man Christ Jesus,*

"One God and one mediator" — God's Son, Jesus. Also the third part of God — the Holy Spirit — abides within us. **This is the Trinity**: the Father, Son, and Holy Spirit — all one, not three separate Gods. Some people have trouble with how one God, as proclaimed in the Bible; can be three entities in one. A popular analogy using water shows it quite well: liquid, steam, and ice are three forms of the same thing with completely different characteristics. But they are all still water. The three parts of the Trinity have specific importance with different characteristics, also: 1) for our eternity — God; 2) for our salvation — Jesus; 3) for our protection and comfort — the Holy Spirit. God's design is brilliant. But do other Gods exist? No. God has told us, **He is the only God**.

As we witness the end times, we need to distrust and disvalue some new upcoming Bible translations during the apostasy period. Some of the most respected Bible translators today have begun to interchange the name of God in new Christian Bibles with the written word, Allah, to satisfy some populations. Their explanation: use this name to keep current with the language certain people understand. But I find it impossible to even consider the use of the name Allah for the God of Abraham, Isaac, and Jacob, and Aja for Jesus, the Son of God in any Christian Bible translation.

These translators' websites profess that Jews and Christians used the name Allah in Arabic communities, all through early history. Their sites claim how we wrongly assume that Allah is not an acceptable name for God, in our Christian Bible. I can accept that in the old days most religions found this generic name acceptable but, for our current time, this thinking causes a serious problem.

The Arabic word for "god" is Allah. Prior to the completion of the Islamic Holy Book, the Quran, in 632 AD, the word "Allah" may have been acceptable as a generic Arabic name for any god. It is believed that Mohamed spoke inspired words to his followers and they scribed all of his thoughts into what is today the Quran.

The Quran has Surahs . . . chapters and verses similar in format to the Bible. Upon the Quran's completion, the Arabic spoken and written word "Allah" was specifically defined as their sole god. To support my thinking I will make reference to some Surahs shortly. If desired, you can read the Quran, online (quran.com).

Mohamed described Allah, in the Quran, as a god specifically different from the God of the Christians and Jews. Explicitly, **a god who has no son**.

It appears that Allah directs the Islamic faithful not to take *"Christians or Jews as allies"* (Quran, 5:51). The Quran also defines Allah as a god superior to all other gods. This includes the God of Abraham, Isaac, and Jacob. Allah is Islam's singular god, the god of Abraham and Ishmael, a god who appears too many to promote Jihad, which is holy war, against people who do not accept only him. This Jihad is happening today. I would even venture to say radical Islam is expanding boldly in an exponential fashion of truly Biblical proportions. And not by chance, but rather, prophetic, and clearly, on God's perfect accurate timeline. The end times are upon us.

Some say it's questionable that Allah requires Jihad in his Quran. If indeed he does not, perhaps his faithful who promote

Jihad purposefully break the tenets of both the Quran and Islam. Regardless, horrible things are happening.

Some of the Islamic faithful seem to imply that Jihad is a self-defense action. The Quran addresses self-defense actions but may indicate that killing nonbelievers without provocation is an act of bravery. Does this imply that Allah desires these actions to prove a person is worthy of him and of heaven? Interestingly, we currently see many Islamic believers killing each other in the Middle East. This appears as a transgression against Allah in the Quran, unless these deaths occur by accident (Quran 4:92-93). It's easy to see that today some people of the Islamic faith are at war with both Jews and Christians, and in some instances, with themselves.

The Bible talks about grace **without requiring works** for salvation. This allows somebody the time to explore and discover their free will selection of a God, within their full natural life span. Nowhere in the Bible does it say Christians must kill somebody as an act required for proving devotion to Jesus or as a work required for entering heaven. Christians, in the recent past, did kill egregiously for religious purposes. They, however, did so in grave error. God did not condone these horrible past actions in any way. Jesus should hold no blame for the incorrect misguided actions of sinful uninformed men.

Now, using the logic of the translators mentioned earlier, who say Allah is one acceptable name for God in the Christian Bible for certain cultures, what are we to think? Based on the two diametrically opposed approaches to faith, listed in the paragraphs above, how can it be justifiable today to accept the name Allah in any format, in any Christian Bible translations, for the God of Abraham, Isaac, and Jacob? It can't.

After the completion of the Quran, the name Allah took on a major change in our lexicon. I understand some Arabic Christians still call God Allah. I have difficulty understanding how, with the severe and defined differences, any Christian—in any geographical location or culture—could use the verbal Arabic word "Allah" so easily for the Father, Son, and the Holy Spirit. In 632 AD, the name Allah took on its current specific meaning and definition and has a clear identity.

As Christians, we must not accept the Arabic spoken or written name Allah, in any format, regardless of past history, as a fair current representation of the God of Abraham, Isaac, and Jacob. The Islamic faith certainly would agree with this statement (Quran 5:72-73) in my estimation, so maybe we should follow their lead and accept their interpretation of god as quite different from a Christian's.

I'm sure sincere Christian people work for these Bible translation organizations, but they truly need to walk cautiously here. The idea of using the written or spoken name Allah in today's Scriptures for the God of Abraham, Isaac, and Jacob is absurd. Some may argue that apostasy is sneaking in on them. As explained above, after the writing of the Quran and the formation of Islam, we can no longer consider this as simply an update of understandable past language. It amounts to dangerous thinking. This current translation controversy, within our faith, indicates a bad sign of the times.

As I see it, we now have an undeniable problem between the Bible and the Quran. I do not see how Islam could ever accept the idea of peace with Israel. A one-world religion, as described in the Christian Bible, would contradict the desires of Islam and the Quran, if Israel, and Christians for that matter, were still involved.

The God of Abraham, Isaac, and Jacob has stated that a perceived world peace with Israel will happen in some form. The tenets of the Quran, on the other hand, dispute this, saying the God of Abraham and Ishmael will destroy Israel. Only one of these two opposing points of view can ultimately be correct. I believe the coming Ezekiel attack will clarify this whole issue. In fact, the Bible tells us, a limited number of Middle East nations will come against Israel at some point in time, attempting to essentially wipe them off the face of the earth (Psalm 83:4). Many followers of Islam truly believe their Quran requires them to destroy Israel also. Looking at the world today, I would venture to say Islam is preparing, right now, to attack Israel in the near future.

Some kind of attack will occur soon, as both the Bible and the Quran predict and our daily news seems to validate. We all need only to wait and watch which side wins. It will be interesting to see how this all plays out.

In the Quran, Allah repeats, many times, he *"does not have a son,"* and he is *"not a part of any three, or triune god entity."* The following list represents Surahs, from the Quran, that back up what I have told you. The following Surahs advocate Islam not accepting the idea of the Trinity (the Father, Son, and Holy Spirit). They are 4:171, 5:57, 5:73, 6:101, 9:30, 17:111, 19:35, 19:36, and 19:88-92. Based on these Surahs, it is impossible for the God of Abraham, Isaac, and Jacob to be the same entity as Allah—or for Aja/Jesus to be the same, either.

The Quran was scribed around 632 AD or about 1,400 years ago. The entire Bible used by Christians today, including both Testaments, finally reached completion by 95 AD, about 1,900 years ago. It fully explains and defines the God of Abraham, Isaac, and Jacob, and establishes all of His prophecies and time-lines—a full five hundred years before the Islamic Quran came into existence.

Many events (not precepts) in the Quran have similar dates, time frames and numerology as the already established and written details in the Christian Bible from five hundred years earlier. In the Quran, however, Allah appears to have removed the God of Abraham, Isaac, and Jacob and adopted these already established time frames for his Quran scribed in 632 AD. Allah, in the younger Quran, appears to have substituted himself and his redefined precepts into the vast majority of already pre-established defined timelines that the Trinity (Father, Son, and Holy Spirit) had already claimed long before.

The Quran disputes that Jesus is the Son of God. In the Quran, Jesus is only a prophet. It appears that Islam believes the Quran — written five hundred years after the Bible — when completed, cleared up errors in the original older Bible. So did God get His Word in the Bible wrong the first time and need to have somebody revise and correct it? No.

Hebrews 6:17-20

17 In the same way God, desiring even more to show to the heirs of the promise the unchangeableness of His purpose, interposed with an oath, 18 so that by two unchangeable things in which it is impossible for God to lie, we who have taken refuge would have strong encouragement to take hold of the hope set before us. 19 This hope we have as an anchor of the soul, a hope both sure and steadfast and one which enters within the veil, 20 where Jesus has entered as a forerunner for us, having become a high priest forever according to the order of Melchizedek.

God has told us *"it is impossible for God to lie"* in Hebrews 6:18. This means God has told us that His Word in the older, original Bible is correct. *"Jesus has entered as a forerunner for us"* so that we may have hope for our future.

Jesus, the son of God, was born, died on the cross, and later resurrected per the Bible — long before Islam was defined. God got it all right the first time. Notice what the Bible tells us about Jesus in Hebrews 13:8.

Hebrews 13:8

8 Jesus Christ is the same yesterday and today and forever.

Jesus and God will never need to modify to catch up with new enlightened times. They are the same, have always been the same, and will always be the same, as they have told us.

They are all-powerful, all-knowing, and have no need to ever evolve or be redefined.

14. FIRST STAGE OF CONVERSION OF THE JEW

Ezekiel 39:7

7 My holy name I will make known in the midst of My people Israel; and I will not let My holy name be profaned anymore. And the nations will know that I am the Lord, the Holy One in Israel.

During the Ezekiel attack, God makes himself known. When the attack is quickly completed, God is victorious for Israel. A short period of revival will occur and many Jews and nonbelievers will profess and accept faith in Jesus. Per the Bible, during this attack, God will remove Islam, creating a large worldwide spiritual and political void. This will clear a path, opening up the door and paving the way for all of the following outstanding remaining prophecies.

15. REBUILDING OF BABYLON (Iraq not Rome)

Zechariah 5:5-11

5 Then the angel who was speaking with me went out and said to me, Lift up now your eyes and see what this is going forth. 6 I said, What is it? And he said, This is the ephah going forth. Again he said, This is their appearance in all the land 7 (and behold, a lead cover was lifted up); and this is a woman sitting inside the ephah. 8 Then he said, This is Wickedness! And he threw her down into the middle of the ephah and cast the lead weight on its opening. 9 Then I lifted up my eyes and looked, and there two women were coming out with the wind in their wings; and they had wings like the wings of a stork, and they lifted up the ephah between the earth and the heavens. 10 I said to the angel who was speaking with me, Where are they taking the ephah? 11 Then he said to me, To build a

*temple for her in the <u>land of Shinar;</u> and when it is
prepared, she will be set there on her own pedestal.*

In the above scripture, God describes the vision of an **ephah**
vessel, which is a measuring container able to hold one ephah
for purchasing and selling. An ephah is a Hebrew unit of dry
measure equal to about a bushel (35 liters). In Zachariah, God
uses an ephah to give us a representation of what will come in
relation to the church and government of the last days' reestablishment in Babylon. Note, the un-capitalized word "ephah"
shows in the above scripture God does not refer to the son of
Midian or any other individual. An ephah is symbolic for **commerce**, and it is also associated with, **gloom**, **darkness**, and
wickedness. God even uses the exact word *"wickedness"* in
verse 8; He has chosen a specific term to make His point.

God shows Zechariah this ephah container with a heavy
lead lid upon it. Zechariah lifts the lid and sees a wicked woman sitting inside the container. The woman sitting within the
ephah vessel signifies the wickedness contained in commerce
and religion, including covetousness and deceit during the future tribulation.

Zechariah describes two women with the appearance of
storks who carry away the ephah container with its heavy lid
and its inhabitant and take them to the *"land of Shinar,"* which
is the real City of Babylon in Iraq. Upon arrival the evil woman
will remain entrapped inside the ephah container until her temple is built. Then, upon her release, *"set on her pedestal."* The
world will soon prepare Babylon as the place for the One World
Church (her pedestal) and Government. I believe we will witness this formation soon after the Ezekiel 38 attack.

After the Ezekiel attack, both the One World Government
and the One World Church start to consolidate. Some incorrectly believe this will happen in the city of Rome. The Antichrist
and his church must be in the *"land of Shinar"* — the actual City

of Babylon in current-day Iraq—categorically not Rome, per Zachariah 5:11.

16. ONE WORLD GOVERNMENT AND ECONOMY

Daniel 7:24
23 "Thus he said: 'The fourth beast will be a fourth kingdom on the earth, which will be different from all the other kingdoms and will devour the whole earth and tread it down and crush it. 24 As for the ten horn, out of this kingdom ten kings will arise; and another will arise after them, and he will be different from the previous ones . . .

After the Ezekiel attack, the One World Government and Economy will quickly form, followed immediately by the One World Government breaking into ten Divisions (**Road Map** prophecy #19). After the ten Divisions form, then and only then will the Antichrist come on the scene (**Road Map** prophecy #20). When we review the verses for these following prophecies, we learn the Antichrist will arrive before the visual Rapture happens, and Tribulation begins. We can also conclude, from prophecy, the One World Government and Economy must be in place before the Tribulation, and before the Antichrist will become known to us. In other words, all world control mechanisms need to be completed and in place before the Tribulation starts.

17. ONE WORLD CHURCH AND FALSE PROPHET

Revelation 17:1-5
1 Then one of the seven angels who had the seven bowls came and spoke with me, saying, Come here, I will show you the judgment of the great harlot who sits on many waters, 2 with whom the kings of the earth committed acts of immorality, and those who dwell on the earth were made drunk with the wine of her immorality. 3 And he

carried me away in the Spirit into a wilderness; and I saw a woman sitting on a scarlet beast, full of blasphemous names, having seven heads and ten horns. ⁴ <u>The woman was clothed in purple and scarlet,</u> and <u>adorned with gold and precious stones and pearls</u>, having <u>in her hand a gold cup</u> full of abominations and of the unclean things of her immorality, ⁵ and on her forehead a name was written, a mystery, BABYLON THE GREAT, <u>THE MOTHER OF HARLOTS </u>AND OF THE ABOMINATIONS OF THE EARTH.

This one intricate and involved prophecy follows closely with **Road Map** prophecy #8 (apostasy). The Deceiver will successfully weaken and marginalize true faith in Jesus. He will achieve this with cunning, and without the majority of the current-day Church knowing it's happening. After the Ezekiel attack, both the One World Church and the False Prophet will smoothly and effortlessly blend onto the scene—not abruptly, but subtly and before the start of the Tribulation.

The Ezekiel attack will create a huge spiritual void, which will quickly be filled by a co-opted version of one major Christian church . . . the current denomination that bears the closest resemblance to the original Babylonian Mystery Religion mentioned in the book of Genesis. This relationship, which I will describe shortly, is a key to what Scripture tells us about the church of the end times in the book of Revelation . . . a crucial piece of end times prophecy.

It will become clear to those who study Bible prophecy what denomination will transform into the Church of the end times after two major things happen: 1) The Ezekiel attack and 2) this specific church physically moves its headquarters to the City of Babylon in current-day Iraq.

God tells us in 1 Timothy 4:1, Christian churches and denominations in the world will fall during the apostasy in the last days.

1 Timothy 4:1
1 But the Spirit explicitly says that in later times some will fall away from the faith, paying attention to <u>deceitful spirits</u> and <u>doctrines</u>...

We all need awareness about the *"falling away"* and must be diligent in watching the actions of our churches to make sure they do not wander away from Jesus.

All Christians, in the last days, are in grave peril. The Deceiver wants everyone to believe the final One World Church will be a wonderful, unified, loving **universal** organization. The Deceiver will essentially kidnap many churches to join into one counterfeit family. For the final One World Church, the Deceiver will also want to take over the denomination with the most influence, wealth, and power. So, which version or denomination of our current Christian family is this church? It will be the **Catholic Church.** Let's take a historical look at this church.

Many of its faithful will totally dismiss that anything such as this could possibly ever happen. Of course, this has not happened yet; but, when soon-to-come world events unfold and dramatic changes rapidly occur, please do not discount this possibility.

The Catholic Church hierarchy does not believe Biblical prophecies should be taken literally. They consider them **allegorical.** This includes the visual Rapture and Biblical Tribulation which we will soon review. But we **are literally seeing** God's prophecies actually happen.

Old Testament Scriptures show us how to know when people (false prophets) teach incorrectly, specifically if we are told something that does not come true. These are issues that do not stand up to Biblical scrutiny.

<u>Deuteronomy 18:20-22</u>
20 <u>But the prophet who speaks a word presumptuously in My name which I have not</u>

<u>commanded him to speak</u>, or which he speaks in the name of other gods, that prophet shall die. '²¹ You may say in your heart, 'How will we know the word which the Lord has not spoken?' ²² When a prophet speaks in the name of the Lord, <u>if the thing does not come about or come true, that is the thing which the Lord has not spoken</u>. The prophet has spoken it presumptuously; you shall not be afraid of him.

God has told us to **look for prophecies** related to His end times scenario. When His expressed plans occur, and we *"see"* them, we must trust God's words. We have to take care not to become mesmerized or taken in by **perilous man-made doctrines**. There is great danger in doing so. And we must not get angry with God when His Word does not line up with incorrect human interpretations.

In **Road Map** prophecy #15, I explained a bit about the rebuilding of the literal real City of Babylon in Iraq. Now, we'll explore this a bit more as it also relates to this coming One World Church, and the establishing of this end times church in the real City of Babylon, in Iraq.

THE BABYLON MYSTERY RELIGION SETS THE MODEL FOR THE FINAL ONE WORLD CHURCH

According to Revelation 17:5 the church of the end times will similarly model the original first Babylon Mystery Religion started by Nimrod's wife, Semiramis, in Iraq. Genesis 10:8-10, classified Nimrod as *"a mighty one on earth"* and ruler of the first world empire after the Flood of Noah, in the *"land of Shinar"* the actual City of Babylon. Nimrod was a real person listed in the Bible. Study of historical resources, independent of the Bible, is required to understand the story of this individual. Some consider Nimrod and his wife to be mythological figures, this is Biblically incorrect. There are a variety of interpretations regarding Nimrod and their Mystery Babylon Religion. I have provided the one that contains the most archeological support for my summary.

Semiramis, Nimrod's wife, a power-hungry individual, schemed to get her husband out of the way so she could take over power. A wild animal conveniently killed Nimrod, and his widow immediately transformed him into a god who had taken possession of the sun (a sun god). She then claimed herself as Ishtar, the queen of heaven and Babylon. A decadent harlot in her private life, she met Nimrod while running a brothel. This must have made for an interesting initial meeting.

Soon after Nimrod's death she claimed that he, in spirit, came and impregnated her—a quasi virgin-like birth scenario. She gave birth to a son named Tammuz . . . supposedly Nimrod reincarnated (a son of a god). This was the beginning of the original Babylon Mystery Religion. All the subsequent temples built for this Mystery Religion had a prominent statue of the mother Ishtar holding in her arms her baby son, Tammuz.

Their new religion needed many priests and priestesses to explain about their false god to the people. Only their priests had access to the **mysteries** of this church. The people had to learn about god through hearsay. As a result, with only limited knowledge of the truth, the supposedly "enlightened" people of that day decided to build a tower to reach the heavens to touch their **false version of god.** They built the Tower of Babel as explained in Genesis 11:1-9. This ignorance about the true God created a kind of arrogance, and the limited false teachings of their priests angered the **true God.** As a punishment, He confused their language.

Through archeological finds we have discovered that mankind created multiple versions of pagan **Babylon Mystery Religions.** They came into existence between 1600 and 2000 BC and, over the following centuries, developed many new cult-like rituals. Some of these included: astrology; idol worship (including the Fish-God Dagon); purgatorial purification after death; salvation by countless sacraments; priestly absolution; and the offering of round cakes to the Queen of heaven. They even created a forty day period called **the Weeping for Tammuz** or the great **Festival of Ishtar**. The egg was sacred to Tammuz. The Easter eggs of today are a lingering result of this festival. An evergreen bush was selected to honor the birth of Tammuz at the winter solstice. We derive the Christmas tree today from this concept.

All of these pagan religious rituals expanded to overtake the world into what is called Babylonianism—created **2,000 years before Christ**. Babylonianism grew rampant in many formats right up to His birth. In fact, when the apostles went out to preach the gospel, Babylonianism in many forms had spread and fought the disciples on every front. At the time of Christ, Rome had already become the center of Babylonianism. Their chief priests wore mitres . . . hats shaped like the head and mouth of a fish honoring the Fish-god Dagon. All this was created **years before Christ lived and Christianity formed**.

The church of the end times will follow this model of operation. We all need awareness of the coming events. The Catholic Church today maintains many similarities and traditions closely related to the original Mystery Babylon Religion model. Look today at the Pope's formal headwear; it resembles a fish's head and from the side an open fish's mouth . . . highly interesting.

Jesus, in the Catholic Church's mother-and-child pairing model is, of course, not counterfeit. He is the real deal. Only He, per the Bible, has the power to save and forgive according to the Biblical Gospels (the first four books of the New Testament), not His mother. From actually reading the Bible personally, I see a main problem: God, in the sixty-six books of the Bible, (Appendix A) does not place any Godly authority on the Virgin Mother. Therefore, treating Mary as a legitimate Biblical intermediary between man and God is inaccurate. Jesus even addresses how to look at His mother:

Luke 11:27-28
*27 While Jesus was saying these things, one of the women
in the crowd raised her voice and said to Him, "Blessed is
the womb that bore You and the breasts at which You
nursed." 28 But He said, "On the contrary, blessed are those
who hear the word of God and observe it."*

From 1962 to 1965 the Catholic Church held the **Second Vatican Council (Vatican II)**—a pastoral convention, convened to update and review the disciplines, policies, and attitudes of the Catholic Church relating to the modern world. The clergy added many new **doctrines** (1 Timothy 4:1) and rules to the church at that time. Even though the modern Catholic Church has chosen not to follow many of their own recorded **doctrines**, they have not revoked them, and the **doctrines** remain a part of their sacred writings.

On November 21, 1964, at the end of the third session of the (Vatican II), when Pope Paul VI proclaimed Mary the **Mother of the Church**, he made the following statement: *"henceforth the Blessed Virgin will be honored and invoked with this title by all Christian people."* Where might this place Christians that do not believe in or accept this premise?

The church of the end times, per the Bible, must have a female orientation or emphasis and God calls it *"the Mother of Harlots."* (Revelation 17:5). Interestingly, this major shift in the Catholic Church regarding placing Mary in such formal high authority occurred only fifty years ago. I must clarify: **in no way** am I suggesting that Mary, the mother of Jesus, was a Harlot. **God blessed her.** I simply think God's description by **gender** regarding the status and general makeup of the final One World Church in Revelation has purposeful significance.

Also, interesting: a negative transition within the Catholic Church, away from literal Bible teachings, occurred in the years 1545-1563 during the Protestant Reformation. The Catholic Church responded to this Reformation with their **Council of**

Trent. They considered the thinking process and beliefs of the Protestants to be blasphemous and wanted to clarify their positions on the Bible.

During this eighteen-year period the Catholic Church pronounced many canons (rules) and decrees as **required doctrines**—some of which affect Christians who hold differing views from the Catholic Church's newly inspired teachings. At this same time in history the Catholic Church added seven separate additional books to their Old Testament version (Appendix A). The current Jewish and Protestant Bible versions do not include those seven books.

There are two types of canons. The books of the Bible are considered canons—the God-inspired books that collectively make up our current complete text. In this section we cover the second kind of canons that are **rules** or **measuring sticks** representing what came out of the Council of Trent. Many of the Church's new **rules** require obedience by <u>**all Christian people**</u> from the Catholic viewpoint.

These newly created canons are not alluded to, described, or explained anywhere in God's written word, the Bible. Some canons totally discount the idea of simple and total instantaneous grace from Jesus. Justification, the subject of the **Seventh Session** of the Council of Trent, generated thirty-three canons and sixteen decrees. Although mandatory for Catholic believers, we must not accept non-Biblical edicts expressed as facts or truth. Also, note that if people do not agree with these stipulations, they become an **anathema**. An **anathema** by definition is *"One that is cursed or damned."*

Four examples of the thirty-three canons:

CANON XII. - If any one saith, that justifying faith is nothing else but confidence in the divine mercy which remits sins for Christ's sake; or, that this confidence alone is that whereby we are justified; **let him be anathema.**

58

CANON XV. - If any one saith, that a man, who is born again and justified, is bound of faith to believe that he is assuredly in the number of the predestinate; **let him be anathema.**

CANON XX. - If any one saith, that the man who is justified and how perfect so ever, is not bound to observe the commandments of God and of the Church, but only to believe; as if indeed the Gospel were a bare and absolute promise of eternal life, without the condition of observing the commandments; **let him be anathema.**

CANON XXIII. - If any one saith, that a man once justified can sin no more, nor lose grace, and that therefore he that falls and sins was never truly justified; or, on the other hand, that he is able, during his whole life, to avoid all sins, even those that are venial, except by a special privilege from God, as the Church holds in regard of the Blessed Virgin; **let him be anathema.**

These man-made Catholic Church interpretations and **doctrines** have no solid basis from within the Bible itself. So did Jesus lie to us? No. Should we assume that non-Catholic Christians are therefore, in fact, **anathemas** for disagreeing with these Catholic Church canons? There can be no other possible conclusion. We all must be careful; as it is highly possible the Catholic Church does not believe you can get to Jesus without their help. If this is true **doctrine**, it is in serious contradiction to what Jesus Himself says in the Bible. Since these canons were direct responses to the Protestants' Biblical views of salvation during the Reformation, this assessment makes a great deal of practical sense.

Now, why am I choosing to address all of this? Because, in my opinion, these Catholic Church canons appear to have come together to divide and separate Christians from one another, not unite us. Who ultimately benefits from this? Not the Christian family, certainly not Jesus; the Deceiver does. These Canons and their use of the term **anathema** appear to be saying Catholics are the only true Christians. If you do not accept their interpretation, you are **"damned"**; not my word, I am quoting. This essentially marginalized and minimized the full unconditional grace of our Lord. Jesus tells us in the Bible, He is the only way and truth. Grace is unmerited favor from Jesus and requires nothing more than simple faith in His promise to us.

Jesus, Himself talks about being **accursed**, only when people seek man's approval or blessings **dispensed by human intermediaries** and not directly, from what we have **"received"** from God **"preached"** by the Lord:

Galatian 1:6-10
6 I am amazed that you are so quickly deserting Him who called you by the grace of Christ, for a different gospel; 7 which is really not another; only there are some who are disturbing you and want to distort the gospel of Christ. But even if we, or an angel from heaven, should preach to you gospel contrary to what <u>we have preached</u> to you, he is to be accursed! 9 As we have said before, so I say again now, if any man is preaching to you a gospel contrary to what you <u>received</u>, he is to be accursed! 10 For am I now seeking the favor of men, or of God? Or am I striving to please men? If I were still trying to please men, I would not be a bond-servant of Christ.

I fear the Catholic Church is on the verge of becoming the One World Church of the end times, and many probably don't know or see it. They have no idea where this is going to lead them and, to me, **this is terrifying**. At the Council of Trent, the Catholic Church basically established that if people do not see things their way, they are not saved.

I feel a need to clarify, emphatically, that I am not trying to pick on Catholics, specifically. Many Christian churches, in the end times, will also fall away from true faith in Jesus if they do not continue to trust in the Lord. The Catholic Church is a huge, visible, established, and wealthy organization owning more land in the world than any other entity. Right now, they have both an established figurehead (a Pope) and a woman intermediary (the Virgin Mary). Of all the Christian churches in existence at this time, I believe the Deceiver has his eyes set directly on this church model due to: its position, its large worldwide wealth, and the fact again that it bears similarity to the original Mystery Babylonian Church model. This all fits in with what God tells us in the book of Revelation. He says look and watch for this to happen and since the Bible is accurate, some church will take control in the last times as the One World entity. It is inevitable.

The Catholic Church tells us that Popes are the guardians and custodians of the Bible, and would never change or teach new doctrine. They even claim **Semper Idem** as their motto, which is **always the same**. The Council of Trent's doctrines and this motto seriously conflict. We all need to carefully watch the spiritual warfare happening all around us. We live in grave times. I earnestly fear that Satan may soon overtake and occupy the Catholic Church in the last days. These subtle and gradual changes will bring danger. Catholics should take great care not to walk on thin ice if you see this happening. Do not compromise your faith in Jesus at any time.

The coming charismatic false profit will appear humble; the majority of mankind will greatly respect him . . . very much like our current Pope, who seems quite charming. Is he currently the prophesied false prophet? I don't think so, but I desire to qualify this opinion. Quite possibly, due to health issues, Pope Francis could resign into unprecedented secondary Emeritus status (Emeritus Pope Benedict XVI being still alive) meaning, the very next Pope could likely be a strong candidate.

During the Council of Trent (1545), the Jesuit order came into existence. Pope Francis is the first Jesuit Pope. Historically, the Jesuits existence, since their formation in 1545, focuses on bringing all Christian religions back into the singular Catholic Church, by any and all means possible.

I believe the majority of these men today have good intentions and good hearts. The leadership—the upper hierarchy—causes the problems. The Jesuits appear loving and humble on the outside, but possibly hide something different within the inner workings of their leadership.

We need to go back into history to identify the Jesuits and their past motives and actions. The Jesuit Order, also known as the **Society of Loyola,** is renowned historically for deception, cruelty, and disruption, as one former President and one former Pope attest:

John Adams (1735-1826) Second President of the United States:

"Shall we not have regular swarms of them here, in as many disguises as only a king of the gypsies can assume, dressed as painters, publishers, writers, and schoolmasters? If ever there was a body of men who merited eternal damnation on earth and in hell it is this Society of Loyola."

Pope Clement XIV, (1705-1774) who had abolished the Jesuit Order, said this upon his likely poisoning (historical cover-up?) in 1773:

"Alas, I knew they [i.e., the Jesuits] would poison me, but I did not expect to die in so slow and cruel a manner."

The idea that a Pontiff could completely change church doctrine was never an issue until now, with the first Jesuit Pope. The Jesuits have the power, and determination, within the church to spearhead a coming universal church reorganization leading to the formation of the prophesied One World Religion. This was and still is their intention, and they may soon achieve their long-desired goal.

The word **Catholic** means **universal**. Some might say the church is not a universal church but merely the Roman Catholic

Church. Look at the two distinctions expressed in Canon XXIX (number twenty-nine of the thirty-three canons) from the Council of Trent under Justification:

CANON XXIX. - *If any one saith, that he, who has fallen after baptism, is not able by the grace of God to rise again; or, that he is able indeed to recover the justice which he has lost, but by faith alone without the sacrament of Penance, contrary to what the* <u>*holy Roman and universal Church*</u>*-instructed by Christ and his Apostles-has hitherto professed, observed, and taught;* **let him be anathema.**

Note: *"holy Roman* **and universal** *Church."* The Catholic Church desires to become the One Church of the world. Exactly what form this will ultimately take is in question.

We can look at the word "universal" both **literally** and **figuratively**. The Catholic Church appears to believe they are the Universal Church in the literal sense. Jesus never used the term "universal church" in His Bible. **He is the Church.** Anyone who simply believes in Him and accepts Him as their Savior is saved and they **become part of Him, the Church. Period.**

John 3:16
16 *For God so loved the world, that He gave His only begotten Son, that whoever believes in Him shall not perish, but have eternal life*

Fairly straightforward. Nowhere does this Scripture regarding Jesus require anyone to become a member of a worldly organization as a secondary prerequisite to obtain or maintain eternal life. People can personally obtain eternal life, and full salvation, from Jesus alone, directly, without intersession. For this interpretation of God's own words, based on Canons XII and XV above, as a Protestant, I appear to be **cursed and damned** according to Catholic Church doctrine.

Right after the completion of the Ezekiel attack—when God eliminates the Islamic influence it will create a large spiritual chasm that will need to be quickly filled. With all the power the Pope holds, we cannot totally count out a possibly infectious desire and opportunity for full religious **universal** dominance. The current or very next Pope might find accepting a new fully dominant world role an enticing prospect.

In Catholicism, the Pope is considered the **Vicar of Christ** or **Christ on earth**. Therefore, we should not consider a strong desire for full total religious control as out of the question. There is a saying: **total power corrupts**, so we need to carefully watch how a transition might happen as prophecy moves forward. Should this spiritual shift occur, it could bring about a Third Vatican Council (Vatican III) to establish how to consolidate all remaining religions into one church system for unity and perceived world peace. Please, pay careful attention, as this could get even more interesting, and dangerous, soon.

Something today called the **Ecumenical Movement** desires to create the One World Church. Many high-level Protestant church leaders will soon tell us how Jesus has always wanted all Christian religions to merge within the Catholic Church. This has no Biblical basis. In 1994 prominent Protestant Church leaders signed a document called *Evangelicals and Catholics Together* basically stating that our differences are insignificant. Per the Bible, the written doctrines of the Catholic Church are inaccurate, so the differences are actually very significant. This document's precepts validate how apostasy is alive and well, and spreading now in the Christian faith. Also, a growing **liberal theology** espouses the Bible is flawed and filled with errors. Then, to go deeper into the Catholic Church, **magisterium** and **ex cathedra** (Papal infallibility) tells us, unconditionally, the **doctrines** of Pope in the Catholic Church are correct, no matter what God tells us directly in our Bibles.

In the near future we again need to attentively watch what happens in our churches. Please do not think the issues I am about to address could never possibly happen. If we see the church accepting behaviors and issues described in the Bible as things God specifically says displease Him, **be careful**. If we see the church indicate someone may get to heaven without Jesus, **be careful**. If we see any Christian leaders tell us we should not use or say the name of Jesus as to not offend anyone, **be careful**. If we see the church also accepting other religions under a proposed mantel of one-God-of-all umbrella, saying we all worship the same loving God, again **be careful**. If we see the church minimizing or trivializing Jesus in any way, to achieve harmony and lumping Him in with all other groups, we need to **be exceptionally careful**. Each of these actions would severely contradict what God has explicitly told us in the Bible.

If you put together all of what I have presented up to now in this section, it creates a recipe for the destruction of the Christian version of the Catholic Church. Our world precariously dances on a dangerous slippery slope. When adding this foundational information to the rest of what I share from the Bible, the entire picture will make more sense.

For Christians, in general, when any church begins to accept all other religions as equals or decides to join or unite within one single church unit for supposed peace, world harmony, and love, **be extremely careful**. <u>**This is apostasy**</u>. If this should occur, within any denomination or church, in the not too distant future, my suggestion and advice: **run away as fast as you can**. God even directs us to watch and then to *"come out of her"* when we see the church abandoning truth:

Revelation 18:4-5
⁴ I heard another voice from heaven, saying, "Come out of her, my people," so that you will not participate in her sins and receive of her plagues; ⁵ for her sins have piled up as high as heaven, and God has remembered <u>her</u> iniquities.

As previously stated, the church of the end times must be female oriented in the model of the original Mystery Babylon

Religion. It must have a predominant female figurehead. The only Church today that has this now is the Catholic Church in the form of the Virgin Mary. It is important to look at the Catholic viewpoints and what the Bible shares about her. This is highly important to understand as it relates to how the Catholic Church is going to severely change soon.

Per the Bible, Mary actually has no high Biblical significance other than God selecting her to bear His Son while still a virgin. She did not choose the role of Jesus' mother; God imparted this blessing on her. All Christians believe in the sixty-six Canonical Books (Appendix A), which do not say this blessing conveyed upon Mary provides any level of superiority or any type of power to mediate for us with God. In fact, praying to the Virgin Mary actually marginalizes what God tells us about His Son Jesus and tends to possibly place more emphasis and honor on the human mother than on God's Son.

1 Timothy 2:3-6
3 This is good and acceptable in the sight of God our Savior, 4 who desires all men to be saved and to come to the knowledge of the truth. 5 For there is one God, and one mediator also between God and men, the man Christ Jesus, 6 who gave Himself as a ransom for all, the testimony given at the proper time.

The Catholic Church hierarchy believes in Mary's **immaculate conception** and, therefore, she as Jesus, was born without sin. The Bible does not say this; it is supposition. By this unsubstantiated action God then made her perfect also as Christ. Consequently, today the Church gives her high authority. However, according to Hebrews 4:15: **Jesus was the only sinless person who ever lived.**

Hebrews 4:14-16
14 Therefore, since we have a great high priest who has passed

through the heavens, Jesus the Son of God, let us hold fast our confession. [15] *For we do not have a high priest who cannot sympathize with our weaknesses, <u>but One</u> who has been tempted in all things as we are, <u>yet without sin</u>.* [16] *Therefore let us draw near with confidence to the throne of grace, so that we may receive mercy and find grace to help in time of need.*

Mary also had natural children with her husband, Joseph, so after Jesus' birth Mary no longer remained a virgin.

Matthew 1:24-25
[24] *And Joseph awoke from his sleep and did as the angel of the Lord commanded him, and took Mary as his wife,* [25] *but <u>kept her a virgin until she gave birth to a Son</u>; and he called His name Jesus.*

Acts 1:14
[14] *These all with one mind were continually devoting themselves to prayer, along with the women, and Mary the mother of Jesus, and with His brothers.*

Galatians 1:19
[19] *But I did not see any other of the apostles except James, the Lord's brother.*

Matthew 13:53-56
[53] *When Jesus had finished these parables, He departed from there.* [54] *He came to His hometown and began teaching them in their synagogue, so that they were astonished, and said, "Where did this man get this wisdom and these miraculous powers?* [55] *Is not this the carpenter's son? Is not <u>His mother called Mary</u>, and <u>His brothers, James and Joseph and Simon and Judas?</u>* [56] *<u>And His sisters</u>, are they not all with us? Where then did this man get all these things?"*

In Acts 1:14, Galatians 1:19, and Matthew 13:53-56, God describes brothers and sisters (six at the very least) of Jesus by both Mary and Joseph. Some people claim these people in the Bible were cousins or Joseph's children from a prior marriage, but they were actual blood half-siblings of Jesus. Here is what the Bible says in Mark 3:31-32 and Luke 8:19-20 for some added specific clarity.

Mark 3:31-32
31 Then His mother and His brothers arrived, and standing outside they sent word to Him and called Him. 32 A crowd was sitting around Him, and they said to Him, "Behold, Your mother and Your brothers are outside looking for You."

Luke 8:19-21
19 And His mother and brothers came to Him, and they were unable to get to Him because of the crowd. 20 And it was reported to Him, "Your mother and Your brothers are standing outside, wishing to see You.

One last point on this issue: remember again, in the book of Revelation, the final Church—inside the Tribulation—is called the *"Mother of Harlots"* (female oriented). This makes it impossible for the Church of the end times to be Islamic. God gave it female gender to assure us.

VERY INTERESTING – CATHOLIC CHURCH'S POSSIBLE MOVE TO THE REAL BABLYON IN IRAQ?

The Church of the end times per prophecy must fully operate inside the actual real City of Babylon, in current-day Iraq. The Catholic Church, once co-opted, may actually move to the real City of Babylon in Iraq, *"the land of Shinar,"* in the not-too-distant future (described in Zachariah 5:11, **Road Map** prophecy #15). If something such as this does occur, and the present Catholic Church moves to Babylon, this will provide **solid proof** of what God shares in His prophecies. The move to Babylon will provide a **tremendous warning sign** for all mankind and would fit perfectly in the Biblical Revelation model regarding the church that will enter the Tribulation.

Now, what might influence the Catholic Church to literally move from Rome, in Italy, to the true City of Babylon in Iraq (Shinar)? What significant thing might possibly occur to make the entire Catholic Church even consider making this move? My Bible teacher came up with a plausible intriguing speculation.

It is my understanding; the Catholic Church fathers purposefully built the Vatican over the site which they claim houses the bones of the Apostle Peter. Peter's bones and his grave site have very profound significance. The Catholic Church considers Peter their first Pope, and understandably holds him in the highest regard. An interesting question: Was Peter ever actually in the physical City of Rome? Are Peter's bones really buried under the Basilica?

From 1940 to 1963 multiple archeological studies took place regarding Peter's bones. A dispute arose between the Vatican archeologist, Antonio Ferrua (1901-2003), and Margherita Guarducci (1902-1999), a classical epigraphist (essentially an inscriptions or graffiti interpreter). Pope Pius XII commissioned Mr. Ferrua to do the first archeological study to verify that Peter's bones were actually buried under St. Peters. After twenty-three years, Pope Paul VI concluded that the bones of Peter are indeed under the Basilica per some findings by Margherita — marginal at best. But Antonio, a trained archeologist, categorically, after the first ten years of in-depth study and research, had said **no**. Peter's bones are not under St. Peters. The tomb was empty. Antonio did find a small box of bone pieces (no coffin) and confirmed the bones were in no way conclusively those of Peter. But, definitely, no full body skeleton existed . . . intriguing for a couple of major reasons:

a. Both Paul and Peter were apostles. Paul was not actually one of the original twelve but, rather, a replacement, and not the 13th apostle as people may think. Paul and Peter had only a few brief meetings because of a conflict in the church, in those early days, related to Grace, through faith in Jesus, and the Law.

b. Paul was the Apostle to the **Gentiles**, predominantly located in the actual city of Rome in Italy.

c. In Paul's letter to the Church of Rome, he greeted twenty-seven different people by name, but with no mention of Peter in the greeting, he was not likely there. Had Peter lived in Rome they would have communicated often.

d. In all the many years Paul resided in Rome (later part of his ministry in prison) and in all his New Testament writings (14 of the 27 New Testament books, if we include Hebrews), he never indicates Peter is present with him in Rome. He does mention a brief visit with Peter in Jerusalem, in the second Chapter of Galatians but, other than that, silence in fourteen books.

e. Christians found it difficult to live in Rome at that time, due to persecution. In the latter part of Paul's ministry, the authorities held him in the Mamertine Prison in Rome until they put him to death. A plaque hangs there today saying both Paul and Peter were there together. Nothing in the Bible supports this. The idea that when God uses the name Babylon in relation to Peter in His Bible (1 Peter 5:13), He actually, symbolically, talks about Rome, is in error. God said Babylon, so He clearly **meant** Babylon. In fact, in 2 Timothy 4:11, Paul says only Luke accompanied him in Rome. Peter never entered the city of Rome. He lived in the City of Babylon as God tells us in the Bible.

f. The Romans sentenced Paul to death because of his faith in Jesus, and they **beheaded** him. It was customary for

Christians to be **beheaded**, at that time **in Rome**. The Romans **did not crucify** Christians **inside the city** in Paul and Peter's time, thirty years plus after Christ's death and resurrection. Keep this in mind as I will address how Peter died in a moment.

g. Also, archeologists actually found Paul's true bones and full skeleton (not just small fragments) in a well-marked grave, outside the city boundary of Rome. The Romans considered Christians unworthy for burial inside the City walls of Rome.

h. Peter was the Apostle to the **Jews**. During all of Peter's ministry years, the majority of the Jews all lived in the real **City of Babylon**, in current-day Iraq.

i. Babylon was located at the very far east of the vastly controlled Roman Empire — nowhere near the actual city of Rome where the Vatican is currently located.

j. The Romans **crucified** Peter on a tree; but remember, they only beheaded Christians in the formal City of Rome, during that period in time.

k. Also, remember, they buried Paul outside of the city walls. Why at the same time in history would they have granted Peter the right of burial inside the city walls? They would have treated him the same as Paul and buried him **outside** the city walls . . . not where the Vatican site is currently located today.

In my follow-up research, I remembered a couple of added interesting things. For many years now, the Catholic Church appears to have purchased large sections of property in the *"land of Shinar,"* the actual area of the real City of Babylon in current-day Iraq. But why?

I learned about this land purchasing about twenty years ago and, at that time, found a great deal of information online. Today when I search this topic, I find nothing. I surmise a complete planned removal from the internet. I find this highly interesting. All of this may actually come into the full light of truth soon through a possible interesting discovery in Iraq.

I have also read additional articles stipulating the Vatican City in Rome is **symbolic Babylon**. The articles talked about the geographic Seven Hills of Rome as proof. The Seven Hills on the other side of the Tiber River in Rome have no relation to the Papal State, the Vatican itself.

Revelation 17:9-11
⁹ Here is the mind which has wisdom. The seven heads are <u>seven mountains</u> on which the woman sits, ¹⁰ <u>and they are seven kings; five have fallen, one is, the other has not yet come</u>; and when he comes, he must remain a little while. ¹¹ The beast which was and is not, is himself also an eighth and is one of the seven, and he goes to destruction.

Revelation 17:10 tell us the *"seven mountains"* (hills) actually represent seven kings, not geography. Five had fallen already when John wrote Revelation, and one existed in his time. And a seventh, by its description in the book of Revelation, depicts the coming One World Government of the end times.

The five types of kings or governments that had already fallen by John's time were:

1. The Tarquin Kings (753 BC – 509 BC)
2. Republican government (509 BC – 300 BC)
3. Plebian government (300 BC – 264 BC)
4. Consular government (264 BC – 60 BC)
5. Triumvirate government (60 BC – 27 BC)

Then, in 27 BC the government of John's day mentioned in Revelation 17:10 as the *"one is"* came as the:

6. Caesarean Imperialism government (A Roman form)

The seventh listed as the *"other yet to come"*:

7. The total One World Government *(The ending of the Roman form)*

The final seventh government version—the ending of the Roman form of government—will reside in Babylon run by the Antichrist. We will learn more about him shortly in **Road Map** prophecy #20.

The city of Rome cannot, and will not, be the correct geographic location for the final World Church during the end times, or during the Tribulation but, rather, in the *"land of Shinar,"* in the actual City of Babylon, in Iraq. The final One World Church will go back to the original ungodly Babylonian model, per the book of Revelation, described as *"The Mother of Harlots,"* and must locate in Babylon in Iraq.

On a side note, why do I keep saying **current-day Iraq**? After the Ezekiel attack, Iraq may become a part of a new larger country. I explore this interesting concept as part of **Road Map** prophecy #22, following shortly.

So, finally, what might possibly make the Catholic Church co-opted in the last days to even consider moving from Rome to Babylon in Iraq? Well, the real City of Babylon is near both the Tigris and the Euphrates rivers. There will be some prophetic significance related to one of these rivers, inside the Tribulation, discussed later in this story. Biblically, the Antichrist will rule the world from Babylon, and the New One World Church needs to accompany him for the first half of the Tribulation.

After the Ezekiel battle we will likely witness an accelerated rebuilding process beginning in the actual City of Babylon, in Iraq, preparing for the future, **Road Map** prophecy #15. During preparations for the new construction, in the early major excavations, the construction teams may likely find something amazing. These teams will find, without any doubt, the true full skeletal remains of Peter in a well-marked and documented grave—in the very land where the Bible says he ministered: Babylon (the plains of Shinar) in Iraq.

Moving the entire newly co-opted One World Church (no longer in reality Christian Catholic) to the location where their claimed first Pope Peter's bones are actually located makes perfect sense.

18.   BUILDING OF THE THIRD TEMPLE IN JERUSALEM

Revelation 11:1-2
¹ Then there was given me a measuring rod like a staff; and someone said, Get up and measure the temple of God and the altar, and those who worship in it. ² Leave out the court which is outside the temple and do not measure it, for it has been given to the nations; and they will tread under foot the holy city for forty-two months.

2 Thessalonians 2:3-4
³ Let no one in any way deceive you, for it will not come unless the apostasy comes first, and the man of lawlessness is revealed, the son of destruction, ⁴ who opposes and exalts himself above every so-called God or object of worship, so that he takes his seat in the temple of God, displaying himself as being God.

In my opinion, the construction of new Third Temple in Jerusalem needs to happen because it will have significance in relation to the end times. I believe the new Third Jewish Temple needs to exist before the Tribulation starts. From my perspective as an architect, builders have the ability to construct the temple quickly. The Ezekiel 38 attack would have resolved the Islamic issue regarding the building site.

When the Antichrist signs his covenant with the Jews, this will officially start the seven-year Tribulation period. This covenant will also allow the Jews to begin sacrificial services in the temple. The Antichrist will allow this for only the first half of the Tribulation—for forty-two months. With the Temple in place at the start of the Tribulation, the sacrificial system can then immediately start. **Sacrifices** need to happen **inside the temple** . . . further verification that the building probably should exist prior to the start of the Tribulation.

As I did my research, I remembered something interesting I'd learned, some years back. The new Third Temple must have an initial blessing before it can open, achieved only through the specific sacrifice of a **red heifer** . . . a detailed **required process**, described in the entire 19th Chapter in the book of Numbers. An excerpt:

Numbers 19:1-2
1 Then the Lord spoke to Moses and Aaron, saying, 2 This is the statute of the law which the Lord has commanded, saying, 'Speak to the sons of Israel that they bring you an unblemished <u>red heifer</u> in which is <u>no defect</u> and on which a yoke has never been placed.

Soon after the destruction of the second temple in 70 AD, this interesting animal, the **red heifer**, basically went dormant, no longer needed because the sacrificial system ended with the destruction of the second temple. Without a temple, sacrifices could no longer happen. Then all of a sudden in 1994 a miraculous event occurred. We have witnessed the birth of a **red heifer**—the first sighted in 1,900 years. After twenty years, they have grown in number and some raised to be kosher—acceptable for the sacrifice to purify and cleanse the new coming Third Temple. An appropriate **red heifer** must be **unblemished** for this sacrifice. Does an unblemished heifer exist today, maybe not yet? But with thousands of them in existence at this time, it will not be long until the correct specimen arrives. God has every detail completely designed.

Finally, according to the Bible, the **abomination of desolation** will occur, inside the temple at the mid-point of the Tribulation, forty-two months, or 1,260 days, or three and a half years into the Tribulation. At this time the Antichrist ends the One

World Religion and takes claim as the only god. The new temple sacrificial system will abruptly end three and one half years into the Tribulation at the Abomination of Desolation (Daniel 12:11).

19.   WORD GOVERNMENT BREAKS INTO 10 KINGDOMS

Daniel 7:24
24 As for the ten horns, out of this kingdom ten kings will arise; and another will arise after them, and he will be different from the previous ones . . .

After the Ezekiel attack, **the entire world** will face bewilderment and disarray. My speculation: due to worldwide confusion, all the countries in the world (through the United Nations) will agree—some reluctantly—to give up all individual sovereignty and to form together into a new unified One World Government. But now what? Due to a total world economic upheaval (not a collapse) caused by this attack, the people will possibly accept unification as inevitable. I also speculate that conceivably, all countries will receive a one-time **debt jubilee** (An Old Testament event forgiving all debts every fifty years, Leviticus 25:8-13) forgiving of all national debts and, in return, cause motivation to give up total individual national sovereignty. In other words, no more elections. It will also appear that we will have no choice and, in exchange, this will lead to world peace. Or will it? I think not. This all sums up **Road Map** prophecy #16.

After all that, it will seem sensible to go to the next level and break up this new One World Government into smaller areas, controlled by kings making local control easier. The ruling authorities at that time will decide that the number of kings will happen to be ten. Daniel 7:24 mentions, "*... ten kings will arise; and another will arise after them, and he will be different from*

the previous ones...." This eleventh king, after the initial ten arrive, is the Antichrist, **Road Map** prophecy #20. Remember, he
needs to be present to sign the covenant with Israel. All of the
One World Government and ten king issues must have reached
completion before the Tribulation can begin.

20. <u>RISE OF THE ANTICHRIST (after the 10 kingdoms)</u>

<u>*Daniel 9:24-27*</u>
[24] *"<u>Seventy weeks</u> have been decreed for your people and
your holy city, to finish the transgression, to make an
end of sin, to make atonement for iniquity, to bring in
everlasting righteousness, to seal up vision and
prophecy and to anoint the most holy place.* [25] *So you
are to know and discern that from the issuing of a
decree to restore and rebuild Jerusalem until Messiah
the Prince there will be <u>seven weeks</u> and <u>sixty-two
weeks;</u> it will be built again, with plaza and moat, even
in times of distress.* [26] *Then <u>after the sixty-two weeks</u>
the Messiah will be cut off and have nothing, and the
people of the prince who is to come will destroy the city
and the sanctuary. And its end will come with a flood;
even to the end there will be war; desolations are
determined.* [27] *And he will make a firm covenant with
the many <u>for one week</u>, but in the middle of the week he
will put a stop to sacrifice and grain offering; and on
the wing of abominations will come one who makes
desolate, even until a complete destruction, one that is
decreed, is poured out on the one who makes desolate.*

In the Bible, Daniel tells us about two issues to look for that
will represent time frames indicating we are about to enter the
Tribulation—the first, **Daniel's 70th week,** the second, the
"fourth kingdom." It's important to have a general understanding of their meanings. Although it seems as if they should tie in

with the One World Government and ten kings, these issues relate, specifically, to how we can know the impending arrival of the Antichrist.

Daniel 9:24-27 tells us the *"seventieth week"* refers to the seven-year Tribulation ruled by the Antichrist. The idea is that God prescribed seventy weeks to complete His work to end all sin. Notice how God defines for us His word *"week"* to mean seven years (Daniel 9:27). He tells us in this *"week"* He makes a Covenant, but in the middle, sacrifices stop and abomination and desolation arrive. This seventieth week is clearly the Tribulation. God does not leave us confused and does make this an actual expressed time comparison. No guesswork needed.

So, sixty-nine weeks (Daniel 9:25) in God's process were completed from the time of Cyrus' decree (Isaiah 44:28) to Christ's crucifixion. Then the world has experienced a long time out. God's assigned **Daniel's seventieth week** represents one major final seven-year period. The coming Tribulation.

Daniel 7:23-24
23 Thus he said: 'The fourth beast will be a <u>fourth kingdom</u> on the earth, which will be different from all the other kingdoms and <u>will devour the whole earth</u> and tread it down and crush it. 24 As for the ten horns, out of this kingdom ten kings will arise; and another will arise after them, and he will be different from the previous ones and will subdue three kings.

Daniel 7:23 talks about a *"fourth kingdom"* that *"will devour the whole earth."* Daniel chapter 2 tells us: the King of Babylon, Nebuchadnezzar, had a troubling dream—one he could not understand. He searched for somebody to help him with an interpretation. Then God gave Daniel direction to provide the interpretation. This prophetic dream relates to the governments of the world that would come from the time of Nebuchadnezzar to the Second coming of Jesus.

In the dream, four different forms of government are explained using the visual of a great statue of an *"extraordinary splendid"* man (Daniel 2:31-33), starting at his head and moving down to his feet. Note the quality of these governments deteriorate based on the use of different metals in this dreams explanation:

1. Head of gold
2. Breast and arms of silver
3. Belly and thighs of bronze
4a. Legs of iron
4b. Feet of iron and clay (the end of #4)

Daniel 2:36-45 lists the four **groups** of people who will control these types of governments. They sound like geographic locations but no, they actually represent four types of governments. In *italics* I list historically the types of governments they represent:

1. Gold, Nebuchadnezzar *(Absolute Monarchy)*
2. Silver, Medo-Persia *(Limited Monarchy)*
3. Bronze, Greece *(Democracy)*
4a. Legs of iron, Rome *(Imperialism, political Rome, still in existence today-ongoing)*
4b. Feet of iron and clay, final form of Political Roman-the One World Government *(Evil final political Rome – dictatorship of the Antichrist soon to come)*

A controversy occurs when we try to place geography into this equation. Geography will have nothing to do with the new coming final fourth **Roman Empire** actually becoming the final version of **Political Rome,** in existence today. The legs of Iron represent a **political Roman form of government** that started just prior to the days of Jesus and has continued in various configurations to our very day. We will soon see the conclusion of this government with the ten toes representing the ten divisions of the coming final One World Government, which came into being in **Road Map** prophecy #19. The Antichrist will rule this final form of government out of Babylon.

As earlier explained, the Antichrist comes on the scene **prior** to the visual Rapture. Jesus stated so in the following verses:

2 Thessalonians 2:1-3
¹ Now we request you, brethren, with regard to the coming of our Lord Jesus Christ and our gathering together to Him, ² that you not be quickly shaken from your composure or be disturbed either by a spirit or a message or a letter as if from us, to the effect that the day of the Lord has come.³ Let no one in any way deceive you, for it will not come <u>unless the apostasy comes first</u>, and <u>the man of lawlessness is revealed</u>, the son of destruction,...

Paul tells us, in these verses, not to be shaken or disturbed to hear that the day of the Lord has come. The day of the Lord is the Tribulation. The Tribulation cannot come until first, the *"apostasy comes;"* and second, *"the man of lawlessness,"* the Antichrist, *"is revealed."*

Only after the One World Government arrives and the Ten World Divisions (Kingdoms) are in place, will the Antichrist be revealed and come on the scene. I believe the visual Rapture happens the day the Tribulation starts. This means we will get to see and know who the Antichrist is for a short time before the visual Rapture occurs.

The majority of people in the world will have no idea of this dynamic leader's identity but, as Christians, we should have no doubts. Others will discover his true identity at the midpoint of the Tribulation. Notice, I said the Antichrist comes on the scene after the Ten Divisions have formed. This clearly means the entire infrastructure for the Antichrist must be physically in place before the Tribulation can start.

21.   TIME OF PEACE & SAFETY IN THE UNBELIEVING WORLD

1 Thessalonians 5:1-3
¹ Now as to the times and the epochs, brethren, you have no need of anything to be written to you. ² For you yourselves know full well that the day of the Lord will come just like a thief in the night. ³ While they are saying, Peace and safety! then destruction will come upon them suddenly like labor pains upon a woman with child, and they will not escape.

In the last days those who will accept the coming One World Government and Religion will feel as if they have finally come into a time of worldwide peace and safety. They will not see what actuality has happened. They will think of Christians as totally insane for not recognizing the good that's happening. However, what appears as peace will, in reality, be just the opposite. The secular world is about to be, literally, caught by surprise. But, Christians should find comfort in the clear knowledge God has given them. We should see and know what He is doing and have confidence He will soon return.

22.   THE APPEARANCE OF ELIJAH

Malachi 4:5-6
⁵ Behold, I am going to send you Elijah the prophet before the coming of the great and terrible day of the Lord. ⁶ He will restore the hearts of the fathers to their children and the hearts of the children to their fathers, so that I will not come and smite the land with a curse.

Before Jesus came the first time, God sent a prophet like Elijah (John the Baptist) into the world to announce the arrival of Jesus. He did this so many people would get an advance notice and know that Jesus was on the way. The announcement also provided a way to prepare people for who Jesus was the Messiah, and His importance to mankind.

Elijah in the Old Testament is considered **the prophet of prophets,** a devoted man of God who did whatever was asked of him, with boldness and great courage. He loved God more than life itself and was a great example for us today. Elisha, Elijah's assistant, ultimately inherited his ministry.

Malachi 4:5-6 tells us something similar will happen before the visual Rapture and the Tribulation, with Elijah coming to provide another bold announcement that Jesus is about to return. God will send Elijah to restore the *"hearts of the fathers"* (the Jews because they came first) *"to their children"* (gentile Christians who came after) so they might restore a heart for Jesus through us. Conversely, he wants to restore the *"hearts of the Children"* (Christians) *"to the father"* (the Jews). Christians are required to love the Jews and do everything we can to help them know that Jesus really was and is still, today, their Messiah. God is gracious and taking yet another step to try to save as many souls as are willing, before the terrible day of the Lord occurs (the Tribulation), but many will still, regrettably, not believe.

According to Revelation 7:4-8, 144,000 Jewish converts to Jesus, the Messiah, will evangelize to the entire world through the majority of the Tribulation . . . 12,000 from each of the twelve tribes of Israel.

Presently, Israel does not control the full extent of the physical geographic land areas promised to them by God. Originally, God provided to each of Jacob's twelve sons (the twelve tribes of Israel) parcels of land currently outside of Israel proper, today. In order to reestablish the tribal system that God will need before He can collect the 144,000, additional land mass must return to Israel. I believe God will reclaim this land Himself with his Ezekiel 38 attack, *"From the river of Egypt as far as the great river, the river Euphrates."* This is the land promised to Israel in Genesis 15:18 — the Abrahamic Covenant.

Genesis 15:18
18 On that day the Lord made a covenant with Abram saying, "To your descendants I have given this land, from the river of Egypt as far as the great river, the river Euphrates."

This is educated speculation on my part. However, notice something interesting on Israel's current Ten Agorot coin. This coin has a seven-candlestick Menorah placed over a map of Israel. With north assumed as up as with all maps and the Mediterranean Sea on the west or left side, we can tell the map shown has a far larger land mass than the small sliver of land Israel controls today.

If we take this shape and align it with the coastline along the Mediterranean Sea, to approximate scale on the following map of the Middle East, we discover something interesting. This footprint would include almost all of the land from the river of

Egypt to the river Euphrates. Exactly the land promised to Israel by God Himself in Genesis 15:18.

Babylon is not shown on the following map; it is about fifty miles south of Baghdad in current-day Iraq. The new capital of the whole world inside the Tribulation will be situated in Babylon, the *"Land of Shinar,"* per Zechariah 5:11 discussed earlier in **Road Map** prophecy #15. If this speculation turns out to be accurate, Babylon will actually be inside this new larger State of Israel.

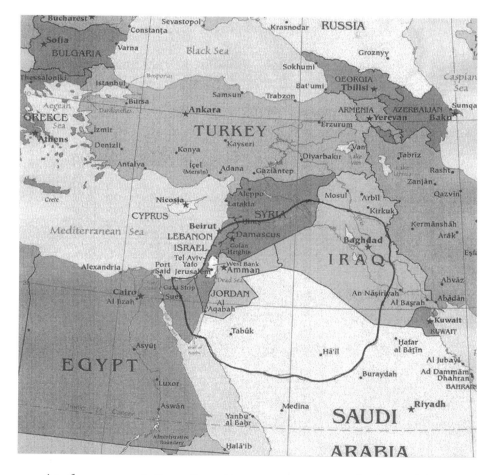

At the current time Israel's enemies control this additional land mass. I believe the Ezekiel 38 attack discussed earlier in **Road Map** prophecy #13 will resolve the situation, as we will soon discover. This also needs to occur before the Tribulation so the 144,000 can come on the scene early, into God's seven-year period of trials.

Very possibly Elijah will also help to reestablish the tribal system in Israel before the Tribulation starts, as we head toward the end of days—vitally important for our Jewish family.

23. FEAR, SCOURGE, THE ANTICHRIST AND HIS COVENANT

Isaiah 28:14-15
[14] Therefore, hear the word of the Lord, O scoffers, who rule this people who are in Jerusalem, [15] Because you have said, We have made a <u>covenant</u> with death, and with Sheol we have made a pact. The <u>overwhelming scourge</u> will not reach us when it passes by, For we have made falsehood our refuge and we have concealed ourselves with deception.

Isaiah 28:18-19
[18] "Your covenant with death will be canceled, and your pact with Sheol will not stand; when the <u>overwhelming scourge</u> passes through. Then you become its trampling place. [19] "As often as it passes through, it will seize you. For morning after morning it will pass through, any time during the day or night. And it will be sheer terror to understand what it means."

Just prior to the start of the Tribulation, the Antichrist will set demons loose on the world . . . the **overwhelming scourge**—Joel 2:1-10. Briefly, demons will march in order and devour, burn, and destroy everything in their path. They can go through windows into and over houses—terrifying to witness. The **overwhelming scourge,** a pivotal detailed warning sign just prior to the visual Rapture, is addressed contextually in greater detail in Chapter 5.

This scourge will start to occur while the people of the world still live in their perceived false peace and safety. The **over-**

whelming scourge will make Israel desire to reluctantly sign a covenant agreement with the Antichrist to protect them from these horrible demons. The covenant signing will start the official seven-year Tribulation. Informed Christians have no need to fear this horrendous event.

24.   SIGNS ON THE DAY OF THE VISUAL RAPTURE

Joel 2:30-32
[30] I will display wonders in the sky and on the earth, blood, fire and columns of smoke. [31] The sun will be turned into darkness and the moon into blood before the great and awesome day of the Lord comes. [32] And it will come about that whoever calls on the name of the Lord will be delivered; For on Mount Zion and in Jerusalem there will be those who escape, as the Lord has said, even among the survivors whom the Lord calls.

Amos 8:9
[9] "It will come about in that day," declares the Lord GOD, "That I will make the sun go down at noon and make the earth dark in broad daylight.

When adding the signs addressed in Joel 2:30-32 along with the **overwhelming scourge (Road Map** prophecy # 23), on that day we get to go home with Jesus in the visual Rapture.

As we continue, I will show how the Bible explains for us (Luke 17:26-32) that the visual Rapture and the start of the Tribulation must happen within the same twenty-four hour day, with no time separation (gap) between these two events. **God has important and profound reasons for these events to happen in this way**. Through the Grace and the promises of God, true, living believers in Jesus will escape in the visual Rapture just hours before the Antichrist signs his covenant with Israel, placing *"the great and awesome day of the Lord,"* the Tribulation into motion.

Matthew 24:32-34

[32] *Now learn the parable from the fig tree: when its branch has already become tender and puts forth its leaves, you know that summer is near;* [33] *so, you too, when you see all these things, recognize that He is near, right at the door.* [34] *Truly I say to you, this generation will not pass away until all these things take place.*

CHAPTER 2

BIRTH PAINS, BIRTH, TIMELINE
PROPHECIES 1-4

We have witnessed the first set of
Biblical end time prophecies.
This witnessing proves, without a doubt, that
imminence is no longer valid thinking.

In Matthew 24:3-8 ,birth pangs and a birth will occur as the first set of end time prophecies confirming Jesus is about to return. God created two major birth pangs (pains, plural) with **specific and significant** purposes corresponding to a birth — the formation of the State of Israel on May 14, 1948. Let's explore the sequence of events and their true purposes.

Matthew 24:3-8

3 As He was sitting on the Mount of Olives, the disciples came to Him privately, saying, Tell us, when will these things happen, and what will be the sign of Your coming, and of the end of the age? 4 And Jesus answered and said to them, see to it that no one misleads you. 5 For many will come in My name, saying, 'I am the Christ,' and will mislead many.6 You will be hearing of <u>wars and rumors of wars</u>. See that you are not frightened, for those things must take place, but that is not yet the end. 7 For <u>nation will rise against nation</u>, and kingdom against kingdom, and in various places there will be <u>famines and earthquakes</u>. 8 But <u>all these things are merely the beginning of birth pangs</u>.

The Bible indicates in these Matthew verses, as we get close to His return, we are to look for some signs. The Lord tells us of *"wars and rumors of wars,"* and that *"nation will rise against nation,"* and we'll experience *"famines, and earthquakes."* Well, this fairly sizes up the twentieth century. Two major *"birth pains"* totally and fully set the stage for God's planned rebirth of Israel. They were WWI and WWII.

Matthew 24:32-34

32 Now learn the parable from the <u>fig tree</u>: <u>when its branch has already become tender and puts forth its leaves</u>, you know that summer is near; 33 so, you too, when you see all these things, recognize that <u>He is near, right at the door</u>. 34 Truly I say to you, <u>this generation will not pass away until all these things take place</u>.

Remember, again, whenever we see a parable related to a *"fig tree,"* we can know that God is talking about Israel, **Road Map** prophesies #3 and #4. In these Matthew verses, God tells us when the fig trees, branches *"become tender,"* as a baby, and it puts forth leaves, becomes alive or born, *"you know that the summer is near."* Also, *"when you see all these things, recognize that He is near."* God is telling us to watch for these signs and prophecies so we, as Christians, will know for certain, that Jesus is coming. Why would God tell us to look for something if He is coming unexpectedly? Also notice again, He is using the word *"see."*

These verses direct us to look for a birth, the prophesied re-birth of Israel. After we witness this birth, Matthew 24:34 tells us the **generation** that will *"see"* this (all of us today) will not pass away until all these things (His prophesies) take place. But what is a **generation** according to the Bible, and how long is it? Here is what God tells us:

Psalm 90:10:
[10] *"As for the days of our life, they contain seventy years, or if due to strength, eighty years."*

God specifically indicates between seventy and eighty years. With this information, we now will discover some interesting things about the two birth pains and the rebirth of the State of Israel. God gives clear direction, so we can understand completely the *"season"* we live in.

When we look at the entire chapter of Matthew 24, many believers say this is telling Christians we might need to live through the Tribulation. This is not an accurate interpretation. To avoid confusion regarding Matthew 24, we use the **Hermeneutical Law of Double Reference** in relation to this Chapters' full context. I did not include the full text of Matthew 24 here due to its size.

The **Hermeneutical Law of Double Reference** is where God talks about His present day and then, for context and example, jumps into the future within the same text. Usually, at some point, after explaining what is coming in the future, He will, in the same text, come back again to the present to finish His explanation and thinking. This is done often in Scriptures. Using this **Hermeneutical Law** let's apply this to Matthew 24.

In verse 3 the disciples ask Jesus a question regarding the signs of His return. In verses 4-8 Jesus tells them about the signs to look for before the start of the future Tribulation. He then jumps into the future in verses 9-31 and, for foundation and emphasis, speaks of the horrors of the future Tribulation period. Jesus then jumps back to their current time in verse 32-51. He answers the initial question asked in verse 3. In these final verses Jesus gives us the answers as to how we, today, will know when **He will be coming back** prior to the Tribulation.

THE TWO MAJOR BIRTH PAINS
PRIOR TO THE BIRTH

The following **significant issues**, relate to the two major birth pains that had major influences on the rebirth of the nation of Israel.

WWI: (1914-1919) Well into the war, the Allies would soon run out of smokeless gunpowder and needed acetone in order to make the explosives needed to fight and achieve victory. Up until WWI, their factories could make acetone from only wood. The English people had cut down most of their forests in the war effort. Their supplies rapidly ran low.

A young Jewish scientist named Chaim Weizmann, knowing the urgency of the situation, developed a way to make acetone using corn mash. This new formula allowed England and the United States to generate enough acetone to make the much-needed smokeless gunpowder to win the war.

England wanted to show their appreciation of Mr. Weizmann's discovery, so at the end of the war, they asked him what they could do to reward him. He told them he would like England (which had control of Israel at that time) to allow the Jewish people the ability to re-establish a country again in their former homeland, Israel. This resulted in the Balfour Declaration dated November 2, 1917 (**Road Map** prophecy #2), which allowed for, but did not form, a revived Jewish homeland, Israel, again after 1,900 years in exile.

WWI was the first major birth pain. After this war, the Jews still felt comfortable living in all the lands where God had scattered them since the destruction of their second temple in Jerusalem in 70 AD. At that time the Jews could not find a good reason to go home to a new and safe Israeli homeland.

WWII: (1939-1945) During the 1930's and through the war, anti-Semitism (hatred of the Jews) in Russia and Europe—particularly Germany—grew exponentially. Adolph Hitler believed the Jews needed to be exterminated from the face of the planet. During WWII, Hitler, through the efforts of one of his senior henchmen, Karl Adolf Eichmann, planned for and systematically killed 50 percent of the Jews living in Europe. After the war, the Jews no longer felt safe in Europe or Russia.

Since the end of the war in 1945, the Second Exodus, returning from the lands where God had scattered them, has accelerated. Jews have returned to Israel from all over the world to live in safety inside their new reestablished homeland.

WWI was the first major birth pain and made the land ready for the Jews. WWII was the second major birth pain and made the Jews ready for the land.

UNITED NATIONS AND THE BIRTH OF ISRAEL

Almost immediately after WWII came the formation of the United Nations on October 24, 1945. One of the first acts of the

United Nations: to ratify Israel as a new country in 1948 the official rebirth of the State of Israel. The United Nations will soon play a pivotal role in ushering in the new One World Government that will rule into the Tribulation. With the rebirth of Israel, the first four of God's twenty-four significant end time prophecies occurred for us to witness.

Note that with every birth, a new *"generation"* begins. Since we have now seen birth pains and a birth, we can equate this to a new *"generation."* Remember, Psalm 90:10 tells us our lives last about eighty years, a generation. An interesting timeline pertaining to this new generation, symbolized by the birth of the new State of Israel, has occurred.

POSSIBLE TIMELINE FOR YET TO COME EVENTS

In Matthew 24:34, the Bible indicates that *"this final generation will not pass away until all these things take place."* Based on Psalm 90:10 along with Matthew 24:34, the birth of Israel started what God intended to be recognized as **His Biblical final generation**. How so?

Let's assume for a moment that the State of Israel is a living person: Israel as a Jewish man, growing up from an infant into manhood. Based on the life cycles of a Jewish human male, some amazing historical events and timing have occurred since this May 14, 1948, rebirth.

The rebirth of the State of Israel started a clear **generational time clock**. It started a literal timeline that all Christians who love the study of end time prophecies, should understand. But has God provided any possible additional indications to validate this? Yes, and it gets interesting.

1. Symbolically, on May 14, 1948, the date of Israel's rebirth, some of the surrounding Arab countries became highly irritated. They decided to fight against Israel on day one of their existence and said they would take them down

quickly. They did not succeed, all of their efforts failed. This irritating action, at birth, can metaphorically relate to a Jewish boy's circumcision.

2. A Jewish boy becomes responsible for his actions, <u>ac-countable</u> at thirteen years of age. He becomes a Bar Mitzvah. The Jewish people hold a Bar Mitzvah ceremony for the young man, to <u>celebrate</u> this event. Remember from earlier, in WWII, the German Karl Adolf Eichmann, the chief architect of the Holocaust? He escaped at the end of the war and was a fugitive until his capture by the Israelis in 1960. On December 11, 1961, he was tried and held <u>accountable</u> for the deaths of millions of Jews. Israel was thirteen years, seven months old when this happened, and I feel sure Israel <u>celebrated</u> this event.

3. Also, a Jewish man becomes eligible to fight in wars while in his twentieth year of life (after his nineteenth birthday.) Adding nineteen years to 5-14-1948 equals 5-14-1967. On 6-7-1967 (Israel was nineteen years twenty-three days old), Israel fought and won the six-day war, and the city of Jerusalem returned back into the control of the Jewish people . . . after over 1,900 years in exile—a fulfillment of prophecy.

4. Symbolically, in the life of a Jewish man, he becomes a man of peace at the age of thirty. Jesus, our Rabbi, started His formal ministry at thirty years of age. Thirty years added to 5-14-1948 equals 5-14-1978. In September of 1978, when Israel was thirty years, four months old, the Camp David Peace Accords were negotiated. Then in March of 1979 (Israel was thirty years, ten months old) Egypt and Israel with Jimmy Carter signed the Camp David Peace (security) Accords. This plan made it possible to keep the borders with Israel and its neighbors safe by agreement—another fulfillment of prophecy. Can this all be chance?

5. On 5-14-2014, the State of Israel celebrated its sixty-sixth birthday.

6. This book was published in late 2014, and we have passed the completion of the sixty-sixth year of a possible eighty-year generation period. Using the Bible as our guide, remember that the entire Tribulation must occur before the completion of the eighty-year generation.

Luke 12:54-56

54 And He was also saying to the crowds, when you see a cloud rising in the west, immediately you say, 'A shower is coming,' and so it turns out. 55 And when you see a south wind blowing, you say, 'It will be a hot day,' and it turns out that way. 56 You hypocrites! You know how to analyze the appearance of the earth and the sky, <u>but why do you not analyze this present time</u>?

I believe we are in the **season** of the Lord's return. Utilizing the full eighty years from Psalm 90:10, I believe the rebirth of Israel started a literal eighty-year **final generation**. God tells us the following regarding this:

Luke 21:32

32 Truly I say to you, <u>this generation</u> will not pass away until all things take place. 33 Heaven and earth will pass away, but My words will not pass away.

This **generation** will not pass away until *"all these things take place."* All these things include the seven-year Tribulation. 5-14-1948, plus eighty years takes us to 5-14-2028. Using the empirical information above, along with the contents of Psalm 90:10 and Luke 21:32, I've created an analogous Biblical timeline of both recent past and yet-to-come end times prophetic events. To recap events:

1. Israel's rebirth May 14, 1948.

2. Attacks by their Arab neighbors from day one, this small irritation, a bit like a circumcision.
3. At age thirteen in 1961, the sentencing and hanging of Eichmann, a celebration occurred similar to a Bar Mitzvah.
4. At nineteen in 1967, symbolically, Israel became of age to fight in wars and took control of Jerusalem in the six-day war.
5. At thirty, in 1978, Israel signed the Camp David Security Accords. They essentially started their ministry (diplomacy) for peace. At the same age, Jesus started His ministry.

Mathematically, per the Bible, let's consider a couple of additional pieces of critical information for God's timeline.

   a. The Bible tells us, at the longest, a generation should be eighty years (Psalm 90:10).
   b. According to the Bible this final Generation will not pass away until *"all these things take place."* Starting with the birth, this includes the balance of the twenty-four prophecies, the visual Rapture and the Tribulation. All these things must take place **before** the eighty-year generation has ended (Luke 21:32).
   c. The Bible says the Tribulation will happen in two, three-and-a-half-year periods of 1,260 days each, for a total of seven years. (Revelation 11:3 and 13:5).
   d. Also from Scriptures: at the midpoint of the Tribulation (three and a half years), all the Jews in Israel, in fear of their lives, will flee the area to get away from the Satan-indwelled Antichrist. (Revelation 13).
   e. The Bible shows us that after the Ezekiel attack; the Jews will burn the fallen instruments of war that fell inside Israel for seven years (Ezekiel 39:9). Per (d) above, no Jews will remain in Israel to burn these items after the first three and a half years. This means

the Ezekiel attack would need to happen at a minimum of **three and a half years before the Tribulation starts.**

So, with all this information, both Biblical and empirical, I'll attempt to show God's possible math as to when to anticipate the *"season"* of visual Rapture.

    f. Israel's birth date, May 14, 1948, plus eighty years equals May 14, 2028. The end of the Tribulation must occur by this date.

    g. Subtracting seven years for the Tribulation takes us back to May 14, 2021. The visual Rapture must happen by this date.

    h. Now subtract three and a half years, minimum, per (e) above, which brings us to **November 14, 2017.** Ezekiel 38 and 39 must occur by this outside date, so this attack could happen at any time now.

Israel is under severe threat of attack from many of their **surrounding neighbors**. It appears today that every country in the world is against them. They are alone. Coincidence? No. Part of God's Devine plan? Yes.

The Bible spends about one-third of its entire text on prophecy, predicting both the first visit of Jesus and our current time the *"season"* of His second return.

God has given us an incredible amount of direction and actual proof of His existence and plans. I cannot see how anybody at this moment in history can still have any honest intellectual doubt about His authenticity.

✶✶✶✶✶✶✶✶✶✶✶✶✶✶✶

God brought the United States into existence at exactly the right time in His historical narrative.

Our young men fought in and won both WWI and WWII. Although others defended their countries from the same enemies, I believe the most credit goes to the United States. Without our country, Japan, Germany, and Italy might have taken over, and the world would have been a much different place.

The benefits Israel derived from the final outcomes of our victories in these two wars would not have materialized, and Israel could not exist today under any other scenario. God's flawless plan continues.

A personal note: My grandfather fought in the Army in WWI. He leaped from trenches to run out and bring wounded soldiers back into safety. For this, he received the United States Distinguished Service Cross and the French Croix de Guerre Medals for gallantry—the second-highest Military awards offered by the two countries. I proudly possess these actual medals today as part of my heritage. I realize, had a bullet taken my grandfather during the war, I would not have had the opportunity to share what I have learned with you. Life hangs on mere threads and God weaves things perfectly.

Psalm 83:1-4

[1] O God, do not remain quiet; do not be silent and, O God, do not be still. [2] For behold, Your enemies make an uproar, and those who hate You have exalted themselves. [3] They make shrewd plans against Your people, and conspire together against Your treasured ones. [4] They have said, Come, and let us wipe them out as a nation, that the name of Israel be remembered no more.

CHAPTER 3

THE
NEXT BIG EVENT
EZEKIEL
38 AND 39
PROPHECY 13

We are currently in the final stage of God's end times prophetical story line regarding His final generation. The Next Big Event will lead us quickly and directly to both the visual Rapture and the Biblical Tribulation.

I believe within the next couple of years we will witness a major attack, per Scriptures, that will come against Israel . . . the Next Big Event, Ezekiel 38 and 39. When this attack happens, it will provide visual proof that God is who the Bible says He is. Israel will be unharmed. This singular event will change the course of human history.

I have included the full Bible text, for both Ezekiel 38 and 39, at the end of this chapter. I quote many verses in this section from Ezekiel. Psalm 83, also included, is a prayer by Asaph, asking God to make the Ezekiel 38 and 39 happen in his future.

The Ezekiel 38 and 39 prophecy is highly controversial. Some say it has already happened. Others think it must occur inside the Tribulation or is the battle of Armageddon. And some consider this prophecy a stand-alone event and do not apply it within the context of God's entire Biblical **Road Map**. In my estimation, this prophecy is a yet-to-come attack, a vital piece of God's larger intricate Biblical puzzle. I propose, and will share, a new way of looking at this great battle. I believe, wholeheartedly, this attack will occur at any time now for us to witness.

Ezekiel 38 and 39 tell us how God's inspired attack on Israel by its neighboring enemies is a different attack than the one currently contemplated by Israel on Iran regarding their nuclear program. Disdain by Islam for the Jews, and Jesus, *"profaning"* His name, will instigate this enemy attack on Israel. Biblically, Ezekiel 38 cannot be a World War (WWIII) or the actual final war, against the Antichrist at the end of the Tribulation, Armageddon.

The Bible clearly shows us how Ezekiel 38 and 39 talk about two different wars and this creates some confusion. Ezekiel 38:1 through 39:16 talks about God's private war with Israel's surrounding enemy neighbors — only a **limited number of nations**. Ezekiel 39:17 through 39:29 talks about Armageddon . . . a different war, **including all the nations** of the world. Two distinctly different wars, in the same verses.

Ezekiel 30:1-5
¹ The word of the Lord came again to me saying, ² Son of man, prophecy and say, 'Thus says the Lord God Wail, Alas for the day! ³ For the day is near, <u>even the day of the Lord is near</u>; It will be a day of clouds, A time of doom for the nations. ⁴ A sword will come upon Egypt, and anguish will be in Ethiopia; when the slain fall in Egypt, they take away her wealth, and her foundations are torn down. ⁵ Ethiopia, Put, Lud, all Arabia, Libya and the people of the land that is in league will fall with them by the sword.

God desires for this Ezekiel attack to occur, for us to witness, before the Tribulation for a couple of profound reasons. How do we know this battle occurs before the Tribulation? The verses in Ezekiel 30:1-5 basically refer to events, soon to follow, in all of Ezekiel 38 and 39. Please pay special attention to Ezekiel 30:3 and note the words *"even the day of the Lord is near."* It says *"near."* This battle is prophesied to happen in the future, just near and **before** the start of *"the day of the Lord."* The term *"the day of the Lord"* is the Tribulation period.

Having Ezekiel 38 and 39 occur prior to both the visual Rapture and Tribulation is the key event that will start to confirm the premise of this entire book. Some people say this attack will never happen and is symbolic. But in Ezekiel 39:8, God makes a declaration stating this attack *"shall"* come.

Ezekiel 39:8
⁸ Behold, it is coming and it <u>shall be done</u>, declares the Lord GOD.

. . . *"it shall be done."* . . . a fairly direct statement I would venture to say.

After the Ezekiel attack we have only a few years left before the visual Rapture and the start of the Tribulation. It is my personal belief that immediately after this Ezekiel attack, some large projects need completion quickly before we depart. We should watch what happens in the near future for God's confirmation.

1. As part of this attack, God will remove the Al-Aqsa Mosque and Dome of the Rock in Jerusalem. Construction of the new Third Jewish Temple must occur on this Temple Mount site. I have learned from other research that plans may already exist for the new third temple. From my viewpoint as an architect, with today's technology, and with an unlimited budget, it won't take long to build.

2. Reconstruction of the city of Babylon will happen rapidly and this will become the new center of the coming One World Government. The United Nations will likely relocate there as well.

3. The One World Church, led by the False Prophet, in my opinion, must be built and in place before the Tribulation starts. This will consolidate all religions into the unified One World Church. The new false church must operate out of Babylon, in current-day Iraq. The One World Government and economy needs to be in place with ten Divisions or Kingdoms established.

These items above are monumental projects. I do not see logistically how any projects of these magnitudes could happen during the first half of the Tribulation. Some Christians talk about how peace will fill the first half of the Tribulation until the Antichrist enters the temple at the midpoint and claims to be the only God. Then at this time, things will get bad. To put this period in some perspective: half of all mankind remaining after the visual Rapture will die (three billion people) in the first half of the Tribulation. Here is how we know this:

Twenty-one judgments come upon the world inside the Tribulation. They occur in three groups of seven events. The first seven are the **Seal** judgments, followed by the seven

Trumpets. The third group of seven is called the **Bowls.** The **Seals** and the **Trumpets** (fourteen) happen in the first half of the Tribulation; the **Bowls** (seven) happen in the second half.

Seal Judgment Four (Revelation 6:7), the fourth of the twenty-one events, will quickly kill off 25 percent of all living beings on earth. Trumpet Judgment Six (Revelation 9:16), the thirteenth of the fourteen events in the first half, will kill another 33 percent of those remaining on earth prior to the midpoint of the Tribulation. Some simple math: start with 1,000 people, kill 25 percent or 250 and you have 750 remaining. Now kill 33 percent of the remaining 750 or 250 and you end up with 500, half of the original number.

The deaths of one half of the world's population will total a staggering, unbelievable number. If three billion people die in the first half of the Tribulation, which lasts 1,260 days, (Revelation 11:2), this would equate to 2,380,000 people per day. We can see from this, no peace of any kind could prevail inside the entire Tribulation. At this death rate, the same total number of people who died in all of WWII (70,000,000 +/-) will have died within the **first thirty days** of the Tribulation.

The second half of the Tribulation will also be devastating. From the analysis above it's clear the Tribulation will be horrendous for the entire seven years. Everybody will struggle to stay alive due to all the horrible punishments God intends, in His judgment period.

No way can any building or large-scale construction projects take place during the Tribulation anywhere in the world. Everything for the Antichrist must be in place first and completed before the Tribulation begins in the pre-Tribulation secular time of peace and safety. In my estimation, this is the main reason why the Ezekiel attack needs to occur at least three and a half years prior to the start of the Tribulation. Secular peace and safety will appear to arrive quickly after this attack. I also surmise the concept of world peace is going to be a key reason, after the Ezekiel attack, for people all over the world to accept the One World Government. I believe the secular world will yearn for total unification. The perception of tangible world peace will motivate everyone. This battle against Israel and God will involve only certain regions and tribes. The Bible refers to the coming Ezekiel event as the battle of **Gog and Magog**. A world war is not comprised of a limited number of nations.

It is my strong belief that Magog is actually Russia. Gog (Russia's president) will be its leader. These limited nations (a coalition) will become emboldened. Did you think that as of 2014 there was any possibility that Russia would ever become aggressive again and start taking over countries for plunder? Does Crimea ring any bells? The world's nations, as a whole, put up only a mild protest. Do you think Russia is beginning to feel emboldened by apparent apathy of the Global Community? Highly likely.

Plunder will be the reason Israel is attacked per Ezekiel 38 and 39. Israel recently found one of the largest and richest natural gas discoveries in the world inside their small country . . . incredible economic value. Most probably some of their enemy neighbors and Gog would like to have this for themselves.

The specific regions in this coming battle against Israel per Ezekiel 38:1-5: Magog, Rosh, Meshach, Tubal, Persia, Ethiopia, Put, Gomer, and Beth-togarma. These regions and/or tribes existed in 571 BC, when the profit Ezekiel, through God's inspiration, wrote about this over 2,600 years ago.

Ezekiel 39:7
⁷My holy name I will make known in the midst of My people Israel; and I will not let My holy name be profaned anymore.

When the enemy states that surround Israel *"profane"* Jesus, it angers God. He has about had it with the name of Jesus being *"profaned"* and will not allow this to continue much longer.

Ezekiel 38:8
8 After many days you will be summoned; in the <u>latter years you will come into the land that is restored from the sword, whose inhabitants have been gathered from many nations</u> to the mountains of <u>Israel which had been a continual waste;</u> but its people were brought out from the nations, <u>and they are living securely,</u> all of them.

In this verse God talks about *"after many days"* and *"in the latter years,"* which I believe is our present time. Also note *"into the land that is restored from the sword."* This occurred on May 14, 1948, with the re-establishment of the State of Israel. Also *"whose inhabitants have been gathered from many nations to the mountains of Israel."* This has happened, largely, for the last sixty-six years. God is talking about the Jews who were scattered to all corners of the earth, by Him, at the destruction of the second Temple, in Jerusalem, in 70 AD. Their descendants today are now, in the latter years, gathering back into Israel. This prophesied re-gathering of the Jews, from all over the world, restores them to their homeland, per Jeremiah 16:15. Also, *"Israel which had been a continual waste"* up until 1948 and mostly abandoned desert for almost 1,900 years. This was because the Jews were not in their homeland. God's land Israel was abandoned and desolate. Since Israel's rebirth in 1948, it has become economically vibrant and beautiful again. Finally, what about living in security? As discussed earlier, Israelites live in security, because they have the most powerful army in the region. They know they can defend themselves. Right now their neighbors also know this and can really do nothing large-scale against Israel on their own. But the building hatred has caused the enemies of Israel to start getting bold.

Jeremiah 16:14-15
14 Therefore behold, days are coming, declares the Lord, when it will no longer be said, 'As the Lord lives, who

brought up the sons of Israel out of the land of Egypt,' [15] *but, 'As the Lord lives, who brought up the sons of Israel from the land of the north and from all the countries where He had banished them.' For I will restore them to their own land which I gave to their fathers.*

In Jeremiah 16:14, during the days of Moses when God delivered Israel out of Egypt into the wilderness, the Jews knew God as **"He who brought up the sons of Israel out of the land of Egypt."** But, in our current time, He is now to be recognized as: **"He who brought the sons of Israel from the land of the north and from all countries where he had banished them."** This is happening today. Israelites should accept God as He who restores them to their own land . . . another sign of the times.

Going back to the enemy lands: each individual surrounding country can do nothing serious against Israel, at this time. They can pester Israel with things such as missile attacks from Hamas. So, Israel lives securely **internally** within **un-walled villages.** But what if these enemies, for some reason, become brazen and all decide, together with Gog of Magog as their leader, to form a coalition and come up with a plan to attack Israel as a large group? Could this happen? Yes. Let's look at Ezekiel 38:10-11.

Ezekiel 38:10-11
[10] *'Thus says the Lord God, It will come about on that day, that thoughts will come into your mind and you will devise an evil plan,* [11] *and you will say, 'I will go up against the land of <u>un-walled villages</u>. I will go against those who are at rest, that live securely, all of them living without walls and having no bars or gates,*

According to these verses, soon the enemy countries surrounding Israel will devise an evil plan, **a coalition** to go against Israel. When I tell you, shortly, what countries, today, match up with the prophesied regions in Ezekiel 38, you will see how they all might soon become a bit embolden: God tells us what will happen to much of the enemy's lands and armies, in this upcoming battle:

Ezekiel 38:16

16 and you will come up against My people Israel like a cloud to cover the land. It shall come about in the <u>last days</u> that I will bring you against My land, so that the nations may know Me when I am sanctified through you before their eyes, O Gog.

Ezekiel 38:18-20

18 It will come about on that day, when Gog comes against the land of Israel, declares the Lord God, that My fury will mount up in My anger. 19 In My zeal and in My blazing wrath I declare that on that day there will surely be a great earthquake in the land of Israel. 20 The fish of the sea, the birds of the heavens, the beasts of the field, all the creeping things that creep on the earth, and all the men who are on the face of the earth will shake at My presence;

Ezekiel 38:22-23

22 With pestilence and with blood I will enter into judgment with him; and I will rain on him and on his troops, and on the many peoples who are with him, a torrential rain, with hailstones, fire and brimstone. 23 I will magnify Myself, sanctify Myself, and make Myself known in the sight of many nations; and they will know that I am the Lord.

Ezekiel 39:3-6

3 I will strike your bow from your left hand and dash down your arrows from your right hand. 4 You will fall on the mountains of Israel, you and all your troops and the peoples who are with you; I will give you as food to every kind of predatory bird and beast of the field. 5 You will fall on the open field; for it is I who have spoken, declares the Lord God. 6 And I will send fire upon Magog and those who inhabit the coastlands in safety;

God, Himself, will destroy all of the armies and governments of the enemy countries He causes to come against Israel. God, on His own, will take all the glory, so the world will know He is Lord. I think God, with this attack, also wants to give all the earth one final clear chance to accept Him before the Tribulation comes. Only a very few will recognize Him or even give Him credit, even after this bold and spectacular event.

Some of you probably think God is talking about this battle happening inside the Tribulation, but is He really? No. It is interesting to note that God often uses the term *"latter years."* *"Latter years"* and *"last days"* refers to the time just prior to and including the Tribulation.

Ezekiel 39:9-10
9 Then those who inhabit the cities of Israel will go out and make fires with the weapons and burn them, both shields and bucklers, bows and arrows, war clubs and spears, and for seven years they will make fires of them. 10 They will not take wood from the field or gather firewood from the forests, for they will make fires with the weapons; and they will take the spoil of those who despoiled them and seize the plunder of those who plundered them, declares the Lord GOD.

We are told Israel will burn all of the destroyed weapons from this Ezekiel attack that fell upon their land for a period of seven years.

Earlier, I mentioned, during the first half of the horrible Tribulation, no one will find it possible to build anything, and one half of the world population will perish. As I stated, most people in the Tribulation will do everything they can to survive. At the midpoint, three and one half years in, everybody will flee from Israel due to fear for their lives from the newly Satan-indwelled Antichrist. Because of this, Israel (the people) will no longer have the ability to burn things inside Israel (the land). This logically means the burning will need to start at a bare minimum of about three and a half years prior to the Tribulation, starting after the Ezekiel attack.

Earlier, I referred to nine territories or tribes God mentions will be involved in the Ezekiel 38 attack. This list represented certain countries and tribes in existence 2,500 years ago. Today, these original geographic areas include many new smaller countries, all with current contemporary names.

Additionally over the years, the tribes within the original land areas expanded and migrated in all directions, including up to Russia and also to Western Europe. Descendants of the original nine tribes live in distant lands due to this migration. Therefore, we can include outside lands today into the Ezekiel equation. So, which countries and tribes today fit within the original nine territories or tribes listed in Ezekiel 38?

Geographical locations where descendants of the tribes from these original areas live today or have migrated indicate the majority of the countries are: Afghanistan, Pakistan, Tajikistan, Turkmenistan, Azerbaijan, Armenia, Georgia, Turkey, Iraq, Iran, Lebanon, UAE, Syria, Jordan, Kuwait, Egypt, Bahrain, Uzbekistan, parts of India, parts of Saudi Arabia, parts of China, parts of Greece, Kyrgyzstan, parts of Eastern Europe—including Germany—also Russia and Libya, and other small countries in Northeastern Africa.

Of course, I am not sure if all these countries will be involved; but they all fit, related to the current-day location of populations from the nine regions listed in Ezekiel 38. Russia, Germany and parts of Eastern Europe are outside of the original geographic areas listed in Ezekiel 38. I find it interesting that their population base consists of the descendants of tribes traced back to Japheth, the Son of Noah originally existing in Persia. Gomer and Magog, Tubal, and Meshach were literal sons of Japheth. Also, a strong Islamic influence and severe anti-Semitism exists in both Russia and Germany at this time. Russia is a strong ally of Iran and other Islamic states. They appear to be arming them now, possibly for some coming military action in the near future. Russia has a major military seaport in Syria. In addition, I think God may still have a score to settle with Germany for WWII. The Germans are descendants of Persia and they still hate the Jews, to this day. With a new German Neo-Nazi movement growing larger by the day, God may want to deal with them Himself. It is currently illegal to be a Nazi in Germany, but a large, rapidly growing, underground movement does exist. Since this underground group also wants to rid the world of the Jews, their destruction by God might make perfect sense.

Saudi Arabia houses the top two of the three most valued and holy locations in the Islamic faith: Mecca and Medina. The Al-Aqsa Mosque and the Dome of the Rock in Jerusalem is the third most holy Islamic site in the world. It currently sits right on top of the Temple Mount site. The new third Jewish Temple must locate on this mount. An inscription on the inside of the Dome of the Rock says, specifically, **god has no son** . . . a clear example of Jesus being *"profaned"* as explained earlier in Ezekiel 39:7. This displeases God.

With all this evidence, it would appear that God intends to deal directly with the Islamic religion that has hated and *"profaned"* His Son so severely. This seems to make sense logistically for a couple of additional reasons. God's Biblical intent, regarding the end of the Islamic influence, is the basis for many factors related to the Ezekiel battle. Also, I do not think the Antichrist can or will be Islamic; God needs them out of the way because Islam would never allow peace with Israel in any form. Also, the Islamic faith would never accept a One World Church that allowed involvement to anyone who was not Islamic.

This Islamic removal by God will open the door for the creation of the One World Government and One World Church so the Antichrist can come on the scene. The Ezekiel attack will, most likely, destroy the Al-Aqsa Mosque and Dome of the Rock in Jerusalem. This will remove all resistance in making the Temple Mount ready for the rebuilding of the new third Jewish Temple. Additionally, if God were to destroy Mecca and Medina in Saudi Arabia, it would decimate the entire Islamic faith system.

God will kill the vast majority of the enemy soldiers involved against Israel. The Islamic influence will not exist any longer in any viable form. Most definitely the Bible and the Quran contradict each other. They do, however, share full agreement about one thing: both say this future battle against Israel will occur, and possibly very soon. There can be only one victor.

Some year's back Iran's former president, Mr. Ahmadinejad, stated openly that Iran desired to *"wipe Israel off the face of the earth."* This statement by Mr. Ahmadinejad is surreal, when reading Psalm 83:4 at the end of this chapter. When the Islamic world attacks Israel, I believe they expect this will usher in the arrival of their **final twelfth Imam,** the **Mahdi**, who, in the Islamic faith, is their Savior of mankind. The God of Abraham, Isaac, and Jacob says He will *"put a hook in their jaws"* and bring them (Islam) against Israel. Could this idea of ushering in their Mahdi possibly be the hook God is talking about in Ezekiel 38:4?

Ezekiel 38:4
⁴ I will turn you about and put hooks into your jaws, and I will bring you out, and all your army, horses and horsemen, all of them splendidly attired, a great company with buckler and shield, all of them wielding swords;

God tells us all this, and everyone needs to pay careful attention to the coming events. I understand that our Islamic friends may totally disagree with this entire assessment of what is to come. Their Quran says something completely different. I understand this. I know Islam has stated a desire to remove Israel from this world and this should not be news to anybody. Until an attack by Islam occurs against Israel, which the Bible says *"shall happen,"* this is all only conjecture on both sides based on different and diametrically opposing individual faith systems.

As previously explained, I believe we will all actually see this attack on Israel between now and mid-2017. The Jewish faith believes in something called the **"Shemitah"** (Sabbatical cycles). They happen in seven-year installments. 2001 and 2008 were Sabbatical years—the Jewish years 5761 and 5768, respectively. The next one will be from the <u>fall of 2014 to the fall 2015</u>, Jewish year 5,775. As we all know, the United States received a Godly wake-up warning in New York back in 2001, and another with the financial crash in 2008—both in Sabbatical years and both in September of those years, at the tail end of each cycle. Note the two events in 2001 and 2008 both related to New York—the financial hub of the world at that time. These events did not only relate to the United States alone. They had world-wide impact.

Presently, many books talk about the four Blood Moons (the tetrad) of 2014-2015. Blood Moons are lunar eclipses that make the moon look reddish (dark orange). Four in quick sequence is a rare astrological event. Originally presented in the book *Blood Moons,* by Pastor Mark Biltz, this idea has created a great deal of enthusiasm. Some commentators say the 2014-2015 moons represent God's key sign of His return. But is this what is really happening?

The Bible talks about *"the moon turning into blood"* as singular events, prior to the Tribulation, in Joel 2:31, Isaiah 13:10, and Acts 2:20. God does not use the terminology **blood moons** in His Bible, but certainly *"the moon turning into blood"* implies something similar. The current books out today on this subject infer that tetrads happen when monumental events occur related to Israel. One supposedly happened in 1948 when Israel was reborn, and another during the six-day war in 1967.

Historical records indicate that the 1948 tetrad actually occurred between 4-13-49 and 9-25-50, a year after the 1948 supposed time frame. One interesting fact is overlooked regarding the 2014–2015 tetrad cycle: if tetrads have great significance related to Israel, note that some of the four blood moon events, in this cycle, will not be visible inside Israel. A rather significant omission.

The Bible **never references** any series of **four consecutive blood moons** happening together, or as a grouping, having any prophetic significance. Additionally, when God talks about *"moons turning into blood"* in the Bible, this phenomenon happens along with, and in conjunction with, other signs. It is never a stand-alone event.

Acts 2:19-21
[19] And I will grant wonders in the sky above, and signs on the earth beneath, blood, and fire, and vapors of smoke. [20] The sun will be turned into darkness, and the <u>moon into blood</u>, before the great and glorious day of the Lord shall come. [21] 'And it shall be, that everyone who calls upon the name of the Lord shall be saved.'

Also, if these events happen at significant historical times related to Israel, why do records not show a tetrad happening at the destruction of the temple in 70 AD, or during the Holocaust? These theories appear to include some selective omissions.

I believe the prophesied *"moon turning into blood"* in the Bible scheduled to happen in the last days just prior to the Rapture will be a **supernatural** God event . . . nothing we can predict. I believe the blood moon God will provide unexpectedly will not be dark orange; it will be **bright blood red,** without any doubt, **seen by the entire world**.

This Ezekiel attack, when quickly completed, will also afford Christians a small bit of remaining time to evangelize. God offers a window of opportunity to share about the love of Jesus, and what He is doing in our world for us to see. This Ezekiel attack will be an incredible eye-opening God event for all of mankind to see for His glory alone.

In Chapter 1, I mentioned how God decides who our leaders will be. He places the right people in power at just the right times, for His purpose. How interesting, that our current president has implied he may have no real desire to assist in any war on behalf of Israel. They are, essentially, abandoned. We have the first president since Israel's rebirth in 1948 to take this position. Also interesting, he plans to end all of our current military conflicts in the Middle East and bring the vast majority of our troops home by the summer of 2015. This very year falls at the end of this current seven-year Sabbatical cycle. God is protecting our country through our president. Our current president fits in perfectly with what the Bible tells us will soon happen. Our president, through his thought process about the world, is actually bringing the majority of our beloved soldiers home to safety before God starts His Ezekiel battle. When the attack on Israel happens, our president will most probably provide only a mild response.

This attack will represent our final Godly warning, not only for Christians, but for all of mankind. Christians will be around, after this attack, for only about another three to four years — pending the completion of all God's other final prophecies, required before the visual Rapture and the start of the Tribulation.

We will see the beginning of Israel burning the destroyed weapons of the losing armies that will fall on their land. This attack will cause a worldwide financial reorganization. Back in **Road Map** prophecy #22, I explained how I believe after Ezekiel 38 the State of Israel will become larger. This has many ramifications. The oil fields in Persia would become a part of Israel as they will have gained back most of the real estate God gave to the Twelve sons of Jacob. Babylon, the ultimate new seat of world government, will be inside a new geographic boundary of the larger Israel. Additionally, Israel with this new land and all the oil fields may become the most wealthy and powerful country in the world, almost overnight—the world's new mega superpower. The Jewish tribal system can then be reestablished. The reestablishment of the twelve tribes of Israel within this newly obtained land mass will need to happen so the 144,000 can come on the scene quickly, and must occur before the Tribulation starts. God will have done all this for Israel and unfortunately will get little or no credit for doing so.

After this major event, the world will appear to need to come together in unity to rebuild as one big global family. This will quickly usher in the prophesied One World Government, the formation of ten world divisions and then, following quickly, the Antichrist will come on the scene. The new capital of the World will soon be in Babylon. Babylon will become the center of commerce, politics, and religion—the new cultural center of the world.

Earlier I told you how the vast majority of the enemy army's soldiers that come against Israel will die in this battle. In fact, so many bodies will lay dead on Israel's ground that God will send predatory birds and beasts of the field to devour them per Ezekiel 39:4-5. An interesting phenomenon is occurring in Israel today. Each season, predatory migrating birds used to fly over Israel to their intended destinations but this has recently changed. Many of these specific predatory birds now take permanent residency inside Israel. No way is this happening by random chance.

Also mentioned earlier: the Christian community seems confused as to when people think the Ezekiel 38 and 39 attack will happen. Revelation 20:7-10 mentions **Gog and Magog** one brief time. **Gog and Magog** is a generally accepted reference to the Ezekiel 38 and 39 battle. Some say this single mention in Revelation indicates this grand attack talked about, in great detail, in

Ezekiel 38 and 39 (two chapters, fifty-two verses) happens during the Tribulation period and not before. When you read Revelation 20:7 carefully, you will notice a significant phrase: *"And when the thousand years are completed."* These Revelation 20:7-10 verses talk about something that will happen at the end of the **Millennium,** not inside the Tribulation. The **Millennium** is a 1,000-year period after the completion of the Tribulation, where Jesus will reign on the entire earth. If the idea that the **Gog and Magog** battle happens inside the Tribulation were true, why didn't God describe this battle inside the book of Revelation, including all its detail, instead of in Ezekiel? Because, at the end of the **Millennium,** it will have already happened over one-thousand years earlier. But how can we know this?

In Revelation 20:7-10 Jesus talks about the final defeat of Satan at the end of the **Millennium.** Satan is briefly freed for a short period of time at the end of the **thousand-year** Reign of Jesus. Remember, we are talking about Satan here and this will become clear, shortly. In the **Millennium,** Christ is with us on earth so why would Ezekiel 38 and 39 need to happen when Jesus is here as the leader of the world? It wouldn't.

Revelation 20:10 tells of the quick final defeat of Satan, with God throwing him into the lake of fire where he *"will be tormented day and night forever and ever."* The reference to **Gog and Magog** in Revelation 20:8 is a **metaphor**. **Gog and Magog** in Revelation 20:8 is representative of how swift and decisive God's final victory over Satan will be, similar to the quick, decisive defeat by God in the Ezekiel 38 and 39 attack that will have happened ages earlier.

The Ezekiel 38 and 39 battle is **not against Satan;** it is against the **enemy armies surrounding Israel**. The Revelation 20:8 event is not against **the surrounding armies of Israel** but, rather, **against Satan**. Two, distinctly different events.

For the people who still say that Ezekiel 38 and 39 must happen inside the Tribulation, here is what the Bible tells us. Let's take another look at Ezekiel 38:8 for clear understanding:

Ezekiel 38:8
⁸ After many days you will be summoned; in the latter years you will come into the land that is restored from the sword, whose inhabitants have been gathered from many nations to the mountains of Israel which had been a continual waste; but its people were brought out from the nations, and they are living securely, all of them.

Note, five specific details mentioned in this verse:
1. *"in the latter years"*
2. *"the land that is restored from the sword"*
3. *"whose inhabitants have been gathered from many nations to the mountains of Israel"*
4. *"(Israel) which had been a continual waste"*
5. *"and they are living securely"*

All five of these items must exist, or be in place, prior to the Tribulation. The Ezekiel attack happens before the start of the Tribulation.

As secularism grows and with Islam neutralized, all the Jesus-believing Christians will be the last people demonized. The growing group of worldwide secularists of the New One World Church and the False Prophets minions will scorn and ridicule us. I classify any supposed Christian members who join or stay within the new One World Church as secularists. Their compromises regarding Jesus will likely put them into the Tribulation.

Mohamed, the founder of the Islamic faith (632 AD), claimed to be an Ishmaelite, a descendant of Ishmael. Ishmael and Isaac are half-brothers, the two sons of Abraham. They have a significant place in both history and what is happening today in the world.

Right after this next section on the Ishmaelites, I have attached the prayer by Asaph in his Psalm 83. This **imprecatory Psalm** is a prayer asking God at some future time to *"bring down vengeance"* on the Ishmaelite wing of Abraham's family, Islam.

SO WHO ARE THE ISHMAELITES?

This goes back to Abraham in the Bible. In Genesis, Abraham receives a promise from God saying he will father many nations and many peoples. But Abraham did not understand this because he had no children, and both he and his wife Sarah were beyond child-bearing years. Because of Sarah's age she decided to offer her maid servant, Hagar, to Abraham so he could create an heir. This was not what God intended, but Abraham did have a son with Hagar. They named him Ishmael.

Genesis 16:15-16
15 So Hagar bore Abram a son; and Abram called the name of his son, whom Hagar bore, <u>Ishmael.</u> 16 Abram was eighty-six years old when Hagar bore Ishmael to him.

God wanted Abraham and Sarah to trust Him, but they decided to take things into their own hands and *"Ishmael"* became an heir. God then **created** a fertile womb for Sarah, in her old age, and she bore Abraham a son named *"Isaac."*

Genesis 21:1-3
1 Then the Lord took note of Sarah as He had said, and the Lord did for Sarah as He had promised. 2 So Sarah conceived and bore a son to Abraham in his old age, at the appointed time of which God had spoken to him. 3 Abraham called the name of his son who was born to him, whom Sarah bore to him, <u>Isaac</u>.

Isaac is the true heir and seed intended by God as mentioned in Genesis 21:12-13.

Genesis 21:12-13
¹² But God said to Abraham, "Do not be distressed because of the lad and your maid; whatever Sarah tells you, listen to her, <u>for through Isaac your descendants shall be named.</u> ¹³ And of the son of the maid I will make a nation also, because he is your descendant."

God also tells Hagar that He will make a nation (large) out of Ishmael in Genesis 16:10-11.

Genesis 16:10-11
¹⁰ Moreover, the angel of the Lord said to her, "<u>I will greatly multiply your descendants so that they will be too many to count.</u>"¹¹ The angel of the Lord said to her further, "behold, you are with child, and you will bear a son and you shall call his name Ishmael, Because the Lord has given heed to your affliction.

Jews and Christians claim relationship with Abraham through Isaac (Jesus also came through the line of Isaac). Genesis 21-12 also makes it clear that through Isaac, Abraham's descendants shall be named.

Those in the Islamic faith claim their lineage to Abraham through Ishmael. The Quran disputes the claim that Isaac is the legitimate heir per the Bible. The Quran also claims that Ishmael is the only true heir, thus the controversy exists to this day. Per the Bible, one Son is legitimate, in the eyes of God, and the other is legitimate in the eyes of the other god. Only one is correct, so these Deities cannot be the same entity. As a matter of fact, per the Bible, God tells us that Ishmael, as the older brother, was born into affliction and God forced Ishmael's hand to be against everyone and everybody would be against him, per Genesis 16:11-12:

Genesis 16:11-12
[11] The angel of the Lord said to her further, "behold,"
you are with child, and you will bear a son; and you
shall call his name Ishmael, because the Lord has given
heed to your affliction.[12] "He will be a wild donkey of a
man, his hand will be against everyone, and everyone's
hand will be against him; and he will live to the east of
all his brothers."

Ishmael (Islam) taunted Isaac (Jews) from the very beginning, and this has followed right through to our current-day.

The Ishmaelite's (Islam) want to wipe out Israel, so their name will be remembered no more. In Psalm 83 below, the writer, Asaph basically prays and asks God to destroy the Ishmaelite's for His glory and their ultimate humiliation.

Some Bible commentators today erroneously tell us that Psalm 83 depicts a **prophesied** attack by Israel on its surrounding enemy nations **prior** to Ezekiel 38 and 39. There are serious flaws with this thinking. But why?

What are Psalms? By definition, in most instances, they are **sacred songs, prayers, or poems.** Asaph was a skilled singer and poet. As mentioned earlier, Jesus Himself spoke about the **Tenach** in Luke 24:44. He made a clear separation between the *"Law of Moses"* the *"Prophets"* and the *"Psalms,"* all distinctly different.

Luke 24:44
[44] Now He said to them, "These are My words which
I spoke to you while I was still with you, that all
things which are written about Me in the Law of Moses
and the Prophets and the Psalms must be fulfilled."

In Psalm 83, below, please pay specific attention to the underlined items in verses 1, 9, 13, 15, and 18. Asaph cannot possibly be asking the State of Israel to do this attack. **He is asking**

God to personally do this for His glory. Psalm 83, specifically, is an **imprecatory prayer, not a prophecy,** asking God to bring His future Ezekiel 38 and 39 battle against the Ishmaelites. Additionally, per Psalm 83:17, only God can fulfill the following: *"Let them be ashamed and dismayed forever, and let them be humiliated and perish. "* Israel does not have this capability; only God does. Also, if the surrounding countries are **dismayed** and **humiliated** *"forever"* and they *"perish,"* the enemy would no longer be around or have the strength to come against Israel for any future secondary Ezekiel 38 and 39 attack. *"Forever"* is forever, and *"perish"* means no more.

Psalm 83

[1] O God, do not remain quiet; do not be silent and, O God, do not be still. [2] For behold, Your enemies make an uproar, And those who hate You have exalted themselves. [3] They make shrewd plans against Your people, And conspire together against Your treasured ones. [4] They have said, Come, and let us wipe them out as a nation, that the name of Israel be remembered no more. [5] For they have conspired together with one mind; against You they make a covenant: [6] The tents of Edom and the Ishmaelites, Moab and the Hagrites; [7] Gebal and Ammon and Amalek, Philistia with the inhabitants of Tyre; [8] Assyria also has joined with them; They have become a help to the children of Lot Selah. [9] Deal with them as with Midian, As with Sisera and Jabin at the torrent of Kishon, [10] who were destroyed at En-dor, Who became as dung for the ground. [11] Make their nobles like Oreb and Zeeb and all their princes like Zebah and Zalmunna, [12] who said, let us possess for ourselves the pastures of God. [13] O my God, make them like the whirling dust, like chaff before the wind. [14] Like fire that burns the forest and like a flame that sets the mountains on fire, [15] So pursue them with Your tempest and terrify them with Your storm. [16] Fill their faces with dishonor, that they may seek your name, O Lord. [17] Let them

be ashamed and dismayed forever, and let them be humiliated and perish, [18] that they may know that You alone, whose name is the Lord, are the Most High over all the earth.

In this text, Asaph clearly asks God (not the State of Israel) to destroy the Ishmaelites for His glory. He gives multiple examples of battles that happened earlier within societies in history and resulted in great victories. They represent what Asaph is asking God to do at some point in the future. The people of that day would have known the type of victory over the Ishmaelites that Asaph asked God to achieve in his prayer, by all the examples he listed in Psalm 83.

We live in an incredible time in history. I strongly believe we will soon witness Ezekiel 38 and 39 as addressed in this chapter and will soon see all of the additional events explained in this book. God will do all of this out of love for us. I only hope that Christians, and maybe even some non-Christians, will pay attention and understand what they witness.

Ezekiel 38

PRIOR TO THE TRIBULATION BATTLE WITH ONLY A LIMITED NUMBER OF NATIONS

[1] And the word of the LORD came to me saying, [2] Son of man, set your face toward Gog of the land of Magog, the prince of Rosh, Meshech, and Tubal, and prophecy against him [3] and say, 'thus says the Lord GOD, Behold, I am against you, O Gog, prince of Rosh, Meshech, and Tubal. [4] I will turn you about and put hooks into your jaws, and I will bring you out, and all your army, horses and horsemen, all of them splendidly attired, a great company with buckler and shield, all of them wielding swords; [5] Persia, Ethiopia, and Put with them, all of them with shield and helmet; [6] Gomer with all its troops; Beth-togarmah from the remote parts of the north with all its troops - many

peoples with you.[7] Be prepared, and prepare yourself, you and all your companies that are assembled about you, and be a guard for them. [8] After many days you will be summoned; in the latter years you will come into the land that is restored from the sword, whose inhabitants have been gathered from many nations to the mountains of Israel which had been a continual waste; but its people were brought out from the nations, and they are living securely, all of them. [9] You will go up, you will come like a storm; you will be like a cloud covering the land, you and all your troops, and many peoples with you.[10] 'Thus says the Lord GOD, It will come about on that day, that thoughts will come into your mind and you will devise an evil plan, [11] and you will say, 'I will go up against the land of un- walled villages. I will go against those who are at rest, that live securely, all of them living without walls and having no bars or gates, [12] to capture spoil and to seize plunder, to turn your hand against the waste places which are now inhabited, and against the people who are gathered from the nations, who have acquired cattle and goods, who live at the center of the world. [13] Sheba and Dedan and the merchants of Tarshish with all its villages will say to you, 'Have you come to capture spoil? Have you assembled your company to seize plunder, to carry away silver and gold, to take away cattle and goods, to capture great spoil? [14] Therefore prophecy, son of man, and say to Gog, 'Thus says the Lord GOD, On that day when My people Israel are living securely, will you not know it? [15] You will come from your place out of the remote parts of the north, you and many peoples with you, all of them riding on horses, a great assembly and a mighty army; [16] and you will come up against My people Israel like a cloud to cover the land. It shall come about in the last days that I will bring you against My land, so that the nations may know Me when I am sanctified through you before their eyes, O Gog.[17] 'Thus says the Lord GOD, Are you the one of whom I spoke in former days through My servants the prophets of Israel, who prophesied in those days for many years that I would bring you against them? [18] It will come about on that day, when Gog comes against the land of Israel, declares the Lord GOD, that My fury will mount up in My anger. [19] In My zeal and in My blazing wrath I declare that on that day there will surely be a great earthquake in the land of Israel. [20] The fish of the sea, the birds of the heavens, the beasts of the field, all the creeping things that creep on the earth, and all the men who are on the face of the earth will shake at My presence; the mountains also will be thrown down, the steep pathways will collapse and every wall will fall to the ground. [21] I will call for a sword against him on all My mountains, declares the Lord GOD. Every man's sword will be against his brother. [22] With pestilence and with blood I will enter into judgment with him; and I will rain on him and on his troops, and on the many peoples who are with him, a torrential rain, with hailstones, fire and brimstone. [23] I will magnify Myself, sanctify Myself, and make Myself known in the sight of many nations; and they will know that I am the LORD.

Ezekiel 39

[1] And you, son of man, prophecy against Gog and say, 'Thus says the Lord GOD, Behold, I am against you, O Gog, prince of Rosh, Meshech and Tubal; [2] and I will turn you around, drive you on, take you up from the remotest parts of the north and bring you against the mountains of Israel. [3] I will strike your bow from your left hand and dash down your arrows from your right hand. [4] You will fall on the mountains of Israel, you and all your troops and the peoples who are with you; <u>I will give you as food to every kind of predatory bird and beast of the field.</u> [5] You will fall on the open field; for it is I who have spoken, declares the Lord GOD. [6] And I will send fire upon Magog and those who inhabit the coastlands in safety; and they will know that I am the LORD. [7] My holy name I will make known in the midst of My people Israel; and I will not let My holy name be profaned anymore. And the nations will know that I am the LORD, the Holy One in Israel. [8] Behold, it is coming and it shall be done, declares the Lord GOD. That is the day of which I have spoken. [9] Then those who inhabit the cities of Israel will go out and make fires with the weapons and burn

them, both shields and bucklers, bows and arrows, war clubs and spears, and for seven years they will make fires of them. [10]They will not take wood from the field or gather firewood from the forests, for they will make fires with the weapons; and they will take the spoil of those who despoiled them and seize the plunder of those who plundered them, declares the Lord GOD.[11] On that day I will give Gog a burial ground there in Israel, the valley of those who pass by east of the sea, and it will block off those who would pass by. So they will bury Gog there with all his horde, and they will call it the valley of Hamon-gog. [12] For seven months the house of Israel will be burying them in order to cleanse the land. [13] Even all the people of the land will bury them; and it will be to their renown on the day that I glorify Myself, declares the Lord GOD. [14] They will set apart men who will constantly pass through the land, burying those who were passing through, even those left on the surface of the ground, in order to cleanse it. At the end of seven months they will make a search. [15] As those who pass through the land pass through and anyone sees a man's bone, then he will set up a marker by it until the buriers have buried it in the valley of Hamon-gog. [16] And even the name of the city will be Hamonah. So they will cleanse the land.

ARMAGEDDON AT THE END OF THE TRIBULATION BATTLE WITH ALL THE NATIONS OF THE EARTH

[17] As for you, son of man, thus says the Lord GOD, 'Speak to every kind of bird and to every beast of the field, Assemble and come, gather from every side to My sacrifice which I am going to sacrifice for you, as a great sacrifice on the mountains of Israel, that you may eat flesh and drink blood. [18] You will eat the flesh of mighty men and drink the blood of the princes of the earth, as though they were rams, lambs, goats and bulls, all of them fatlings of Bashan. [19] So you will eat fat until you are glutted, and drink blood until you are drunk, from My sacrifice which I have sacrificed for you. [20] You will be glutted at My

table with horses and charioteers, with mighty men and all the men of war, declares the Lord GOD. 21 And I will set My glory among the nations; and all the nations will see My judgment which I have executed and My hand which I have laid on them. 22 And the house of Israel will know that I am the LORD their God from that day onward. 23 The nations will know that the house of Israel went into exile for their iniquity because they acted treacherously against Me, and I hid My face from them; so I gave them into the hand of their adversaries, and all of them fell by the sword. 24 According to their uncleanness and according to their transgressions I dealt with them, and I hid My face from them. 25 Therefore thus says the Lord GOD, Now I will restore the fortunes of Jacob and have mercy on the whole house of Israel; and I will be jealous for My holy name. 26 They will forget their disgrace and all their treachery which they perpetrated against Me, when they live securely on their own land with no one to make them afraid. 27 When I bring them back from the peoples and gather them from the lands of their enemies, then I shall be sanctified through them in the sight of the many nations. 28 Then they will know that I am the LORD their God because I made them go into exile among the nations, and then gathered them again to their own land; and I will leave none of them there any longer. 29 I will not hide My face from them any longer, for I will have poured out My Spirit on the house of Israel, declares the Lord GOD.

2 Timothy 4:3-4

[3] *For the time will come when they will not endure sound doctrine; but wanting to have their ears tickled, they will accumulate for themselves teachers in accordance to their own desires,* [4] *and will turn away their ears from the truth and will turn aside to myths.*

CHAPTER 4

DECEPTIONS

The Deceiver knows we are close to the Lord's return at the visual Rapture. He does not want people to recognize this, so he uses multiple, subtle deceptions and myths to fool many. God tells all of us to . . . take great care in these last days.

Biblical deceptions are actions or theories where the creation, or man, begins to think and believe they know more than their Creator. At this time in history, humanity—with the guidance and support of the Deceiver—rebels against the Creator more than ever. God warns about this happening in the last days. He battles against His fallen creation, the Deceiver. The Deceiver has only one goal: to keep as many people from God as possible. He knows he will not get to heaven and he knows God's supremacy has power. He also understands he will ultimately lose both the battles and the war. In spite of his awareness, he still arrogantly thinks he can change the outcome. He perceives the possibility of a victory.

Right now, one of the biggest deceptions of all faces us daily. Everything in our world regarding right and wrong is backward. What God tells us is right and moral is now ignored and discounted in the eyes of the majority. Unfortunately, the secular world now compassionately tolerates and accepts what God considers sin. The Deceiver would have us think if we are truly intelligent, we should have no problem seeing things his way. In fact, when a Christian tries to denounce an action or theory because of Biblical teachings, many people immediately marginalize and label us as intolerant or phobic.

Isaiah 5:20-21
20 Woe to those who call evil good, and good evil; who substitute darkness for light and light for darkness; who substitute bitter for sweet and sweet for bitter! 21 Woe to those who are wise in their own eyes and clever in their own sight!

God tells us to act cautiously when we see this happening. He even says those who accept evil as good should take great care. God specifically tells us in Isaiah 5:20-21 *"woe to those who call evil good..."*

So, our nemesis deceives man in many ways. He uses indifference and proclaims that errors and cultural myths fill the Bible. The Deceiver uses the opinions and the beliefs of alleged Bible scholars. He uses only those who agree with him as the authenticators of his new corrupt truth—not the truth of the all-knowing original author, God. If anyone perceives the Bible as containing only stories and myths, the Deceiver can tell them that he (Satan) isn't real, but rather a figment of their imaginations, and to think he exists borders on lunacy.

2 Timothy 4:3-4
³ For the time will come when they will not endure sound doctrine; but wanting to have their <u>ears tickled</u>, they will accumulate for themselves teachers in accordance to their own desires, ⁴ and will turn away their ears from the truth and will turn aside to <u>myths</u>.

"Ears tickled," "myths." Secular man has great difficulty perceiving God's tremendous power. I believe God holds the universe in the palms of His hands. Most of the secular world cannot accept the grandeur of God.

Ephesians 4:17-18
¹⁷ So this I say, and affirm together with the Lord, that you walk no longer just as the Gentiles also walk, in the futility of their mind, ¹⁸ being darkened in their understanding, excluded from the life of God because of the ignorance that is in them, because of the hardness of their heart;

To achieve his goals the Deceiver uses ignorance, which comes from a lack of true knowledge, true information, and true education. He does this with a great sense of pride. The secular world, his realm, calls Christians ignorant for not accepting, supposedly, proven scientific findings of things such as natural selection and the evolvement of man. God, however, is supernatural, and not bound by the limited amount of natural things He has selected to allow man to discover. He has not allowed us to know everything, yet.

Luke 21:34
34 *Be on guard, so that your hearts will not be weighted down with dissipation and drunkenness and the worries of life, and that day will not come on you suddenly like a trap;*

The Deceiver uses infiltration with diversions such as keeping us busy all day striving and searching for external pleasures in our lives. He tries to convince us that personal desires for wealth, lust, power, careers and success will make us happy. All at the cost of lost family, relationships, joy, and time with God. Faith loses out when the Deceiver successfully makes his enticing pleasures more attractive to us than what God offers.

Ephesians 6:10-13
10 *Finally, be strong in the Lord and in the strength of His might.* 11 *Put on the full armor of God, so that you will be able to stand firm against the schemes of the devil.* 12 *For our struggle is not against flesh and blood, but against the rulers, against the powers, against the world forces of this darkness, against the spiritual forces of wickedness in the heavenly places.* 13 *Therefore, take up the full armor of God, so that you will be able to resist in the evil day, and having done everything, to stand firm.*

God warns us about the perpetual spiritual warfare all around us. He provides the Bible to help us know what in our world comes from Him—everything sound, good, and true. He tells us to *"Put on the full armor of God."* He also gave us His Bible to inform us how to know the difference between His Holy Bible and the Deceiver's humanistic Bible. The humanistic Bible is the Deceiver's plan. Individually, we all need to choose which version to accept.

Many additional issues fall into the category of deception. One highly controversial topic I explore in this chapter brings about a grand deception: man's theory of natural evolution. Non-Christians may accept evolution . . . a free will choice. I directed the arguments made here at Christians who have accepted what I truly believe to be a flawed concept from a Biblical standpoint.

If we follow the literal genealogies in the Bible, God shows us that mankind, by His design, has lived on earth for only about 6,000 years. How can we know this? The Bible provides a full chronology of mankind from the first man Adam up to the birth of Christ. Genesis Chapter 5, Genesis 11:10-32 and Matthew 1:1-16 list by name the genealogies and the specific ages of Adam's descendants. A review of these scriptures reveals that God provides actual ages for each successive individual and, when summed up, this represents 4,000 years, from Adam to Christ's birth. Add the 2,000 years since Christ's first visit and the result is 6,000 years. This period of time relates to **only mankind,** and **not the earth itself.** This gets a bit complicated, but please follow my thinking.

If we do not accept what God says about **creating** Adam and Eve but, instead, choose to think that He used some non-stated alternate path, this creates a problem. A problem related to all faith in Jesus, in general. I have looked at both sides of this evolution question and feel confident with what the Bible says, and not what man has created as their new recently accepted alternate path, evolution.

I think the time will soon come when we'll walk on dangerous ground if we even talk about the creation view. Biblical thinking will indicate to secularists that a person lacks intellect and clings to outdated fables as only a fool would do. The time has, essentially, already arrived.

I find it interesting how, today, the evolution issue — even for Christians — appears divisive . . . a topic that generates heated debates even to the point of confrontation between believers. For some reason, it seems as if some Christians have drawn battle lines on this topic. But why? Why should a controversy regarding this subject even exist within the Christian family? The Deceiver wants this to happen.

Mark 3:25
25 *If a house is divided against itself, that house will not be able to stand.*

Satan wants division to happen within the Christian community, causing strife and infighting. This evolution issue is but one valid sample of a divide that will grow much worse in the faith community. God expects all Christians to use the Bible alone as our sole basis for theological learning and teaching. He says not to employ speculation (theory) or to accept the scientific interpretations of man, in this endeavor. As mankind becomes more prideful and arrogant and believes they are getting as smart as, or even possibly smarter, than some fictional God, this creates a much bigger problem. As this happens, mankind will make the very same deadly error Satan made through his pride. The need for the Bible or God's word or any need to rely on Him alone will become more and more deluded. God becomes excluded. If a theory created by mankind, in any form, causes even one person to walk away from God due to a false perception that God may be weak, the Deceiver succeeds.

I encourage any Christian who accepts the possibility of evolution to further explore the findings of supposed archeology and scientific interpretations. If you believe God could have used evolution to achieve life from the beginning, then please take the following steps:

- Find the specific Bible text proving evolution is something God has literally shown us in His word.
- Provide a full and complete outline of all the verses that clearly indicate God's intention to convey evolution as His desired design vehicle.

You will find this does not exist.

Some people will insist that science has proven the Theory of Evolution. We are told the Big Bang theory, for instance, helps to prove the concept. Because we can see the universe expanding in deep space through our great telescopes, supposedly over billions of years—doing mathematical calculations—they even go so far as to postulate how God had nothing to do with it.

Did you know, the Catholic Church diligently tries to discover extraterrestrial life? But why? It appears the Catholic Church, in this time of apostasy, has accepted a modern belief system leading to the conclusion that the solar system is one set of worlds around a single star with life on one of its planets. Since there are trillions of stars in the universe, they say it is arrogant for mankind not to believe that a big God has created life in only one place.

It is my understanding, on May 14, 2014, during his morning mass, Pope Francis was asked a question essentially as follows:

If — for example — tomorrow an expedition of Martians came, and some of them came to us, here … and one says, 'But I want to be baptized!' What would happen?

The Pope answered and said the church does not have a closed door and would baptize them. A tongue-in-cheek answer, right? Today, possibly, but soon, maybe not. Why diligently look for extraterrestrial life? Who actually benefits from this since God never mentions this in the Bible, anywhere? The Deceiver benefits.

This extraterrestrial search, however, seems severely flawed because of God's omnipotence. He can create anything to any size, at will. The size of the universe is, in fact, daunting in scale from our small limited human perspective, but its size means nothing to God. In His scale it is both immense and at the same time very small because He has no limits. God provides the universe to reveal His grandeur and unlimited nature.

The Catholic Jesuits operate, and the Vatican owns a majority interest in one of the best telescopes in the world located on the top of Mt. Graham, in Arizona. The group of Vatican scientists who run this equipment have come to the conclusion that the Big Bang (theory) is the most probable explanation for the formation of our world and universe. This all occurred over billions of years. So logically, we can no longer consider the six days of creation which God talks about in Genesis, the only serious possibility; it is allegorical.

A few interesting facts about the two Arizona telescopes: the Jesuits (the Catholic Church) own the VATT (Vatican Advanced Technology Telescope). There is also a grand second unit the LBT (Large Binocular Telescope). They form a consortium. The Jesuits can use the LBT at any time. The LBT telescope and its sophisticated, deep-space camera has a rather lengthy name. It is called a **Large, Binocular Telescope with Near Infrared Utility, with Camera, and Integral, Field unit for Extragalactic Research.** Take note of the underlined letters in the words in italics to see an interesting acronym. It is my understanding that the Catholic Church did not have anything to do with the naming of the LBT unit and has no responsibility for its nickname: **Lucifer.**

One of the lead Institutes on board to build the LBT telescope in Arizona was the Heidelberg University in the German State of Baden-Württemberg. The governor of this state, at that time, Erwin Teufel, was instrumental in obtaining funding for its construction. So, it is believed the telescope was nicknamed in his honor. Do you know what the German word or name **Teufel** translates to in the English language? It translates as the

Devil, Satan, or <u>Lucifer</u>. The intriguing thing: Teufel is a common name in Germany, right now. Nobody there understands what the fuss might be about. (Remember we talked about Germany in the Ezekiel 38 and 39 section.) After all, Lucifer is the fabled fallen angel in the Bible. The Germans actually say, **fabled**. Interestingly, the Catholic Church did not make much of a protest to this naming.

Germans with the surname Teufel tell us not to worry about this because Lucifer (Satan) in Latin is defined as the **bearer of light**, or the **"star of the morning."** In the Bible, the **"Morning Star"** does refer to both Satan and Jesus, but with a large separation and distinction. Satan was God's most beautiful **creation** and the highest possible angel. Jesus however; is God. When Satan fell, due to his arrogance and pride present in Isaiah 14:12-15, he was no longer the **"star of the morning"** in God's kingdom. After Satan's fall, all future references to the **"Morning Star"** always refer to the Messiah, the Christ, which of course, is Jesus, not the Devil. Remember, the Devil wants to be god, so he counterfeits everything and still believes he qualifies as a **"star of the morning."** It's interesting that the LBT telescope is right next door to the Catholic Church's VATT unit, and the Catholics use it often. One of the very tools they use on a regular basis to discredit what God says in His Bible is nicknamed **Lucifer**. The irony is palpable. How can this all be chance? It can't.

Only four-hundred years ago the Catholic Church did not allow research of the heavens for truth regarding the nature of the universe. In 1592 an astrologer by the name of Giordano Bruno came up with a theory that the earth revolved around the sun. The Catholic Church did not like this and lured him to Rome under the guise of giving him a job. When he arrived in Rome, Mr. Bruno was imprisoned. He withstood eight years of torture because he would not denounce his theory. The Catholic Hierarchy considered Mr. Bruno's theory as heresy and put him on trial. On February 19, 1600, his judge, Cardinal Robert Bellarmine, sentenced him to death. Not a simple, kind death, but a brutal barbaric death—all for his lack of penance related to Catholic doctrine. So how did he die? First, Mr. Bruno had his jaw clamped shut with an iron gag. Torturers drove spikes through his tongue and palate. They stripped him naked, and paraded him through the streets of Rome, then publically burned him at the stake. In **Road Map** prophecy #17, I made reference to the possibility that the Jesuits may not be as nice and kind as they want us to believe. The horrible, cruel, sadistic death that Mr. Bruno experienced was brought about by Cardinal Bellarmine—a Jesuit.

In the years following this event, between 1616 and 1633, Cardinal Ballarmine, who died in 1621, was initially a key player in trying Galileo for heresy, due to his new astrological discoveries. On July 22, 1633, the Catholic Church found Galileo **"gravely suspect of heresy"** and ordered him to indefinite imprisonment. He remained under house arrest until his death, in 1642.

Science is "systemic knowledge of the physical or material world gained through observation and experimentation." God has allowed us the ability to discover small pieces of the perfect design and harmony He put into existence. He did this so we can live and enjoy our daily lives productively. Let's be clear on this and not be fooled. God (the creator) is not bound to what we (the creation) have enjoyed as scientific constants regarding the universe. He established them. I will even venture to speculate that on the day of the visual Rapture and the start of the literal Tribulation, all the scientific norms God has allowed mankind to discover, up to that point, will be turned upside down. How can living humans visually rise into the sky (defying gravity) and disappear into the clouds never to be seen again? Remember those telescopes? After the Rapture, maybe the co-opted Catholic Church will say they found extraterrestrials and they removed all the looney Christians to cleanse the earth of a problem . . . a logical possibility, as the Deceiver will need a way to explain away to the world what they just saw happen.

After the visual Rapture, not all remaining people will remain deceived. Many will start to realize the science they thought proved things are constant and in harmony was flawed and that man really did not get to know everything. Should this really come as a surprise to informed Christians living today? No. I still take God's words literally, as spoken, and do not feel comfortable going down any path that deviates from His clear and simple stated concepts. I trust the literal words in the Bible.

The Bible has not changed for over 3,500 years and, intellectually, as mentioned before, we must decide whether or not the Bible is perfect. We cannot twist the words to make it fit our needs or our new enlightened scientific intelligence. We all know through observation, that all science, in our time, constantly changes almost on a daily basis, based on new information unknown yesterday. Since man is not perfect, who is to say scientific theories discovered by man are completely correct? Issues we thought factual only one-hundred years ago, have since been debunked and updated. I do agree, the science of man has evolved because it is man's creation (educated speculation). The Bible, however, is a constant, created by the perfect creator and not flawed in any way.

1 Corinthians 15: 12-19

[12] Now if Christ is preached, that He has been raised from the dead, how do some among you say that there is no resurrection of the dead? [13] But if there is no resurrection of the dead, not even Christ has been raised; [14] and if Christ has not been raised, then our preaching is vain, your faith also is vain. [15] Moreover we are even found to be false witnesses of God, because we testified against God that He raised Christ, whom He did not raise, if in fact the dead are not raised. [16] For if the dead are not raised, not

even Christ has been raised; [17] and if Christ has not been raised, your faith is worthless; you are still in your sins. [18]Then those also who have fallen asleep in Christ have perished. [19] If we have hoped in Christ in this life only, we are of all men most to be pitied.

Romans 12: 3
[3] *For through the grace given to me I say to everyone among you not to think more highly of himself than he ought to think; but to think so as to have sound judgment, as God has allotted to each a measure of faith.*

Romans 16: 17
[17] *Now I urge you, brethren, keep your eye on those who cause dissensions and hindrances contrary to the teaching which you learned, and turn away from them.*

2 Corinthians 4: 3-4
[3] *And even if our gospel is veiled, it is veiled to those who are perishing, [4] in whose case the God of this world has blinded the minds of the unbelieving so that they might not see the light of the gospel of the glory of Christ, who is the image of God.*

In the preceding set of verses, notice that God tells us some things about humility, and what a world without faith can do to people. Were the people who came up with and continue to propagate evolution mainly strong believers in Jesus Christ? No. Is this theory now taught as fact inspired by men of God, or men of this world? Men of this world. The answers to these questions will determine where people place their faith, either with imperfect man, or with God the Creator.

So, does the Bible speak of **creation** or **evolution**? Clearly **creation**. If we choose to say that God is not literal in what He tells us in His Bible and that we, His creation, have discovered the truths about the world, beware. If Christians accept evolution as a fact based on new scientific assumptions and expanding levels of human enlightenment in contradiction to God's stated words, it creates a dilemma. Using this form of reasoning, we cannot accept with certainty, the resurrection of Jesus as stated by God. It places all convictions in doubt. The people who say evolution is now a fact provide what they think is full justification for questioning the resurrection. According to them, humans would no longer need full knowledge and faith in God because the resurrection of Jesus is not scientifically plausible. Jesus, under this line of reasoning, has no real value. He was simply a nice man and no salvation is required. Through his deception the Deceiver has succeeded in squelching faith leading to salvation for many. This is his goal.

Does God have any limits? No. Is He limited by time, space, or dimensions? No. Is spiritual warfare going on in the world right now? Yes. This occurrence indicates the Deceiver actually does plan to get many things going to discredit God by claiming myths and fables, so he can keep as many souls as possible away from God. The idea of evolution demeans God and creates doubt in the minds of some people about who God really is — the resurrection of His Son — and His power over creation.

In Genesis, God talks about His six days of creation. I will soon show how He explains to us the actuality of six literal (twenty-four hour) days. If these days of creation prove to be factual, could Satan achieve any benefit for himself from this as a reality? No, because a quick-creation process proves God's supremacy and power. If God were not powerful enough to do His works in six literal days, as the Bible tell us in the book of Genesis, and actually needed billions of years for this process, is it possible God might appear weak to those who do not yet believe? Yes. Who benefits the most from this perceived weakness? The Deceiver does not want Christians to take literally God's use of the word: **"day"** in the Bible. Understanding its high significance will be critical.

Revelation 22:18-19

[18] *I testify to everyone who hears the words of the prophecy of this book: if anyone adds to them, God will add to him the plagues which are written in this book;* [19] *and if anyone takes away from the words of the book of this prophecy, God will take away his part from the tree of life and from the holy city, which are written in this book.*

Although this Scripture comes from the book of Revelation, it is also true for the whole Bible. It does tell us, the Word of God is precise. We are not to add to it, or subtract from it, or it will result in severe consequences.

When I have verbal disagreements with Christian friends on this evolution issue, something interesting happens. They often tell me I am narrow-minded for sticking up for what is stated, by God Himself, in His word. Evolutionists must entirely take away God's expressed written words in Genesis for their point of view to gain any consideration. Am I wrong here? No. Isn't this exactly what God asks people not to do, per Revelation 22:18-19 above? Yes. I desire to make a strong effort to let the Bible speak for itself. What the Bible says counts — not scientists or even me, for that matter. Only what God says and means has lifesaving value.

Colossians 1:16

[16] *For by Him all things were <u>created</u>, both in the heavens and on earth, visible and invisible, whether thrones or dominions or rulers or authorities <u>all things have been created</u> through Him and for Him.* [17] *He is before all things, and in Him all things hold together.*

God created all things with emphasis on *"created"* and *"all"* — not <u>some</u>. He did not **evolve** all things, or He would have said **evolve** using a correct Hebrew or Greek word of the day. But He purposefully did not do this.

144

Hebrews 1:1-2

¹ God, after He spoke long ago to the fathers in the prophets in many portions and in many ways, ² in these last days has spoken to us in His Son, whom He appointed heir of all things, through whom also He made the world.

Hebrews 11:3

³ By faith we understand that the worlds were prepared by the word of God, <u>so that what is seen was not made out of things which are visible</u>.

"So that what is seen was not made from things which are visible." This is an incredible statement. *"Seeing is believing"* is for agnostics; but *"believing without seeing"* is for Christians.

As for people who still believe evolution might have occurred, versus creation by God in Genesis 1, a fabricated narrative follows that might be a way to replace portions of the basic original Genesis 1 story with basic evolution concepts in mind. How might the Genesis 1 story be rewritten to explain and justify the evolution option had God originally intended such a thing? It is not my intention to sound sarcastic in the modified narrative. It was difficult to attempt this, because it goes against my spirit. However, here is a pass at an alternate evolution narrative:

In the beginning God commenced with the evolution process. After about six billion years of evolving and forming, the earth finally came to its appointed time, to a threshold point that was pleasing to God. Adam had now evolved from a lower primate to the point where man was acceptable to God in His evolutionary cycle. With man at the correct evolutionary stage, God now declared Adam ready to be called the first official man #1 (human) that had evolved to be in God's image, in the line of God's specific species. Adam now, at this correct point in God's perfect evolutionary plan, had sufficiently evolved in full wisdom, intellect, and knowledge, and had already developed the communications skills needed to proceed in God's creation narrative. All the animals of the world have now, also, at the same exact moment in time, evolved (male and female of all like kinds) to their correct and perfect forms, to be assembled all at one time, for their naming ceremony, to be done by Adam. With Adam and all the animals now in their acceptable stages in God's evolutionary process, God was now comfortable to use one of Adam's ribs to create Eve. This, of course, is symbolic because Eve also came to being through the evolutionary process and also evolved as God had planned. Since Adam did not have a helpmate, was lonely, and did not know she existed, God decided the time had come to no longer hide Eve from him. God introduced Adam to Eve for the first time. Adam joyfully met her.

I accept the literal six-day creation version exactly as God describes in Genesis. I understand what He wanted to originally convey. By reading the fabricated version provided above, assuming a way to explain the Theory of Evolution, it is unrealistic to assume Adam could have come to his form by any direct creation process. The Theory of Evolution supposedly proves that man evolved from some series of primal predecessors. So with evolution, any creation event could not be possible if God had really chosen the evolution path. So in essence, it needs to be all creation or all evolution—one or the other, but it cannot be both. Why would God do part evolution and part creation when that would make absolutely no sense at all? He didn't and it would be improbable. God literally calls it *"creation"* and "made" in Genesis 1. So, is this a lie? No. Remember, *"it is impossible for God to lie."* God requires us to trust only Him for the answers as He tells us.

Hebrews 6:18
[18] *so that by two unchangeable things in which <u>it is impossible for God to lie</u>, we who have taken refuge would have strong encouragement to take hold of the hope set before us.*

When we go into Genesis 1 and look at the genealogies of the people who lived from Adam to Noah, we find the men, at that time, did not have children until they were about one-hundred-twenty years old. According to the Bible, originally, all of these early men lived about eight-hundred years. But, if at that time man had evolved — and evolution usually means we adapt in a positive direction to our environment and not regressively — why do we not live this long today, or even a great deal longer?

The Bible, in Genesis, indicates that until Adam and Eve sinned there was no death in the world — no physical, bodily death. According to the Bible God's original desired plan did not include worldly death for all living creatures. This did not come into play until Adam and Eve, enticed by Satan, sinned in the Garden of Eden. They transgressed by eating fruit from the tree of the knowledge of good and evil. According to the Bible, this one action, by Adam and Eve, brought sin and death into the world. This created the entire reason and our need for the Bible. The Bible makes it possible for God to tell and show us that He needed to send His Son, Jesus, to correct this sin-and-death issue caused by Adam and Eve's folly.

Evolution invalidates this account by God regarding death, because it would have necessitated animals and plants to evolve and die for billions of years prior to Adam and Eve's evolutionary point of acceptance. All previous iterations of early man would have died prior to Adam and Eve, as seen in fossil records, supposedly proving the long evolution period. But the very first two sentences in the Bible, in the book of Genesis, tell us the earth was void and formless and covered with water.

Genesis 1:1-2
[1] In the beginning God created the heavens and the earth.
[2] The earth was formless and void, and darkness was over the surface of the deep, and the Spirit of God was moving over the surface of the waters.

How could any living things exist in this stated environment? They couldn't. So logically then, using evolution would mean God must have told us about death more like a fable in Genesis 1, and only symbolically because His original plan was not to consider anything prior to Adam and Eve's sin as death. It was only evolution. Death can occur and be considered death only after God accepted Adam and Eve as the first evolutionary acceptable humans in God's image. Does this all seem realistically logical? Not even close.

In the last days the Deceiver must fully discredit the Bible by making adjustments to the smallest things God talks about in the Scripture. One example: the true understanding of the word *"day"* in Genesis. It seems small, and insignificant, but it is consequential.

What assurances has God given us to verify that He really talks about six literal (twenty-four hour) days of creation and reconstruction or restoration in Genesis 1? It is my understanding the Hebrew word for **day** in the original Hebrew manuscript for Genesis is **yom**. I know this word has been made controversial, and some say this can be a variety of periods of time. If people study this in detail, they will discover that this word has been highly overanalyzed to a point of full confusion. I believe this was done on purpose to discredit the word **yom**. God actually gave us a very simple way to prove this word is meant to be one actual day within His Genesis text. God is quite brilliant.

Mankind is not perfect, but God is. So let me postulate an idea from the Bible that I think God has provided as proof for us. God did not expect the majority of the readers of the Bible to be scholars. He knew the majority of us who would read the Scriptures for our current time would be regular folks. God spoke clearly in a way we would understand. Even in the parables. If you have accepted Jesus as your personal Savior and have the Holy Spirit for help, amazingly the parables become quite clear. God uses His Hebrew word for **day** in the original text of Genesis over 350 times—the majority of the time with a literal number attached. Here are a couple of examples: six **days,** or seventeen **days,** or one **day** etc., all in simple, understandable language.

When we look at the accounts of Noah and the flood in Genesis 7:11, God says that Noah entered the Ark when he was *"six-hundred years, two-months, and seventeen-days"* old—quite specific. And the word **days** is used with both months and years. This leaves no room for confusion as to literal days being mentioned. Why didn't God say Noah entered the ark when at an old age? God knew exactly what He was doing. He wanted the word **day** in Genesis to convey an actual calendar day.

These Noah verses and Genesis 1 use the same Hebrew words for **day**. When God used this Hebrew word **(yom)** for Noah in Genesis 7:11, along with the number seventeen, which represents seventeen units of the word day, could this possibly represent longer periods of time? No. Also, why then would the exact same words used for both Noah's age and the Creation days mean different segments of time? They wouldn't.

In Genesis 1, the six days of creation and regeneration or realignment also include the attachment of the words *"evening and morning."* Two more Scriptures that reference *"morning and evening"*:

Exodus 16:8

8 Moses said, This will happen when the Lord gives you meat to eat in the evening, and bread to the full in the morning; for the Lord hears your grumblings which you grumble against Him. And what are we? Your grumblings are not against us but against the Lord.

Exodus 18:13

13 It came about the next day that Moses sat to judge the people, and the people stood about Moses from the morning until the evening.

The clear intention is for these **day time frames** to be **one literal twenty-four-hour day period**. God always chooses to be straightforward and direct with us. So my simple conclusion: God wants us to take Him literally.

Mark 10:15
15 Truly I say to you, whoever does not receive the kingdom of God like a child will not enter it at all.

God wants us to accept the Bible at face value, and read it with the simplicity of a child. Mankind must not try to read so much more into the Bible than what God provided in the text, created perfectly for the common man.

Evolution speculation has resulted in dissension. The Bible again tells us God *"created"* man and He never intended death . . . for Adam and Eve—or any of us, for that matter. With the help of the evil Deceiver, Adam and Eve disobeyed God, which brought both sin and death into the world. So, God needed to fix this serious situation. When Jesus comes the second time, the removal of both sin and death will soon take place. God has almost finished His process. We are the fortunate generation, for we shall see this in our time.

What about ancient fossil records as proof of evolution? This viewpoint depends on whether or not people accept God at His Word. Is the Bible literal or representative? There may be a strong correlation to fossil records and the flood of Noah. Let's explore this flood event:

Genesis 7:4-6
4 For after seven more days, I will send rain on the earth forty days and forty nights; and I will <u>blot out</u> from the face of the land <u>every living thing</u> that I have made. 6 Now Noah was six hundred years old when the flood of water came upon the earth.

150

Genesis 7:10-11

¹⁰ It came about after the seven days, that the water of the flood came upon the earth. ¹¹ In the six hundredth year of Noah's life, in the second month, on the <u>seventeenth day</u> of the month, <u>on the same day</u> all the fountains of the great deep burst open, and the floodgates of the sky were opened.

Genesis 8:3-5

³ and the water receded steadily from the earth, and at the end of one hundred and fifty days the water decreased. ⁴ In the seventh month, on the seventeenth day of the month, the ark rested upon the mountains of Ararat. ⁵ The water decreased steadily until the tenth month; in the tenth month, on the first day of the month, the tops of the mountains became visible.

Genesis 8:13-14

¹³ Now it came about in the six hundred and first year, in the first month, on the first of the month, the water was dried up from the earth. Then Noah removed the covering of the ark, and looked, and behold, the surface of the ground was dried up. ¹⁴ In the second month, on the twenty-seventh day of the month, the earth was dry.

Genesis 7:17-24

¹⁷ Then the flood came upon the earth for forty days, and the water increased and lifted up the ark, so that it rose above the earth. ¹⁸ The water prevailed and increased greatly upon the earth, and the ark floated on the surface of the water. ¹⁹ The water prevailed more and more upon the earth, so that <u>all the high mountains everywhere under the heavens were covered.</u> ²⁰<u>The water prevailed fifteen cubits higher, and the mountains were covered.</u> ²¹ All flesh that moved on the earth perished, birds and cattle and beasts and every swarming thing that swarms upon the earth, and all mankind; ²² of all that was on the dry land, all in whose nostrils was the breath of the spirit of life, died. ²³ <u>Thus He blotted out every living thing that was upon the face of the land, from man to animals to creeping things and to</u>

birds of the sky, and they were blotted out from the earth; and only Noah was left, together with those that were with him in the ark. ²⁴ *The water prevailed upon the earth one hundred and fifty days.*

This was not a localized flood. **It filled the entire world**. The entire earth became a giant raging sea for over a year. Every living thing, other than those on the ark, died. The earth dried up when Noah was six-hundred-one years, two-months and twenty-seven days old . . . the second time God details time frames using in combination years, months, and days. There is absolutely no confusion here regarding the word **day**.

Can we even comprehend how much water came upon the earth from both below and from above? God's flood rose higher than all the mountains . . . enough water to cover the entire earth in a mere forty days. The quantity of water needed would have been unbelievably torrential with velocity greater than the largest known historical tsunamis. Look at the debris and death that occurred from the thirty foot tsunami waves that recently hit in Asia. They killed many people and buried them below a great deal of mud. This flood in Noah's time would have easily buried all destroyed life under a tremendous amount of sludge and sediment—precisely why today, all over the world, archeologists find so many animal bones, close together in groups, buried under the earth's surfaces—and also why they find whale bones in the middle of continents.

Some people still say God's flood was localized and not worldwide. Do the Bible verses we reviewed tell us this? No. Why would God have Noah build an Ark over many years (God gave him one-hundred-twenty years advance warning) for a small, localized flood? It took Noah a very long time to build the Ark. Would this be logical for only a localized flood that would not come for **twelve decades**? If localized, God could have simply had Noah migrate to some land outside of the localized flood zone. Noah, his family, and all the animals could have moved somewhere to safety with no need for an Ark. But, in reality, when the flood waters came, people continued going to higher and higher ground until no higher place existed. Also, had the flood been localized many would have found dry land. But this did not occur. The worldwide flood **killed all life** on earth per Genesis 7:23.

According to evolutionists, creation must be scientifically logical, or it didn't occur. This thinking does not require faith in a higher power, but rather faith in man's own science. Mankind's scientific analysis says the evolution theory cannot be wrong. The next logical step, in these last days, will entail forcing people to accept this theory as the only truth, through threats, intimidation, and fear, demanding acquiescence. Think this cannot happen? Well, it worked for Hitler, and the Antichrist will make Hitler look like a choir boy.

God always gives us His absolute clear intentions, and He does it for a reason. God specifically used His Hebrew word for a **day**, as previously explained in each of the six days in His creation reconstruction narrative. To nail the point home, as mentioned earlier, God also says at the end of each day in His Genesis Scriptures *"and then there was evening and morning one day, then day two..."* etc.

Let me try one more verse modification to see how this *"evening and morning one day"* issue might work related to evolution. Let's assume this supposed evolution view of the creation events took six-billion years. Then logically we should be able to modify some verses based on, let's say, a day being likened to a literal one-billion-year period of time. Using this analogy, if God did choose evolution, He probably should have told us the following in Genesis 1:5:

Genesis 1:3-5
3 Then God said, let there be light; and there was light. 4 God saw that the light was good; and God

separated the light from the darkness. ⁵ *God called the light day, and the darkness He called night. And there was evening and there was morning, one billion years.*

Could this one change representing an evolution long day make any sense in God's text? No. The problem: God did not say this, or even allude to this type of long day as an expressly desired extended period of time.

The six days of creation, talked about in Genesis 1:3-31, are actually really six literal days of **reconstruction** or **restoration**. I will address this shortly. As mentioned earlier, God talks about the conditions of the earth before His six days of reconstruction or restoration occurred. No biological life could exist on a void, dark earth filled by water. Here again the first two sentences of Genesis address profound issues and answer many questions:

Genesis 1:1-2
¹ *In the beginning God created the heavens and the earth.* ² *The earth was formless and void, and darkness was over the surface of the deep, and the Spirit of God was moving over the surface of the waters.*

In Genesis 1:1, God says, *"In the beginning God created the heavens and the earth."* So, what does God say here and why? Does Genesis 1:1 say He *"created the heavens and earth"* in the beginning, then He *"created"* it all over again in the six days explained in Genesis 1:3-31? It makes no logical sense. So, why are these first two sentences even in the Bible if they do not have great significance? It is because they actually do have great significance.

The heavens and earth existed from the beginning as God stated in Genesis 1:1. The earth was originally only a place where angels dwelt, as described in portions of the Old Testament (Ezekiel 28:11-19). God allowed angelic beings to freely go back and forth between heaven and earth. They had a perfect form of society until Lucifer challenged God's supremacy and brought evil into existence. Due to Satan's arrogance and pride, God needed separation. God threw Lucifer out of heaven *"down to the earth"* and, as a result severely punished the planet. God was angry.

Isaiah 14:12

12 *"How you have fallen from heaven, O star of the morning, son of the dawn! You have been cut down to the earth, ...*

One third of all the angels in heaven sided with Lucifer, and God threw them down to Earth also. God's anger, and this action, took away all the earth's original beauty. In the Beginning, the earth did exist as God tells us in Genesis 1-1 . . . made up of minerals and precious stones . . . quite magnificent (Ezekiel 28:13-16). The eternal kingdom will look similar to this after the completion of the Millennium as described in Revelation 21:18-21. The early beautiful mineral earth *"had not yet had vegetation"* and biological life per Genesis 2:5-8 and Ezekiel 28:11-19. This early earth had nothing to do with evolution.

Because of Satan's arrogance and pride, God placed a full punishment on His beautiful earth when He cast down from heaven, Satan and the fallen angels. God made the earth *"formless,"* *"void"* and *"darkness was over the surface of the deep"* — the consequence of Satan bringing evil and sin into existence. God put Satan and his angels on a punished earth, banished there in darkness. God tells us again the *"heavens and the earth"* existed long ago" in 2 Peter 3:3-6:

2 Peter 3:3-6

3 *Know this first of all, that in the last days mockers will come with their mocking, following after their own lusts,*
4 *and saying, "Where is the promise of His coming? Forever since the fathers fell asleep, all continues just as*

it was from the beginning of creation." [5] For when they maintain this, it escapes their notice that by the word of God the heavens existed long ago and the earth was formed out of water and by water, [6] through which the world at that time was destroyed, being flooded with water. [7] But by His word the present heavens and earth are being reserved for fire, kept for the day of judgment and destruction of ungodly men.

Earlier in Genesis 1:1-2 God talks about *"the surface of the deep."* What deep? What waters? God makes this absolutely clear at this point in Genesis 1:2. The Scripture indicates the earth had no dry land, no light, and had a full surface of water. It was severely dark, empty, without form, and completely **flooded**—completely uninhabitable, unorganized, and hostile. God then tells us He was personally *"moving over the surface of the waters."* But why? Because He was getting ready to do something wonderful. He would repair the damage He had placed on the earth because of Satan's sinful pride. The coming six days of **reconstruction** or **restoration** were about to take place. Some creation also occurs within this six-day time frame.

Please note: In Genesis 1:1, God says He *"created"* everything, *"in the beginning."* In Genesis 1:2 the already-**created** earth was now void and formless due to sin, almost like a lump of potter's clay waiting for the artist to make something beautiful. The word *"made"* was used for all the physical attributes of the restoration process of the world itself: the reorganization of elements already created earlier, *"in the beginning."* But in the **six-day process** the word *"create"* has new significance. During this period God uses the word *"create"* for all the plants, animals, sea monsters, and for man, himself, **all new creations** to the existing world. Prior to God's six-day restoration cycle, everything created from the beginning had been seriously dismantled. This is clear from Genesis 1:2. So, even though the earth had existed from the beginning, per Genesis 1:1, mankind—

including all the plants, animals, and sea creatures that God *"created"* and placed on the earth—has existed in the world for only about 6,000 years as explained earlier.

Currently, in Christianity, a group of well-intentioned people strongly believe in a full literal total creation of everything, including the universe, in six literal days. They believe in the **young-earth** concept, where all the heavens and the earth are only 6,000 years old. I do not believe the Bible tells us this. These people believe, if we do not accept that God did all creation in six days, we have a theological problem because, if the earth existed from the beginning as God tells us in Genesis 1:1 this **old-earth** thinking opens the door for the credibility of evolution.

Our all-knowing God knew from the beginning, the Theory of Evolution would come in our day. To dispel this future evolution concept, God boldly cleared up all this for us in the first two sentences in the Bible. I strongly believe God purposely chose these first two sentences in Genesis to clearly show us the myth of evolution. The environment God talks about in Genesis 1:2 leaves out the possibility of any biological life of any kind. God provided no logical way to justify the evolution path.

Another major problem with the theory of the literal six days for the full creation (non-restoration view) of all the heavens and all the earth: Where in these six literal days described in Genesis 1:3-31 are Lucifer, his fall, and his fallen angels addressed? How and when did Satan come into existence within these six days and still have time to battle with God, fall away, and be thrown down to the earth? God shows us this all happened, on earth, long before man existed.

We can either accept that the world was void, formless, and covered with water, as God has specifically told us, or we can believe in evolution. Everyone, individually, must decide for themselves. I choose to take God at His literal word and believe the earth existed from the beginning, as God tells us directly.

The Bible teaches us about Satan's attributes, and how the earth existed long ago for only angelic beings:

1. Ezekiel 28:1-10 talks about the arrogant prideful King of Tyre. Then in Ezekiel 28:11-19 God compares this King of Tyre's similarities to the characteristics of Lucifer. In verses 1-10 God clearly talks about this human king. Verses 11-19, by comparison, could in no way refer to a human, rather to the most beautiful fallen prideful angel: Lucifer (or Satan the Deceiver). But how do we know this? Three excerpts of the many items talked about in Ezekiel 28:11-19 tell us the entity being referred to is not the literal human King of Tyre. These traits can be attributed to only the angelic being of Lucifer himself.

   a. Verse 12, *"You had the seal of perfection"*
   b. Verse 12, *"Full of wisdom and perfect in beauty."*
   c. Verse 14, *"You were the anointed cherub."*

2. Isaiah 14:12-15 explains about the fall of God's most beautiful angel.

As the cancer of apostasy keeps growing in our world, many people will try to say Satan, as described in the Bible, does not exist. They will also say this quasi, old-earth view means evolution actually happened, not the story about Satan's fall. Satan actually does exist. Do not be deceived.

Here are all the verses in Genesis 1:3-23 that refer to the six days of restoration or reconstruction and the use of *"evening and morning"* for each day. God **reorganized** the earth and then added new things to it in the following verses.

Genesis 1:3-31
³ Then God said, "Let there be light"; and there was light.
⁴ God saw that the light was good; and God <u>separated</u> the light from the darkness ⁵ God called the light day,

and the darkness He called night. And there was evening and there was morning, <u>one day</u>.

[6] Then God said, "Let there be an expanse in the midst of the waters, and let it <u>separate</u> the waters from the waters." [7] God <u>made</u> the expanse, and <u>separated</u> the waters which were below the expanse from the waters which were above the expanse; and it was so. [8] God called the expanse heaven. And there was evening and there was morning, a <u>second day</u>.

[9] Then God said, "Let the waters below the heavens be gathered into one place, and let the dry land appear"; and it was so. [10] God called the dry land earth, and the gathering of the waters He called seas; and God saw that it was good. [11] Then God said, "Let the earth sprout vegetation, plants yielding seed, and fruit trees on the earth bearing fruit after their kind with seed in them"; and it was so [12] The earth brought forth vegetation, plants yielding seed after their kind, and trees bearing fruit with seed in them, after their kind; and God saw that it was good. [13] There was evening and there was morning, a <u>third day</u>.

[14] Then God said, "Let there be lights in the expanse of the heavens to <u>separate</u> the day from the night, and let them be for signs and for seasons and for days and years; [15] and let them be for lights in the expanse of the heavens to give light on the earth"; and it was so. [16] God <u>made</u> the two great lights, the greater light to govern the day, and the lesser light to govern the night; He made the stars also [17] God placed them in the expanse of the heavens to give light on the earth, [18] and to govern the day and the night, and to <u>separate</u> the light from the darkness; and God saw that it was good. [19] There was evening and there was morning, a <u>fourth day</u>.

 20 Then God said, "Let the waters teem with swarms of living creatures, and let birds fly above the earth in the open expanse of the heaven. 21 God *created* the great sea monsters and every living creature that moves, with which the waters swarmed after their kind, and every winged bird after its kind; and God saw that it was good. 22 God blessed them, saying, Be fruitful and multiply, and fill the waters in the seas, and let birds multiply on the earth. 23 There was evening and there was morning, a *fifth day*.

 24 Then God said, "Let the earth bring forth living creatures after their kind: cattle and creeping things and beasts of the earth after their kind"; and it was so. 25 God made the beasts of the earth after their kind, and the cattle after their kind, and everything that creeps on the ground after its kind; and God saw that it was good. 26 Then God said, "Let Us make man in Our image, according to Our likeness; and let them rule over the fish of the sea and over the birds of the sky and over the cattle and over all the earth, and over every creeping thing that creeps on the earth."27 God *created* man in His own image, in the image of God He *created* him; male and female He *created* them. 28 God blessed them; and God said to them, "Be fruitful and multiply, and fill the earth, and subdue it; and rule over the fish of the sea and over the birds of the sky and over every living thing that moves on the earth." 29 Then God said, "Behold, I have given you every plant yielding seed that is on the surface of all the earth, and every tree which has fruit yielding seed; it shall be food for you; 30 and to every beast of the earth and to every bird of the sky and to everything that moves on the earth which has life, I have given every green plant for food"; and it was so. 31 God saw all that He had made, and behold, it was very good. And there was evening and there was morning, the *sixth day*.

Now, I have mentioned that, prior to the six days of **regeneration**, no biological life existed on the earth. Without biological life, how could evolution be possible? It could not. Plants, animals, and people are all biological, and all animal life would need plants and other animals as food to sustain life and an evolutionary process. So, how can we possibly know that no biological life existed on earth prior to God's explanation about how life came to be in Genesis 1? God tells us directly:

Genesis 2:5-8

⁵ Now <u>no shrub</u> of the field was yet in the earth, and <u>no plant</u> of the field <u>had yet sprouted</u>, for the L<small>ORD</small> God had not sent rain upon the earth, and <u>there was no man to cultivate the ground</u>. ⁶ But a mist used to rise from the earth and water the whole surface of the ground.⁷ Then the Lord God formed man of dust from the ground, and breathed into his nostrils the breath of life; and man became a living being. ⁸ The Lord God planted a garden toward the east, in Eden; and there He placed the man whom He had formed.

In Genesis 1:3-31, God explains how He *"created"* animals, and then *"plants,"* and *"man"* in day six of this process. In Genesis 2:7 He tells us again, without any room for doubt, that man was *"created"* and did not evolve. Note, God shares with us: *"no shrub of the field was yet in the earth, and no plant of the field had yet sprouted"* . . . clear evidence that evolution did not occur. This Scripture points out the reason no plants had yet existed: *"there was no man to cultivate the ground."* Interesting, no man yet? How can this verse be explained away by Christian evolutionists? It can't.

Psalm 33:6-9

⁶ By the word of the Lord the heavens were made, and by the <u>breath of His mouth</u> all their host. ⁷ He gathers the waters of the sea together as a heap; He lays up the deeps in storehouses. ⁸ Let all the earth fear the Lord; let all the inhabitants of the world stand in awe of

Him. [9] For He spoke, and it was done; He commanded,
and it stood fast.

By His word and *"the breath of His mouth"* the heavens and all in them were made . . . paraphrased, but it kind of makes my point. The precepts of man must not limit God's teachings. Human beings—part of the creation and not the creator—must not assume we are smarter than what His word tells us.

Genesis 2:7
[7] Then the LORD God formed man of dust from the ground, and breathed into his nostrils the breath of life; and man became a living being.

God formed man from the dust of the ground—not some single cell creatures. He tells it like it is and will not abide with us trying to figure out some mysterious alternate path.

Genesis 2:19-23
[19] Out of the ground the LORD God formed every beast of the field and every bird of the sky, and brought them to the man to see what he would call them; and whatever the man called a living creature, that was its name. [20] The man gave names to all the cattle, and to the birds of the sky, and to every beast of the field, [21] So the LORD God caused a deep sleep to fall upon the man, and he slept; then He took one of his ribs and closed up the flesh at that place. [22] The LORD God fashioned into a woman the rib which He had taken from the man, and brought her to the man. [23] The man said, This is now bone of my bones, and flesh of my flesh; She shall be called Woman, because she was taken out of Man.

God formed all animals out of the ground, also, and had Adam name them. Then he formed Eve from one of Adam's ribs and named her *"woman, because she was taken out of man."* Why would God use so many details if this were all not literal?

162

Using evolution as an answer to creation would make this account a lie, which is not possible for God.

Genesis 3:17-19

[17] Then to Adam He said, Because you have listened to the voice of your wife, and have eaten from the tree about which I commanded you, saying, 'You shall not eat from it'; Cursed is the ground because of you; In toil you will eat of it. All the days of your life.[18] Both thorns and thistles it shall grow for you; and you will eat the plants of the field; [19] By the sweat of your face. You will eat bread, Till you return to the ground, Because from it you were taken; For you are dust, and to dust you shall return.

God never intended for man to either labor or to die an earthly death. Adam lived in a perfect world until sin entered him. The entire situation and fallen condition we live with now results from Adam and Eve's original sin. The good news: God corrected this through His Son, Jesus.

Exodus 31:15-17

[15] For six days work may be done, but on the seventh day there is a Sabbath of complete rest, holy to the Lord; whoever does any work on the Sabbath day shall surely be put to death. [16] So the sons of Israel shall observe the Sabbath, to celebrate the Sabbath throughout their generations as a perpetual covenant.' [17] It is a sign between Me and the sons of Israel forever; for in six days the Lord made heaven and earth, but on the seventh day He ceased from labor, and was refreshed.

God *"made"* all this in six literal days and rested on the seventh. He intended this also as an example for man to do the same. Work for six days and rest on the seventh. This is also why we have seven-day weeks today. God established seven real and consistent literal twenty-four-hour day periods. God then enlisted twelve-month years. It all goes back to God's example for us. Again, is God capable enough to do His Genesis work in six literal twenty-four-hour days? Yes. I find it interesting that God has special numbers that are important to him: three, seven, twelve, and twenty-four are used all throughout the Bible.

John 1:3
3 All things came into being through Him, and apart from Him nothing came into being that has come into being.

Hebrews 11:3
3 By faith we understand that the worlds were prepared by the word of God, so that what is seen was not made out of things which are visible.

Romans 3:4
4 May it never be! Rather, let God be found true, though every man be found a liar.

To reiterate, some people will tell us all logic points to God creating the world through evolution over about six billion years. After all, He is God and He can do anything, right? Yes, I agree God can do anything. So, by using the same logic, in the other direction: His power makes it possible to have easily created everything in six-billionths of a second because, yes, He is God and, yes, He can do anything. So, we can all agree that almighty God, is **all mighty**. He could have done it very slowly or incredibly fast, because He has no limits. It becomes **more logical** to accept, at face value, God's six (twenty-four hour) days of restoration as He described in His own Words, in Genesis, and to accept it literally.

Then, how about dinosaurs? For nonbelievers and even some Christians alike, when somebody tells them dinosaurs could have existed along with man, the concept is often laughed at and mocked as stupidity. Well, I still stand on my belief in

God and the Genesis view of *"all animals"* being *"created"* by Him. This means the dinosaurs also. I can find nothing in God's word that tells me otherwise. Intellectually, could a God with no limits have created and placed the dinosaurs here with man? Absolutely, He could have. If you lived in the early days of Adam, you would have lived with the dinosaurs and have no need to explain them to the people of that day. God says, Adam controlled *"all animals."* The Bible does not exclude the animals we refer to as dinosaurs (a term created by man in 1841). It said **all animals**. I believe God referred to what we call dinosaurs today as beasts. God also uses the term *"Behemoth"* in the Bible:

Job 40:15-18
15 Behold now, <u>Behemoth,</u> which I made as well as you; He eats grass like an ox. 16 Behold now, his strength in his loins and his power in the muscles of his belly. 17 <u>He bends his tail like a cedar;</u> the sinews of his thighs are knit together. 18 His bones are tubes of bronze; His limbs are like bars of iron.

God describes a *"Behemoth"* a huge beast—some say a sea monster or whale. But notice something interesting in Job 40:17: *"he bends his tail like a cedar"* . . . one really big animal tail. Controversial? Yes. Possible? Yes. I believe this illustrates that what we call dinosaurs today actually lived with man. The Bible tells us God gave Adam complete dominion over **all** living things, not some.

So, what does God say about living creatures?

Genesis 1:24-25
24 Then God said, "Let the earth bring forth living creatures after their kind: cattle and creeping things and <u>beasts of the earth</u> after their kind"; and it was so. 25 <u>God made the beasts of the earth</u> after their kind, and the cattle after their kind, and everything that creeps on the ground after its kind; and God saw that it was good.

But some might say, what about those massive Tyranno-saurus Rex teeth, and those vicious Velociraptors? How could man survive living with such vicious beasts that could eat or kill them through their overpowering strength? Think about this a bit. We still have lions, alligators, tigers, bears, and sharks, so we have living animals right now that could both eat us or kill us for sport, but we all manage to co-exist. Mankind is actually a bigger threat to mankind than any of these animals, if you really give it fair consideration.

Whales are huge: in fact, the blue whale is still the largest animal that ever existed in this world. They are still here and they have no desire to harm us. In reality, we are more of a potential threat to them. This whole section on the dinosaurs becomes a bit more honest when you think about it in these terms.

In 2012, a scientist, Mark Armitage, from the California State University at Northridge discovered a triceratops horn at the Hell Creek Formation in Montana. Archeologists have found many dinosaur fossils at this location. In his study of this fossil under a high-powered microscope, he found something amaz-ing—soft tissue that had not yet fossilized. This essentially means this fossil could not be more than about 4,000 years old. This goes back to about the time of the great flood of Noah . . . a major surprise to paleontologists. This discovery had mixed re-actions. Mr. Armitage believes in creation and this discovery actually supported what God has told us all along. The univer-sity fired Mr. Armitage for exposing this information, and his findings have seen little light. I understand that other similar discoveries have occurred, but the secular world will not acknowledge them as they do not fit in with a desired narrative. This reaction should not surprise Christians; but rather, we should anticipate it.

The Deceiver's deceptions are rampant in our world and can easily grow within each of us. One must search out God's truth and become aware of His loving direction to avoid deception.

I have used evolution as a main example of how the Deceiver wants to do everything he can to make man speculate and change the subject away from God. Satan also wants to suppress the truth from honoring the Bible as-is and to create doubt in both God's Word, as literal truth, and His supreme sovereignty. Paul tells us in Romans about those who suppress His truth:

Romans 1:18-21

[18] *For the wrath of God is revealed from heaven against all un-Godliness and unrighteousness of men who suppress the truth in unrighteousness,* [19] *because that which is known about God is evident within them; for God made it evident to them.* [20] *For since the creation of the world His invisible attributes, His eternal power and divine nature, have been clearly seen, being understood through what has been made, so that they are without excuse.* [21] *For even though they knew God, they did not honor Him as God or give thanks, but they became futile in their speculations, and their foolish heart was darkened.*

Romans 1:28-32

[28] *And just as they did not see fit to acknowledge God any longer, God gave them over to a depraved mind, to do those things which are not proper,* [29] *being filled with all unrighteousness, wickedness, greed, evil; full of envy, murder, strife, deceit, malice; they are gossips,* [30] *slanderers, haters of God, insolent, arrogant, boastful, inventors of evil, disobedient to parents,* [31] *without understanding, untrustworthy, unloving, unmerciful;* [32] *and although they know the ordinance of God, that those who practice such things are worthy of death, they not only do the same, but also give hearty approval to those who practice them.*

I have provided the verses above, prepared for us 1,900 years ago by God Himself, so we will all know what to expect for our current time in history. The majority of the secular world considers God's views expressed in Romans 1 as diatribe. These verses essentially explain exactly what is happening in our world today. God knew what would occur in the last days, and how people would respond. God has told us exactly what to expect.

Looking at the news each night, we can see how the world is shaping up. I think we can see from these verses that as we continue into these end times, we have a larger battle coming. Not only will mankind abandon God for full secular thinking in violation of God's Word, they will do it arrogantly in God's face. So much so that God will not discourage them, but He Himself will give them over to their lusts. This is like God heaping hot coals on them, for their arrogance. Notice how the Apostle Paul addresses this further for us in both Romans 2:5-8, and Ephesians 6:10-13:

Romans 2:5-8

5 But because of your stubbornness and unrepentant heart you are storing up wrath for yourself in the day of wrath and revelation of the righteous judgment of God, 6 who will render to each person according to his deeds: 7 to those who by perseverance in doing good seek for glory and honor and immortality, eternal life; 8 but to those who are selfishly ambitious and do not obey the truth, but obey unrighteousness, wrath and indignation.

Ephesians 6:10-13

10 Finally, be strong in the Lord and in the strength of His might. 11 Put on the full armor of God, so that you will be able to stand firm against the schemes of the devil. 12 For our struggle is not against flesh and blood, but against the rulers, against the powers, against the world forces of this darkness, against the spiritual forces of wickedness in the heavenly places. 13 Therefore, take up the full armor of God, so that you will be able to resist in the evil day, and having done everything, to stand firm.

For Christians who have accepted Jesus as their personal Lord and Savior and know they are truly saved, they needn't worry about their salvation because it is secure. The Deceiver is working hard to prevent our unbelieving and doubting friends and family members from coming to a loving knowledge about Jesus.

Some people have trouble accepting the literal resurrection of Christ, because it does not fit in with the scientific created norms of mankind. The supernatural aspects that one must accept regarding the resurrection seems incomprehensible to people who have a set regulated orderly view of how science and physics work . . . almost like some people are too smart for their own good. This is unfortunate and plays right into the Deceiver hands.

Ephesians 6:12 explains the struggles all around us with wickedness in heavenly places. This deception causes a quandary in the minds of nonbelievers. In reality, they have only two choices. Will they place their eternal destiny in the loving hands of Jesus, or in the theories and evolving sciences of imperfect mankind? Both of these options require faith. It's a question of where someone chooses to place it. I understand it is a complicated choice, but this choice has severe and profound eternal consequences.

Here is a major question to think about. Is Satan real? Let's explore what God Himself has to say regarding this:

1 John 5:18-19
18 We know that no one who is born of God sins; but He who was born of God keeps him, and the evil one does not touch him. 19 We know that we are of God, and that the whole world lies in the power of the evil one.

Ephesians 6:11-12
11 Put on the full armor of God, so that you will be able to stand firm against the schemes of the devil. 12 For our struggle is not

against flesh and blood, but against the rulers, against the powers, against the world forces of this darkness, against the spiritual forces of wickedness in the heavenly places.

Job 1:6-7
6 Now there was a day when the sons of God came to present themselves before the Lord, and Satan also came among them. 7 The Lord said to Satan, from where do you come? Then Satan answered the Lord and said, from roaming about on the earth and walking around on it.

Matthew 4:8-11
8 Again, the devil took Him to a very high mountain and showed Him all the kingdoms of the world and their glory; 9 and he said to Him, all these things I will give You, if You fall down and worship me.10 Then Jesus said to him, Go, Satan! For it is written, 'You shall worship the Lord your God and serve Him only.' 11 Then the devil left Him; and behold, angels came and began to minister to Him.

1 Peter 5:8
8 Be of sober spirit, be on the alert. Your adversary, the devil, prowls around like a roaring lion, seeking someone to devour.

God tells us Satan (the Deceiver) is real, so I will let the Bible speak for itself and trust God at His own assessment.

Can you imagine what it would be like if all Bible readers could take the Word of God literally instead of trying to always read between the lines for hidden meanings? I cannot believe our God wanted to hide the truth from us. So many false ideas and theories of faith exist today. Anyone can pick whichever interpretation matches their own personal comfort zone and lifestyle. This unfortunately diminishes the greatness of our God. When the Ezekiel attack happens, I sincerely hope every-thing will become a bit clearer. God has given us the Bible for our comfort, guidance, and protection.

Deceptions

I love God, and I know He loves me.

For my readers who are parents: Would you purposefully try to make life more difficult for your children, or would you try to give them sound direction and guidance? If you knew difficult times were coming, wouldn't you do your best to warn, protect, and even show them how to escape dangers? If needed, wouldn't you even die for them if the choice were either them or you? The Bible and Jesus have done all of that for us. But some try so hard to read things into the Bible that are not there and dismiss the real story. It saddens me that some Christians diminish God by accepting so many deceptions that contradict the Bible. Sadly, the Deceiver is winning this battle. The Bible tells us the Deceiver will appear to win for a short time, and to not be discouraged. The story has a good ending and so will we.

As Christians, we need to stand with the Lord and keep our eyes keenly focused on everything that goes on in the world. In the next couple of years, things will get even more challenging for us. It will become much harder for current nonbelievers to know Jesus because their hearts will grow colder. Many will willingly choose to stay solidly with secularism right into the Tribulation.

Please remember, as I have continually said, after the Ezekiel attack happens, and after the shock wears off, the Deceiver will go into full gear. Mankind will quickly start to look as if they are finally getting their world act together. It will begin to look as if all of us will enter into the Age of Aquarius, with harmony and understanding.

This will be the ultimate deception!

Revelation 3: 10-11

[10] *Because you have kept the word of My perseverance, I also will keep you from the hour of testing, that hour which is about to come upon the whole world, to test those who dwell on the earth.* [11] *I am coming quickly; hold fast what you have, so that no one will take your crown.*

CHAPTER 5

THE VISUAL RAPTURE
PROPHECIES 21-24

At some time in the near future the entire world will see Christians leaving earth in God's visual Rapture. He has incredible reasons for the Rapture to occur for everybody to witness. It will be an EPIC event.

When I discovered what God appears to tell us about this topic, it gave me a rejuvenated vigor and passion for the Lord. Understanding what must actually happen in the next couple of years has given my life new tranquility, peace, and comfort. I know many commentators have written hundreds of different ideas regarding what will happen in the end times. What I have learned through Biblical teaching and research represents a beautiful, spectacular, and awesome view of our magnificent caring Lord.

I believe the second coming will take place over seven years. Two separate Jesus events will **bookend** the tribulation. The visual Rapture will **reveal** the Son of Man per Luke 17:30, but not **physically** to the earth. The actual physical return-to- the-earth portion of the Second Coming happens at the end of the Tribulation and denotes the time when God comes to fix the broken world.

According to Scriptures, during the end times any believing Christian will have the opportunity to be **caught up alive** to be with the Lord in a literal visual Rapture. I have discovered God requires some **specific actions** on our part to fulfill this. Not all living Christians will go up alive at the final trumpet. This may sound confusing; however, I am going to elaborate.

Some Bible scholars today tell us they believe the Bible shows us the Rapture and the Tribulation occurred around the time of the second Jewish Temple's destruction in the year 70 AD. This however is not possible, but how can we know this? John did not write the book that explains these events until around 95 A.D., a **full twenty-five years after** the temple had been destroyed.

One of the reasons God instructed John to write the book of Revelation was to help and comfort those who will enter the Tribulation period. I see Revelation as literal because it specifi-cally mentions 1,260 days from the start of the Tribulation to the mid-point, when the Antichrist claims to be God. Then another second set of 1,260 days, until Jesus physically returns . . . the literal second coming. Why would God define specific periods of time in the Tribulation if it will not be a real event?

These future days of the Tribulation will bring horror (outlined provided in Chapter 6), and God wants the people living during this time to know how long they must wait until the finish line. This will give them hope and strength to make it through this defined set period of time. Using these two 1,260 numbers, we can know, with specificity, when the literal Second Coming of the Lord to the earth (to the ground) will occur. It will not be an unknown event. This dispels the notion by some that the Rapture happens at the middle, or at the end of the Tribulation.

The Bible explains everything, from the time of Jesus' first visit to His second coming. God has told us a long time would pass before Christ's return, and uses letters representing examples of the characteristics within seven churches of his day.

They represent snapshots of seven future time periods that explain how we will be able to know Jesus is about to return. All seven letters/time periods are described in Revelation 2 and 3. The first five took 1,792 years to complete. The final two church letters/time periods, Philadelphia and Laodicea (six and seven), have relevancy for our study:

Letter to the Church of Philadelphia (6th Church Time Period)

Revelation 3:7-13
7 And to the angel of the church in Philadelphia write: He who is holy, who is true, who has the key of David, who opens and no one will shut, and who shuts and no one opens, says this: 8 'I know your deeds. Behold, I have put before you an open door which no one can shut, because you have a little power, and have kept My word, and have not denied My name. 9 Behold, I will cause those of the synagogue of Satan, who say that they are Jews and are

not, but lie - I will make them come and bow down at your feet, and make them know that I have loved you. [10]Because you have kept the word of My perseverance, <u>I also will keep you from the hour of testing</u>, that hour which is about to come upon the whole world, to test those who dwell on the earth. [11] I am coming quickly; hold fast what you have, so that no one will take your crown. [12] He who overcomes, I will make him a pillar in the temple of My God, and he will not go out from it anymore; and I will write on him the name of My God, and the name of the city of My God, the new Jerusalem, which comes down out of heaven from My God, and My new name. [13] He who has an ear, let him hear what the Spirit says to the churches.'

Letter to the Church of Laodicea (7th Church Time Period)

Revelation 3:14-22

[14] To the angel of the church in Laodicea write The Amen, the faithful and true Witness, the Beginning of the creation of God, says this: [15] 'I know your deeds, that you are neither cold nor hot; I wish that you were cold or hot. [16] So because you are lukewarm, and neither hot nor cold, <u>I will spit you out of My mouth.</u> [17] Because you say, I am rich, and have become wealthy, and have need of nothing, and you do not know that you are wretched and miserable and poor and blind and naked, [18] I advise you to buy from Me gold refined by fire so that you may become rich, and white garments so that you may clothe yourself, and that the shame of your nakedness will not be revealed; and eye salve to anoint your eyes so that you may see. [19] Those whom I love, I reprove and discipline; therefore be zealous and repent. [20] Behold, I stand at the door and knock; if anyone hears My voice and opens the door, I will come in to him and will dine with him, and he with Me.[21] He who overcomes, I will grant to him to sit down with Me on My throne, as I also overcame and sat down with My Father

on His throne. [22] *He who has an ear, let him hear what the Spirit says to the churches.*

The sixth letter to the church of Philadelphia (Revelation 3:7-13) represents the time period that started in 1792 when William Carey sailed to India and became the first foreign missionary. This sixth church, in Eschatology, is referred to as **the loving church** because it represents the group that has a heart for the Lord and shares the truth about Jesus with others. In Revelations 3:9 God says He loves the Church of Philadelphia because it keeps His word. He even says those who remain faithful will have the name of God written on them by Jesus (sealed). Faithful Christian believers today comprise this group. The Church of Philadelphia's time period will end at the visual Rapture.

Additional evidence in the Scriptures also indicates that believing Christians fall within the sixth church period of Philadelphia. Revelation 3:10 states: Jesus, will keep this group *"from the hour of testing"* (the Tribulation). Also, Christ does not want anyone to take our *"Crown,"* Revelation 3:11, the *"Crown of Righteousness,"* 2 Timothy 4:8. We can lose this one particular crown if we do not remain strong and fall short in our faith during the apostasy, we experience today. We also cannot attain this crown if we do not follow some specific instructions the Lord has for us prior to the visual Rapture. God offers five crown rewards for superior obedience. I will share more about all five crowns at the end of this chapter.

The seventh letter to the Church of Laodicea (Revelation 3:14-22) represents the time period that came into being in the late 1800's and purposefully overlaps with Philadelphia. This is the *"Lukewarm"* Church as God calls it in Revelation 3:16 . . . it is neither *"hot"* nor *"cold"* and drifts away from accepting both Jesus and His Bible as the only truth. This group compromises and accepts **man-made doctrines** and morality in direct contradiction to the Bible. They do not agree to absolutes required by

God; if they've decided something is right for them it is right. They condone it as enlightenment, regardless of what God thinks. Since the *"Lukewarm"* church does not believe in the Tribulation as a future reality, they will not, for the most part, recognize God's warning signs (His prophecies) and will dismiss them. For this reason the final seventh church will go into the Tribulation. They will wander off God's true path, accepting concepts and doctrines that believe having faith in Jesus alone has no real specific, major defining significance.

The Antichrist will eventually take over and control the seventh church period, Laodicea. Unfortunately, again, the Deceiver will use the church of this period to steal as many people away from God as possible, before the beginning and into the Tribulation. We can see this all happening today. The Deceiver will achieve this through secular deceptions, as explained earlier in Chapter 4. In Revelation 3:17, God tells us the rich will say they have need for nothing, including God, because they are self-sufficient. What folly, dismissing God as irrelevant . . . just another example of arrogance engrained in the members of the seventh church time period. God, due to this arrogance, will *"spit them out of His mouth"* per Revelation 3:16. This wayward seventh church group will spearhead the formation of the One World Church, led by the False Prophet, prior to the start of the Tribulation.

After the visual Rapture, many people who remain will instantly know they made a serious mistake by listening to the king of all lies, the Deceiver. In Revelation 3:14-22, notice the absence of talk about the seventh church time period, Laodicea, *"being kept"* from the hour of testing. The reason: because the people who did not accept Jesus whole-heartedly before the visual Rapture, or pretended God had no absolutes, or marginalized Him, will enter the Tribulation for God's period of testing. Hope prevails, however. Jesus, though rejected before the visual Rapture, still wants all people to be with Him, per Revelation 3:20. During the Tribulation, the Lord will stand at the door knocking, hoping people will open their hearts and let Him in.

Some Christians do not accept this time period's viewpoint of the seven churches in Revelation 2 and 3. They think of these seven churches as literally real congregations in existence, when God inspired John to write the book of Revelation. Well, they're absolutely correct. But yet God in His all-knowing wisdom knew that an enormous amount of time would pass before Jesus' second return. Many more than seven types or forms of churches existed at the time John wrote Revelation 2 and 3 by God's inspiration. But God selected only these particular seven literal churches as specific examples of the seven forms of time periods coming in the future before Jesus' second coming. God uses these time period examples as an additional clear prophetic guide for us to see and know about how history would progress leading right up to the last days.

Can we logically assume these specific, seven existing churches in John's day would have seen the second coming of Jesus? Can we logically assume the Tribulation would occur in their lifetimes? The answer to both of these questions is no. So, what must we think? The answers rest within the letter to the church of Philadelphia, Revelation 3:10-11:

Revelation 3:10-11
10 Because you have kept the word of My perseverance, <u>I also will keep you from the hour of testing</u>, <u>that hour which is about to come upon</u> the whole world, to test those who dwell on the earth. 11 I am coming quickly; hold fast what you have, so that no one will take your crown.

If God intended the letters to the churches of Philadelphia and Laodicea for the actual literal congregations of John's day (Revelation 1:4 through 3:22), we have a dilemma. Why would God choose to keep only the people living and attending the actual real Church of Philadelphia from the *"hour of testing,"* the Tribulation? Why not also save the other six churches as well? Then what about all the other churches of that day He chose not to use as examples in the Bible? Makes no sense.

It appears clear to me that God did indeed use the existing seven church models as examples of future time periods to come in sequence and to explain what future ages will look like. All the actual seven church periods in history have historical precedence and line up with God's church/time period models. What God has shared allows us to see, through Scriptures, how the sixth and seventh church time periods match up perfectly with the two church models in our present day. The **loving church** that trusts solely in Jesus, and the **lukewarm church,** the final church that will soon come together into the false One World Religion.

This final church/time period today, the one that accepts issues in conflict with God's laws and does not repent, will be the church that enters the Tribulation. These parallels are quite compelling and another validation of God's **Road Map** for us to see and know His season and to confirm, without doubt, that we currently live in the last days.

2 Thessalonians 2:3-7
[3] Let no one in any way deceive you, for it will not come unless the apostasy comes first, and the <u>man of lawlessness is revealed</u>, the son of destruction, [4] who opposes and exalts himself above every so-called god or object of worship, so that <u>he takes his seat in the temple of God, displaying himself as being God</u>. [5] Do you not remember that while I was still with you, I was telling you these things? [6] And <u>you know what restrains him now</u>, so that <u>in his time he will be revealed</u>. [7] For the mystery of lawlessness is already at work; <u>only he who now restrains</u> will do so until he <u>is taken out of the way</u>.

2 Thessalonians 2:3-7 talks about removing the restrainer. The restrainer is not the Holy Spirit, because God will do all He can through His coming 144,000 evangelists to save as many people as possible during the entire seven-year Tribulation. But how can we know the Holy Spirit won't leave the world at the visual Rapture? The book of Mark answers this question. In the following verses, Mark 13:11 talks about the persecution of believers inside the Tribulation:

Mark 13:9-11
⁹ *"But be on your guard; for they will deliver you to the courts, and you will be flogged in the synagogues, and you will stand before governors and kings for My sake, as a testimony to them.* ¹⁰ *The gospel must first be preached to all the nations.*¹¹ *When they arrest you and hand you over, do not worry beforehand about what you are to say, but say whatever is given you in that hour; for it is not you who speak, but it is the Holy Spirit.*

Let's get back to the previous 2 Thessalonians 2:3-7 verses. Note something significant in these verses. People will not know the Antichrist is Satan (revealed) until he takes his seat in the temple **at the midpoint of the Tribulation.** He is restrained for the entire first half of the Tribulation. So, who is the restrainer? Clearly the Holy Spirit works inside the Tribulation, so it cannot be Him. Remember in the last days, ten World Divisions (with ten Kings) will exist at the beginning and into the first half of the Tribulation. Three of the ten Kings dislike what the Antichrist tries to do. They **restrain** him for a time from the full evil he has planned but ultimately fail and suffer defeat **at the midpoint of the Tribulation.** After this defeat, the three Kings will no longer **restrain** the Antichrist. He then has full Satanic authority, and away he goes on his final three and a half years of sheer terror. The restrainer is also not the church; we left three and one half years earlier. **The restrainer** is actually the **three Kings** of the defeated divisions.

Another thing all Christians should remember: As I mentioned earlier, God requires us to love Israel and do our best to help our Jewish brothers and sisters understand who Jesus is. Do you realize while we are still here, we have an opportunity to provide our Jewish family with the Scriptures and tools they will need to discover Jesus—after the visual Rapture? Christians today might, in the end, be the catalyst for assisting the 144,000 Jewish leaders to become believers in the Messiah, Jesus, during the Tribulation. These 144,000 are the people who will ultimately help save billions of souls during the Tribulation.

At the end of this book I provide additional information regarding how Christians today could possibly become God's future catalyst through something called **The 144,000 Project**.

DELIVER US FROM EVIL

Another verse similar to Revelation 3:10-11 says God does not want us to fall from grace due to current evil in the world.

Matthew 6:13
13 *'And do not lead us into temptation, but deliver us from evil. For Yours is the kingdom and the power and the glory forever. Amen.'*

Our God will not allow us—His current faithful church—to go into the Tribulation. Those of us who have accepted Him before the shout at the visual Rapture event get special protection from our Father.

SIGNS, SHOUTS, TRUMPETS:
SEVEN STAGE OF THE VISUAL RAPTURE

Joel 2:30-32
30 *I will display wonders in the sky and on the earth, Blood, fire and columns of smoke.* 31 *The sun will be turned*

into darkness and the moon into blood <u>before the great</u> <u>and awesome day of the Lord</u> comes. [32] And it will come about that whoever calls on the name of the Lord will be delivered; for on Mount Zion and in Jerusalem there will be those who escape, as the Lord has said, even among the survivors whom the Lord calls.

<u>Luke 21:25-28</u>
[25] There will be signs in sun and moon and stars, and on the earth dismay among nations, in perplexity at the roaring of the sea and the waves, [26] men fainting from fear and the expectation of the things which are coming upon the world; for the powers of the heavens will be shaken. [27] Then they will see the Son of Man coming in the cloud with power and great glory. [28] But when these things begin to take place, <u>straighten up and lift up your heads</u>, because your redemption is drawing near.

<u>1 Thessalonians 4:13-18</u>
[13] But we do not want you to be uninformed, brethren, about those who are asleep, so that you will not grieve as do the rest who have no hope. [14] For if we believe that Jesus died and rose again, even so God will bring with Him those who have fallen asleep in Jesus. [15] For this we say to you by the word of the Lord, that we who are alive and remain until the coming of the Lord, will not precede those who have fallen asleep. [16] For the Lord Himself will descend from heaven <u>with a shout</u>, with the voice of the archangel and with the trumpet of God, and the dead in Christ will rise first. [17] Then we who are alive and remain will be caught up together with them in the clouds to meet the Lord in the air, and so we shall always be with the Lord. [18] Therefore comfort one another with these words.

1 Corinthians 15:51-52
51 Behold, I tell you a mystery; we will not all sleep, but we will all be changed, 52 in a moment, in the twinkling of an eye, at the last trumpet; for the trumpet will sound, and the dead will be raised imperishable, and we will be changed.

Joel 2:1
1 Blow a trumpet in Zion, and sound an alarm on My holy mountain! Let all the inhabitants of the land tremble, for the day of the Lord is coming; Surely it is near,

Now, if God had designed the entire Rapture event to happen unexpectedly, without any warning or fanfare, why would He give us so many additional explicit instructions in all these verses? God may also tell us in Luke 21:25-26 how the early signs indicating the arrival of the visual Rapture may actually also be the beginning stages of the Tribulation. The Tribulation will start in full force the same day the Lord takes us home in the visual Rapture. Luke 21:27 tells us *"they"* (everyone) will *"see"* the Son of Man coming in the cloud with great power and great glory. The troubling signs God will use to show us the visual Rapture is about to begin will then continue and escalate into the Tribulation.

Now, some might say that Luke 17:20 tells us **no signs** will precede the Rapture and this is **partially** true:

Luke 17:20
20 Now having been questioned by the <u>Pharisees</u> as to when the kingdom of God was coming, He answered them and said, "<u>The kingdom of God is not coming with signs to be observed</u>; 21 nor will they say, 'Look, here it is!' or, 'There it is!' For behold, the kingdom of God is in your midst."

Who is God talking to? The **Pharisees,** who were the **bad guys** in His time. The coming signs of the Rapture listed in this section are for **believers, <u>not unbelievers</u>**. This is what God tells us as Christians regarding being **in the light** and **not in the darkness**. The unbelieving world has **no desire to look for signs,** so none will be provided. The Rapture will catch them totally off guard.

The following verses provide some partial answers to our actually hearing these trumpets in the visual Rapture sequence.

Numbers 10:9

⁹ When you go to war in your land against the adversary who attacks you, then you shall sound an alarm with the trumpets, that you may be remembered before the LORD your God, and be saved from your enemies.

Numbers 10:3-6

³ When both are blown, all the congregation shall gather themselves to you at the doorway of the tent of meeting. ⁴ Yet if only one is blown, then the leaders, the heads of the divisions of Israel, shall assemble before you. ⁵ But when you blow an alarm, the camps that are pitched on the east side shall set out. ⁶ When you blow an alarm the second time, the camps that are pitched on the south side shall set out; an alarm is to be blown for them to set out.

God used trumpets in the Old Testament to announce battles, wars, remembrance, and deliverance to safety. The verses above show us a precedent of how God uses trumpets as loud and audible announcements, in a variety of ways. At the Rapture, I believe the whole world will hear the trumpets. This may also serve as a loud formal announcement, by God, verifying the beginning of His Tribulation is about to arrive.

The visual Rapture will likely take several minutes to complete. God seems to do almost everything in a big way, so I believe He designed the visual Rapture to make a grand, visual, worldwide announcement to all of mankind. Can you imagine the statement God will make when all of mankind views the

Rapture, actually seeing us all leaving up into the sky when Jesus takes us to safety, to join Him in Heaven? . . . a spectacular sight, for sure.

Earlier, I mentioned how God in His word shares stories about specific events that also explain about His overall character and thought process. They describe the nature of Jesus. Please, keep this overall concept in mind as we proceed.

Numbers 10:9, although written for a specific event, states: at the sound of a trumpet His people are *"remembered before the Lord your God, and saved from your enemies."* At the visual Rapture the trumpet will warn Christians and save us from our enemy, the Deceiver. Our incredible God provides us with direction. Many people remaining after the visual Rapture will realize, without a doubt, they made a grave error in judgment. By sharing with everyone we know the events explained in this book, those who scoff at all this may come to realize, as we depart, this information was accurate and, hopefully, many will then accept the Lord.

WE CAN KNOW THE RAPTURE TIMING BY GOD'S ADVANCE WARNING

The following verses make it clear that God does not leave His beloved people wondering about His plans. He tells us, His children, everything in advance as any loving parent does. These next verses show how He does things:

Amos 3:7
⁷ *Surely the Lord God does nothing unless He reveals His secret counsel to His servants the prophets.*

Mark 13:23
²³ *But take heed; behold, I have told you everything in advance.*

Luke 8:16-17

16 Now no one after lighting a lamp covers it over with a container, or puts it under a bed; but he puts it on a lampstand, so that those who come in may see the light. 17 For nothing is hidden that will not become evident, nor anything secret that will not be known and come to light.

Luke 12:35-37

35 Be dressed in readiness, and keep your lamps lit. 36 Be like men who are waiting for their master when he returns from the wedding feast, so that they may immediately <u>open the door to him </u>when he comes and knocks. 37 Blessed are those slaves whom the master will find on the <u>alert</u> when he comes;

God wants us to keep our lamps on and to know what the Bible tells us about the visual Rapture event, so we can stay alert in readiness to open the door for Him, so-to-speak, upon His return. But how can we know the process necessary to stay *"alert"* and ready to *"open the door to him?"* If God meant to hide the Rapture from us or not to expect it, He wouldn't have told us to prepare. Why would He have us stay alert, if the Rapture were a hidden surprise event? Putting our lamps on the lampstands means God is asking us to share this light with others. This includes telling our Christian friends to understand what will soon come upon the world.

Luke 21:34-36

34 <u>Be on guard</u>, so that your hearts will not be weighted down with dissipation and drunkenness and the <u>worries of life</u>, and that day will not come on you suddenly like a trap; 35 for it will come upon all those who dwell on the face of <u>all the earth.</u> 36 But keep on the alert at all times, praying that you may have strength to escape all these *things that are about to take place, and to stand before the Son of Man.*

"Be on guard." Do not let our earthly problems allow us to keep our eyes off the ball. Stay alert and stand strong because God has given us all the information we need, to know exactly when He will return. The Bible lights our way. God also wants us to pray for the strength to escape the horrors of the Tribulation.

1 Thessalonians 5:1-11

¹ Now as to the times and the epochs, brethren, you have no need of anything to be written to you. ² For you yourselves know full well that the day of the Lord will come just like a thief in the night. ³ While they are saying, Peace and safety! Then destruction will come upon them suddenly like labor pains upon a woman with child, and they will not escape. ⁴ But you, brethren, are not in darkness, that the day would overtake you like a thief; ⁵ for you are all sons of light and sons of day. We are not of night nor of darkness; ⁶ so then let us not sleep as others do, but let us be alert and sober. ⁷ For those who sleep do their sleeping at night, and those who get drunk get drunk at night. ⁸ But since we are of the day, let us be sober, having put on the breastplate of faith and love, and as a helmet, the hope of salvation. ⁹ For God has not destined us for wrath, but for obtaining salvation through our Lord Jesus Christ,¹⁰ who died for us, so that whether we are awake or asleep, we will live together with Him. ¹¹ Therefore encourage one another and build up one another, just as you also are doing.

The *"thief in the night"* does not refer to God taking Christians in the Rapture, but rather, specifically, to the start of the Tribulation. The visual Rapture will be part of the announcement to the world that the Tribulation has arrived. These verses tell us that, as believers, we should know, full well, the day of the Lord (the Tribulation) **will come like a thief** in the night, but only to the **unbelieving world**. 1 Thessalonians 5:3 tell us clearly while *"they"* are saying ... well, who are **"they?"** These *"they"* are all the **unbelievers** who will have **unexpected punishments** coming upon them. God says Christians are not of the darkness, but of the light. God has given us all the signs we need to know and as believers to understand this assessment is correct. We are not destined for wrath. God even tells us to *"encourage and build up one another"* with this information.

God specifically asks all living believers *"not to sleep,"* which means staying aware, per Thessalonians 5:7-8. This word *"sleeping"* in those verses will have some major significance soon in this story.

After we see God's signs, we need to comprehend what God wants us to do and know. The visual Rapture appears to contain **SEVEN** distinct explicit events on a grand scale:

FIRST, per Luke 21:25-26, signs and a visible display of wonders in the sky and on the earth will appear and the unbelieving people of the world, including **uninformed Christians,** will tremble with fear. About this time, the Christians who have studied and understand end times prophecy will get a clear **gift** a warning from God in their hearts, the *"day star,"* per 2 Peter 1:19, sharing with us, in advance, that the Rapture is about to begin.

2 Peter 1:19
19 So we have the prophetic word made more sure, to which you do well to pay attention as to a lamp shining in a dark place, until the day dawns and the day star (*) arises in your hearts.

(*) The term "day star" comes from the King James Version KJV

Per Luke 21:27-28 when these signs *"begin,"* at this point we need to *"look up"* as *"our redemption is drawing near."* This is not symbolic but literal. The visual Rapture is about to begin.

Luke 21:27-28
[27] Then they will see the Son of Man coming in the cloud with power and great glory. [28] But when these things begin to take place, <u>straighten up and lift up your heads</u>, because <u>your redemption is drawing near.</u>

In the **SECOND** event, the Lord descends from Heaven in the clouds with a shout.

In the **THIRD** event, we will hear the sound of the first trumpet.

In the **FOURTH** event, the dead in Christ rise first—the reuniting of the **souls** of **those who died** between Christ's ascension and the visual Rapture. Those souls currently in heaven with the Lord will now reunite with their earthly bodies. Graves will open and empty. The sea will give up its dead. Ashes will be transformed into their original form. Additionally, certain uninformed living Christians who do not know to *"look up"* may be raptured with this group, by an **alternate path** through death. I will explain this Biblical concept shortly. At this point all souls and their bodies have rejoined. They are still imperfect, reconstructed, human bodies and not in heavenly form **yet.**

In the **FIFTH** event, living Christians who did *"look up"* upon seeing God's warning signs (first event) and received the **"day star"** warning in their hearts, still alive, will rise into the sky to join those who started rising at the beginning of the <u>fourth event</u>. I believe we will do this in our current earthly bodies also, until the <u>seventh event</u> occurs.

In the **SIXTH** event, we will hear the final trumpet, which causes the seventh event to occur.

And, in the **SEVENTH** event of the visual Rapture, at the final trumpet, we will *"all be changed, in a moment in the twin-*

kling of an eye" into our new heavenly bodies (1 Corinthians 15: 52). This seventh event is the only part of the Rapture that happens instantaneously.

SIGNS JUST BEFORE THE VISUAL RAPTURE AND THE COMMAND TO "LOOK UP"

Luke 21:25-28
25 There will be signs in sun and moon and stars, and on the earth dismay among nations, in perplexity at the roaring of the sea and the waves, 26 men fainting from fear and the expectation of the things which are coming upon the world; for the powers of the heavens will be shaken. 27 Then they will see the Son of Man coming in the cloud with power and great glory. 28 But when these things begin to take place, straighten up and lift up your heads, because your redemption is drawing near.

Joel 2:30-31 The Day of the Lord
30 I will display wonders in the sky and on the earth, Blood, fire and columns of smoke. 31 The sun will be turned into darkness and the moon into blood before the great and awesome day of the Lord comes.

We are directed to look for His **visual signs** prior to the visual Rapture. As in the time of Christ's crucifixion, the world turned dark, stormy, gloomy and horrifying, because God showed His anger related to His Son's death on the cross. At the time of Christ's death, loud thunder roared, an earthquake came, and the world turned dark and terrifying. The people of that day realized the true Son of God had just died.

The Bible tells us in Luke 21:25-28, a **similar situation** will occur just prior to the Tribulation because God, again, reacts in anger. When these signs begin to happen, everyone on earth will feel terrified by what they see and sense. As informed Christians we needn't fear, because we can know from the Bible what God is really doing.

Prior to the visual Rapture, we will see signs in the sun, moon (not the Blood Moons from an earlier chapter), and stars. Those who do not know what is happening will feel perplexity at the roaring of the sea and the waves and men fainting with fear. In addition we may witness the ghastly **overwhelming scourge** the Antichrist sets loose on the world (Joel 2:1-10). As Christians it's **mandatory** to understand about the scourge so if we do see it, we won't feel afraid.

Luke 17:31
³¹ *On <u>that day</u>, the one who is on the housetop and whose goods are in the house must not go down to take them out; ...*

This scourge, another sign of our impending departure, will cause fearful people to attempt to leave their housetops to get their goods, and possibly save their lives due to the sheer terror. The next verses define the scourge in brilliant detail. As believers in Jesus, when we see this scourge, our deliverance is guaranteed and nothing will harm us. The scourge:

Joel 2:1-10
¹ *Blow a trumpet in Zion, and sound an alarm on My holy mountain! Let all the inhabitants of the land tremble, <u>For the day of the Lord is coming; Surely it is near,</u> ² A day of <u>darkness and gloom, a day of clouds and thick darkness. As the dawn is spread</u> over the mountains, so there is a great and mighty people; there has never been anything like it, nor will there be again after it to the years of many generations. ³ A fire consumes before them and behind them a flame burns. The land is like the garden of Eden before them but a desolate wilderness behind them, And nothing at all escapes them. ⁴ Their appearance is like the appearance of horses; And like war horses, so they run. ⁵ With a noise as of chariots they leap on the tops of the mountains, like the crackling of a flame of fire consuming the stubble, like a mighty people arranged for battle. ⁶ Before them the people*

are in anguish; all faces turn pale. ⁷ They run like mighty men, they climb the wall like soldiers; and they each march in line, nor do they deviate from their paths. ⁸ They do not crowd each other, they march everyone in his path; When they burst through the defenses, they do not break ranks. ⁹They rush on the city, they run on the wall; they climb into the houses, they enter through the windows like a thief. ¹⁰Before them the earth quakes, the heavens tremble, the sun and the moon grow dark and the stars lose their brightness.

The Antichrist places the overflowing scourge on the world just prior to the start of the Tribulation. In Joel 2:1; *"for the day of the Lord is coming; surely it is near."* So, the day of the Lord, the Tribulation, has not yet started. I think the signs mentioned in Luke 21:25-26 — in the stars, the sun, the moon, and the oceans — will occur soon after the scourge arrives. The scourge will be a pivotal event prior to the visual Rapture.

In **Road Map**, prophecies #17 and #22, I speculate that after the Ezekiel attack the physical land mass of Israel will actually become much larger than its current geographic footprint. After the Ezekiel battle, Israel's land mass will return to its original size, the full land area God had originally provided for Jacob's twelve sons per Genesis 13:14-15 and Genesis 15:18.

I believe the Antichrist uses the scourge as a power of persuasion. In Joel 2:3 we can see, as the scourge marches, it destroys everything in its path behind them and nothing escapes. The whole world will hear about this happening and the news will terrify them. Most of the world will not understand what is happening. Also, again, notice in Joel 2:1-2 the mention of the following:

Joel 2:1-2
¹ ... "For the day of the Lord is coming; Surely it is near, ² A day of darkness and gloom, a day of clouds and thick darkness. As the dawn is spreading...."

Please make note to the reference of *"dawn"* as it may have an interesting correlation to the sequence of events as we proceed.

Israel will quickly surmise this scourge comes for them, with no way to stop it. Then this new charismatic leader, who recently came on the scene (the Antichrist), tells Israel he has a way to protect them from the impending terrors and effects of this scourge. Israel knows they cannot stop it and they believe this new leader can. Reluctantly, Israel signs a **covenant** with the Antichrist to allow this scourge to pass over them . . . actually, a deception.

Isaiah 28:14-15
14 Therefore, hear the word of the Lord, O scoffers, who rule this people who are in Jerusalem, 15 Because you have said, We have made a <u>covenant</u> with death, and with Sheol we have made a pact. The overwhelming scourge will not reach us when it passes by, For we have made falsehood our refuge and we have concealed ourselves with deception.

Isaiah 28:18-19
18 Your <u>covenant</u> with death <u>will be canceled</u>, and your pact with Sheol will not stand; When the overwhelming scourge passes through, Then you become its trampling place. 19 As often as it passes through, it will seize you; For morning after morning it will pass through, any time during the day or night, and it will be sheer terror to understand what it means.

This covenant signed by Israel with the Antichrist will prove to be false, and this *"covenant"* agreement *"will be canceled."* Israel will then have the scourge come upon them over and over again causing incredible horror.

When we see the imposing signs, mentioned in Luke 21:25-26, along with the events in Joel 2:1-10, we can anticipate with certainty we will soon hear the shout from the Lord. The first trumpet and the visual Rapture begins.

Many Bible commentators falsely believe the overwhelming scourge is actually the army of two-hundred million from the east, explained in the Sixth Trumpet judgment inside the Tribulation, Revelation 9:13-21. The overwhelming scourge talked about in Joel 2 is an entirely different event and will start shortly before the Tribulation begins.

2 Peter 1:19-21
19 So we have the prophetic word made more sure, to which you do well to pay attention as to a lamp shining in a dark place, until the <u>day dawns</u> and the <u>day star (*) arises in your hearts</u>. 20 But know this first of all, that no prophecy of Scripture is a matter of one's own interpretation, 21 for no prophecy was ever made by an act of human will, but men moved by the Holy Spirit spoke from God.

(*) The term "day star" comes from the King James Version KJV

Luke 21:25-28
25 There will be signs in sun and moon and stars, and on the earth dismay among nations, in perplexity at the roaring of the sea and the waves, 26 men fainting from fear and the expectation of the things which are coming upon the world; for the powers of the heavens will be shaken. 27 Then they will see the Son of Man coming in the cloud with power and great glory. 28 But when these things begin to take place, <u>straighten up and lift up your heads</u>, because your redemption is drawing near.

Again, Luke 21:28 tells us, specifically, to **"lift up your heads,"** in other words, **look up.** But how do we know when to do this? How can we do this precise command if the Rapture is to happen without any warning? We can't. Those of us who understand end times prophecy and truly comprehend the signs God has given us will get our special **gift** from God when the *"day dawns,"* and *"the <u>day star</u> arises in our hearts."* 2 Peter 1:19. But what does God tell us here? He will give us the gift, within our hearts, of a kind of **heads up** (pardon the pun), telling us without a doubt that He is on the way. This will alert us to have our lamps on, giving us the foreknowledge to actually know the visual Rapture is about to take place, so we will be able to **look up** with certainty. This also answers the question many people have regarding how we can know when the visual Rapture comes if we are asleep in our beds. God has provided us with the answer for all those who understand what is happening. He will wake us so we can then fully prepare and stay alert with certainty to know when to **look up** and see Him coming for us. **I find this glorious.**

Back in Joel 2:2, it said the scourge starts *"As the dawn is spreading..."* This sounds similar to the sun starting to rise in the morning. In 2 Peter 1:19, when *"the day dawns,"* or after the sun has completely risen in the morning, we will get the warning from God Himself that He is coming and *"the day star arises in your hearts."* These verses seem to tell us, when we see the scourge starting, we won't need to worry about it because, at about the same time, we need to get ready to go home with Jesus in the visual Rapture. Note: *"As the dawn is spreading..."* and then *"the day dawns,"* seem to refer to the same day as events unfold. This laces all these events into a defined sequence.

We will hear about the scourge, receive the warning in our hearts by God, begin to see the signs in the sky and on the earth and, at this point, we **look up.** We hear the shout of the archangel, hear the first trumpet and, while still alive, witness all the dead in Christ rise first. We all need to keep looking up and then, prior to the final trumpet, those of us alive are also taken up. For the Biblical and spiritual obedience of knowing all this, we get **our special reward: the Crown of Righteousness,** for loving His appearing—as promised in 2 Timothy 4:8:

2 Timothy 4:8
8 in the future there is laid up for me the <u>crown of righteousness</u>, which the Lord, the righteous Judge, will award to me on that day; and not only to me, but also <u>to all who have loved His appearing</u>.

Christians who seriously understand end time prophecies, who have longed for His appearing and are **looking up,** as God directs us to do, will get our **crown.** Do you want your crown for this action at the visual Rapture? If God wanted the Rapture unknown to us, why would He give such a wonderful blessing and reward for **looking up?** We are commanded to know about all this as God directs each of us.

We really need to understand, after 1,900 years, a great deal of prophecy has been, and is still being, fulfilled today. Because of this, it is obvious that Jesus appears to be on the way. We truly need to know what to anticipate, and what the Bible does tell us. We do not want anybody to give us wrong information. We don't want to lose our crown. Time is running out. We need to choose wisely with the help of the Lord.

Revelation 3:3
3 So remember what you have received and heard; and keep it, and repent. Therefore if you do not wake up, I will come like a thief, and you will not know at what hour I will come to you.

The Lord is telling us to **stay awake.** Do not keep too busy with worldly things or lack the information to both see and know the signs He has graciously given us to determine when to **look up. Sleeping** Christians, unaware of God's signs, will not receive the *"day star."* Do not allow yourself to be afraid of these coming signs due to lack of study and understanding. Certainly, ignorance can make one terrified of these events — something God does not want informed Christians to experience.

TWINKLING OF AN EYE

1 Corinthians 15:51-52
[51] Behold, I tell you a mystery; we will not all sleep, but we will all be changed, [52] in a moment, in the twinkling of an eye, at the last trumpet; for the trumpet will sound, and the dead will be raised imperishable, and we will be changed.

Verse 51 **does not tell us** the Rapture will happen in a moment, in the twinkling of an eye but, rather we will all change (bodily) *"in a moment, in the twinkling of an eye, at the last trumpet."*

THE VISUAL RAPTURE THE SAME LITERAL DAY AS THE START OF TRIBULATION

Luke 17:26-27
[26] And just as it happened in the days of Noah, so it will be also <u>in the days of the Son of Man:</u> [27] they were eating, they were drinking, they were marrying, they were being given in marriage, until <u>the day</u> that Noah entered the ark, and the flood came and destroyed them all.

In the Bible, God uses many different terms to describe the seven-year Tribulation. He uses: the Tribulation, the great Tribulation, the time of Jacob's trouble, the day of wrath, *"the days of the Son of Man,"* Daniel's Seventieth week, and the day of the Lord's vengeance. He provides a time frame regarding Noah and the flood to make a comparison as to what will happen *"in the days of the Son of Man."* The two specific words *"the day"* (yom) in the verses above hold significance:

Luke 17:26-27 mentions a couple of profound things. People lived their lives normally and peacefully until *"the day"* Noah entered the ark. On that same day (a twenty-four-hour period) the flood caught **the unbelieving world** by surprise and destroyed them. But Noah expected it. God had given him, and all the people of his day, one hundred and twenty years of foreknowledge about what would come, so they could prepare . . . very similar to what God does for us now through His prophecies regarding the end times and visual Rapture, all intended as preparation for us to witness. Even with one-hundred and twenty years of warnings, the people of Noah's day scoffed at the idea of a flood happening—even as they all daily looked upon Noah's huge boat. They considered Noah crazy. God delivered Noah and his family to safety on the **very same day** His punishment came upon the rest of the world.

God now provides yet another example in Luke of the complacency of mankind prior to an event that also happens in **one day,** with catastrophic ramifications:

Luke 17:28-29
[28] *It was the same as happened in the days of Lot: they were eating, they were drinking, they were buying, they were selling, they were planting, they were building;* [29] *but on the day that Lot went out from Sodom it rained fire and brimstone from heaven and destroyed them all.*

Everybody in the days of Lot lived their lives in perceived peace and normalcy until **the day** Lot went out of Sodom. During the same day (a twenty-four-hour period) fire and brimstone from heaven caught everyone by surprise and destroyed them. But again, God delivered Lot and his family to safety on the very same day that His punishment came upon Sodom.

Two angels forewarned Lot and his wife to take God's explicit instructions **not to look back** at what was going to take place. Lot's wife, however, upon their departure from Sodom, did not obey what God requested of them. She looked back and paid a penalty. God turned her into a pillar of salt.

Luke 17:30-36
30 It will be just the same <u>on the day</u> that the Son of Man is revealed. 31 On <u>that day</u>, the one who is on the housetop and whose goods are in the house must not go down to take them out; and likewise the one who is in the field must not turn back. 32<u>Remember Lot's wife</u>. 33Whoever seeks to keep his life will lose it, and whoever loses his life will preserve it. 34 I tell you, on that night there will be two in one bed; <u>one will be taken</u> and the other will be left. 35 There will be two women grinding at the same place; <u>one will be taken</u> and the other will be left. 36 Two men will be in the field; <u>one will be taken</u> and the other will be left."

Since God specifically asks us to *"remember Lot's wife"* related to our last days, this may have a significant parallel during the visual Rapture.

Luke 17:30 says *"It will be just the same <u>on the day</u> that the Son of Man is revealed."* The Son of Man *"revealed"* happens again at the visual Rapture just prior to the start of the Tribulation. In Luke 17:34-36, in three different examples, God talks about *"one will being taken"* and the other left. These verses mention nothing to imply these *"takings"* will be spontaneous hidden events, in a moment or twinkling. More than likely the three *"takings"* will be blatantly obvious.

Based on all these verses, when Christ comes to visually Rapture us into the clouds and takes us home, the world should expect the Tribulation to start within, literally, twenty-four hours of our departure. We will know the day and the approximate hour when all of this will come upon us by God's hand and not by any prognostication on our part. Only God knows the day and the hour. Prophecy students will know, in our hearts, when God reveals to us the approximate time of the Rapture.

We will all go to bed one night and when we awaken the following day, the signs will start, bringing the actual day of the visual Rapture. We should know, with certainty, the day has come because God has provided us with His full and complete prophetic **Road Map** along with His specific warnings.

The Bible tells us **we** cannot know the day or the hour of His return, so this all probably sounds like a contradiction when I say we can and will know the Rapture is **about to occur**. However in reality, we will not be able to say with certainty, **the day before** the visual Rapture happens, that tomorrow is the day.

THE WORLD WILL APPEAR AT PEACE UP TO THE DAY OF THE VISUAL RAPTURE

Our world will get crazy in the near future and difficult to watch, for Christians especially. Did you pick up on something quite interesting in both the singular **day** concepts in the Noah and Lot verses? From these verses we can know the world will appear peaceful or normal to nonbelievers right up until the visual Rapture. Both Noah and Lot lived in a spiritually decadent world; yet it did not appear so to the outside secular masses. The people of the world at that time lived what they believed to be good, productive, profitable lives in counterfeit peace and harmony.

The world at that time had no idea that God was about to remove their so-called peace. Noah entered the Ark, and Lot left Sodom, and on those specific individual days, God came suddenly and **stole** everyone's false peace. He came like a **thief**.

God's arrival in no way surprised either Noah or Lot, because God provided detailed foreknowledge of what would come. This is a model for us for our time; be fully aware of what God is showing us.

These Noah and Lot verses indicate to me that we will not see WWIII or any other terrible cataclysmic punishments before the visual Rapture occurs. Our hurt and despair as Christians comes in seeing the world has basically lost Biblical morality and faith in Jesus. We need to take caution in order to survive in a degenerative and unfriendly world.

Having the world seem to appear at peace and prosperous right up to the visual Rapture gives the Deceiver a great opportunity. It offers a masterful way for Him to convince the secular world that when certain Christians today talk about impending gloom and doom, and survivalist type issues, they are crazy. Satan will insist there is no need to prepare for anarchy; nothing is going to happen. The world will accept this wholeheartedly. I personally believe the horrible survivalist type of events in the world **will not occur** until the start of the Tribulation period. All of the cataclysmic happenings will touch only those who live into the Tribulation. Worried Christians today, showing fear, play right into the Deceiver's hands and make Christians in general look like frightened children. The Deceiver can then easily use this against us and say something like this to the world:

> *"Why can't Jesus believers stop being so fearful and negative, and truly see how great and wonderful the world has become. Jesus believers are all unjustifiably fearful. Something must be wrong with them. They need my help and retraining. Pay no attention to their delusions."*

Fortunately, Christians may get to benefit from this perceived peaceful world. God will remove us all in the visual Rapture right before He makes things on earth devastatingly horrible. Right after nonbelievers see us leave, in the visual Rapture, as I have mentioned before, many left behind will immediately figure out the deception. We need only to trust in the Lord, heed His warnings, follow His instructions, and we will get to go home with Him just hours before God's serious punishments come upon the world.

ADDED SUPPORT REGARDING THE VALIDITY OF BELIEVING IN A VISUAL RAPTURE

Well, actually, **THREE** Raptures will occur within the seven-year Tribulation period. The **FIRST** one on the day the Tribulation starts (just prior to the covenant signing) is for all Christians who, by faith, accepted Jesus as their Savior prior to this initial visual Rapture. In the **SECOND**, God has two witnesses who minister for Him during the first half of the Tribulation (Revelation 11:1-14). For background, these two witnesses will be sent by God to prophesy for him during the entire first half of the Tribulation. It is thought the two witnesses God sends might be Moses and Elijah (Matthew 17:3-4). Note: Elijah may already be here, per **Road Map** prophecy #22. They have tremendous powers and can control the entire earth's environmental systems at will. We are told they can breathe fire out of their mouths. They are indestructible until their ministry is completed at the midpoint of the Tribulation. God now allows the Antichrist to kill them. They lay dead in the street for three and a half days. God then resurrects them, lifting them up to heaven. God literally, visually Raptures these two men. The world is terrified by this.

The **THIRD** will happen when the <u>Tribulation saints</u>, the people who accepted Jesus during the entire seven-year Tribulation and died for their faith, are reunited with their bodies, Matthew 24:31. This occurs at the end of the Tribulation. Events **TWO** and **THREE** could not possibly happen at an unspecified time.

The visual Rapture of God's two witnesses is a Godly statement that will terrify those still living on earth at the middle of the Tribulation—another bold way God will use to try to awaken everybody a second time during the Tribulation.

Revelation 11:11-13
[11] But after the three and a half days, the breath of life from God came into them, and they stood on their feet; and great fear fell upon those who were watching them. [12] And they heard a loud voice from heaven saying to them, "Come up here." Then they went up into heaven in the cloud, and their enemies watched them. [13] And in that hour there was a great earthquake, and a tenth of the city fell; seven thousand people were killed in the earthquake, and the rest were terrified and gave glory to the God of heaven.

God talks about His two witnesses and their death at the middle of the Tribulation (Revelation 11). Three days after their deaths, the world will hear the voice from heaven saying *"Come up here"*—similar to how the first visual Rapture starts to happen. Something vital is missing at this second visual Rapture event, which indicates this is not the first visual Rapture of the whole church. Did you pick up on this? No trumpets sound in this sequence. The first visual Rapture with trumpets must certainly be visible also to gain the very same desired effect, as this small second visual Rapture.

Beyond the three events mentioned above that take place at the Tribulation, there is another Biblical event: God taking up Elijah into heaven in the Old Testament. 2 Kings 2:9-12, provides an account of Elisha witnessing Elijah going into heaven in a whirlwind and a chariot of fire. Elisha saw this as it happened:

2 Kings 2:9-12

⁹ When they had crossed over, Elijah said to Elisha, "Ask what I shall do for you before I am taken from you." And Elisha said, "Please, let a double portion of your spirit be upon me." ¹⁰ He said, "You have asked a hard thing. Nevertheless, if you see me when I am taken from you, it shall be so for you; but if not, it shall not be so." ¹¹ As they were going along and talking, behold, there appeared a chariot of fire and horses of fire which separated the two of them. And Elijah went up by a whirlwind to heaven.¹² Elisha saw it and cried out, "My father, my father, the chariots of Israel and its horsemen!" And he saw Elijah no more

Our majestic God truly loves showing who He is to the people of the world. I see this also happening within our visual Rapture in the official Godly announcement to the world that His Tribulation has arrived.

God's Bible tells of yet another likely visual Rapture event just after the resurrection of Jesus:

Matthew 27:50-53

⁵⁰ And Jesus cried out again with a loud voice, and yielded up His spirit.⁵¹ And behold, the veil of the temple was torn in two from top to bottom; and the earth shook and the rocks were split. ⁵² The tombs were opened, and many bodies of the saints who had fallen asleep were raised; ⁵³<u>and coming out of the tombs after His resurrection they entered the holy city and appeared to many.</u>

Matthew tells how Jesus collected and resurrected all believers—from the time of Adam up to the time of His resurrection—to join their souls and enter the Holy city. God tells us they *"appeared to many."* But to whom did they appear? Likely, the people in Jerusalem, the Holy city, and did the people witness their departure to heaven with Jesus . . . some speculation at this point, but highly possible.

God refers to all who accept Him as *"saints"*, multiple times in the New Testament. The following verses talk about *"saints."* Notice these were all average, living believers:

Philippians 1:1-2
¹ Paul and Timothy, bond-servants of Christ Jesus, to all the saints in Christ Jesus who are in Philippi, including the overseers and deacons: ² Grace to you and peace from God our Father and the Lord Jesus Christ.

Hebrews 6:10
⁹ But, beloved, we are convinced of better things concerning you, and things that accompany salvation, though we are speaking in this way. ¹⁰ For God is not unjust so as to forget your work and the love which you have shown toward His name, in having ministered and in still ministering to the saints.

Ephesians 4:11-12
¹¹ And He gave some as apostles, and some as prophets, and some as evangelists, and some as pastors and teachers, ¹² for the equipping of the saints for the work of service, to the building up of the body of Christ;

This term *"saint,"* according to the Bible, refers to **every common believer**, both deceased and alive today. In the Catholic Church **saints** are only those people selected and appointed by the **world church** (man's concepts not God's) as worthy of this status, in their human opinion. Regular believers are not considered worthy of sainthood. The **world church** cannot assign or convey saint status to anyone. God has granted this status already to all believers.

ALTERNATE PATHS FOR LIVING CHRISTIANS ON THE DAY OF THE VISUAL RAPTURE

Christians who don't know about God's signs just prior to the visual Rapture and the scourge will feel frightened. Terrified at what they see, they will try to hide; but only because they did not study the information God provided, regarding what to know and do. These Christians may suffer a small penalty. Earlier in Luke 17:31 we are told *"the ones who are on the housetops must not go down into their houses."* Also, Luke 17:33, said **"Whoever seeks to keep his life will lose it, and whoever loses his life will preserve it."** I see a clear significance to these verses because God has shared with us everything we need to know.

1 Thessalonians 5:6-7
6 so then let us not sleep as others do, but let us be alert and sober. 7 For those who sleep do their sleeping at night, and those who get drunk get drunk at night.

1 Corinthians 15:51-52
51 Behold, I tell you a mystery; we will not all sleep, but we will all be changed,

Revelation 3:3
3 So remember what you have received and heard; and keep it, and repent. Therefore if you do not wake up, I will come like a thief, and you will not know at what hour I will come to you.

Luke 17:33-36
33 Whoever seeks to keep his life will lose it, and whoever loses his life will preserve it. 34 I tell you, on that night there will be two in one bed; one will be taken and the other will be left. 35 There will be two women grinding at the same place; one will be taken

and the other will be left. [36] Two men will be in the field; one will be taken and the other will be left.

Luke 17:33 may just be telling us: all living Christians, on the day of the visual Rapture, may experience the event slightly different. Our personal obedience to God's Word and His final directions and requests through prophecy will determine how we get Raptured.

God provides something special for those of us who have loved and seek His coming. God takes those of us who trust and understand His prophecies, know about His specific signs, and actually do **look up** as commanded, up alive in the visual Rapture at the **final trumpet**. All of the horrifying signs we see will look like something that would kill us. God has requested us to **look up** so we will neither see nor concentrate on the scourge, and the horror of it. Maybe as with Lot's wife, God does not want us to look upon the punishments coming on the world for our ultimate blessing. Perhaps this is why God specifically tells us to remember Lot's wife and to be **looking up.** God told Lot's wife and now possibly those of us living today **where to place our eyes**, on Him.

The Christians who have not studied end time prophecies may, basically, run and hide for their lives, down into their houses when they see these signs and the scourge. These Christians who have not learned about this prophecy regarding Gods' final request for us to **look up**, but are still faithful Christians, might have to deal with something else. Due only to the lack of end time's knowledge, these Christians who are afraid and try to hide when these terrifying signs happen, and do not **look up,** may enter heaven by a different path. Remember Lots' wife? She died because she did not specifically follow God's required direction regarding what to do upon leaving Sodom. She immediately went to heaven, but she went the hard way, through death.

The Bible appears to tell us that if a Christian does not know to **look up**, prior to the very first trumpet blast, their bodies will die here on earth, first. God will then instantly Rapture those people with the first group, who have died on earth, from Pentecost up to the time of the Rapture. Those of us who know the signs, and obey, will recognize them and **look up**; we will go up alive at the final trumpet and then receive **our crown** from the Lord for a job well done. We still all go together, but the paths and the rewards differ. Those of us who enter the Kingdom alive in the visual Rapture just prior to the final trumpet might get one additional wonderful blessing. This amazing blessing will occur just before God transforms us. He will allow us to see the masses of the entire body of the church, rising into the sky to join Him. God will allow us to witness all the Christians' souls already with the Lord, those who died an earthly death reunited with their bodies rising up into the sky just before we join into this event. I hold a magnificent mental visual picture of this.

The visual Rapture of the church will begin the second largest series of Godly events in all of human history. The first of course was Christ's birth, death, resurrection, and ascension into heaven. Why would God desire to have a secretive and hidden Rapture? Based on all Bible history and God's very nature, this would make absolutely no logical sense.

Revelation 1:7-8
[7] Behold, He is coming with the clouds, <u>and every eye will see Him</u>, even those who pierced Him; and all the tribes of the earth will mourn over Him. So it is to be. Amen. [8] "I am the Alpha and the Omega," says the Lord God, "who is and who was and who is to come, the Almighty."

An interesting, final thought to ponder on this topic: By God allowing the whole world *"every eye"* to see us actually physically depart in the visual Rapture, something wonderful will happen. God, in this one visual action, will have saved millions upon millions of unbelievers, still on earth, within minutes of our departure. If we simply disappeared unexpectedly, this would not happen and would be a severely wasted opportunity to save many quickly. All of our doubting friends who thought us strange and crazy, for sharing the information in this book, will understand immediately that we had provided them with the truth and had **given them the correct information**. God will not waste this opportunity and wants everybody to find Him. Therefore, it is important to offer this information to our friends for thoughtful consideration. What one event could do more for God's ultimate glory than the visual Rapture? It will be an EPIC event.

THE FIVE CROWNS WE CAN WIN FOR THE LORD

God has five crown rewards for excellent service during our life on earth. I didn't list them in any particular order but start with the one we discussed in this chapter.

1. The Crown of Righteousness for those who love His appearing.

2 Timothy 4:7-8
7 I have fought the good fight, I have finished the course, I have kept the faith; 8 in the future there is laid up for me the crown of righteousness, which the Lord, the righteous Judge, will award to me on that day; and not only to me, but also to all who have loved His appearing.

Timothy understood about God and loved the concept of His appearing in the second coming. He also knew he would not be living when this happened. All believers who love the study of end time prophecies, and anticipated Jesus appearing whether living or having died prior to the visual Rapture, will receive this crown. Some Bible teachers state that God offers this crown to all people who accept Jesus as their Savior; this is incorrect.

Those of us alive who have studied Bible prophecy and love the concept of His appearing, and understand to literally look up at the Rapture, will get this crown as part of the visual Rapture.

2. The Crown of Life is the Martyr's crown

James 1:12
¹² *Blessed is a man who perseveres under trial; for once he has been approved, he will receive the crown of life which the Lord has promised to those who love Him.*

Revelation 2:10
¹⁰ *Do not fear what you are about to suffer. Behold, the devil is about to cast some of you into prison, so that you will be tested, and you will have Tribulation for ten days. Be faithful until death, and I will give you the crown of life.*

The ten days listed above define a time limit for those who accept Jesus during the Tribulation. This comforting verse tells the new Christians in the Tribulation that Satan may imprison them before he puts them to death, but any suffering will last for a limited time.

3. The Crown of Glory for Godly people who have served Christ quietly and with a good heart and pure motives.

1 Peter 5:1-5
¹ *Therefore, I exhort the elders among you, as your fellow elder and witness of the sufferings of Christ, and a partaker also of the glory that is to be revealed, ² shepherd the flock of God among you, exercising oversight not*

under compulsion, but voluntarily, according to the will of God; and not for sordid gain, but with eagerness; [3] nor yet as Lording it over those allotted to your charge, but proving to be examples to the flock. [4] And when the Chief Shepherd appears, you will receive the unfading crown of glory. [5] You younger men, likewise, be subject to your elders; and all of you, clothe yourselves with humility toward one another, for God is opposed to the proud, but gives grace to the humble.

4. The **Crown of Exultation** (**Rejoicing**) is the soul winner's crown, for ministers and evangelists: those who teach the word and go out to try to help people find Jesus.

1 Thessalonians 2:19
[19] For who is our hope or joy or crown of exultation? Is it not even you, in the presence of our Lord Jesus at His coming?

5. The **Incorruptible Crown** is for those who have control over their lusts which is the spirit of self-denial.

1 Corinthians 9:25-27 (New King James Version)
[25] And every man that striveth for the mastery is temperate in all things. Now they do it to obtain a corruptible crown; but we an incorruptible.

Romans 2:5-9

5 *But because of your stubbornness and unrepentant heart you are storing up wrath for yourself in the day of wrath and revelation of the righteous judgment of God,* 6*who will render to each person according to his deeds:* 7 *to those who by perseverance in doing good seek for glory and honor and immortality, eternal life;* 8 *but to those who are selfishly ambitious and do not obey the truth, but obey unrighteousness, wrath and indignation.* 9 *There will be tribulation...*

CHAPTER 6

THE TRIBULATION
GOD'S
21 JUDGMENTS

Some Christians falsely believe we'll have a peaceful first half of the Tribulation. This is categorically incorrect. Instead it creates seven years of hell on earth. The Tribulation will happen, and nobody should want to live through any portion of this seven-year period of God's judgments.

Some might find this chapter to be a bit disconcerting, but I feel it necessitates understanding. God loves us so much; He does not want believers to experience His coming judgments. He tells us vividly what they will be . . . all very horrible and offers us a loving way to escape the Tribulation. We can achieve this by personally accepting Jesus.

The book of Revelation (Apokalypsis) **reveals** God's will to put an end to evil in the world and bring the knowledge of Jesus to Israel. This final special book in the Bible explains the last scenes of God's great play. John the Apostle wrote the book of Revelation purposefully for God to share what must take place to fulfill and complete all the Old Testament prophecies regarding the Messiah. This will occur in the *"latter days"* . . . our time. These Biblical concepts tell us to fully understand what God requires of us and heed the warnings. The Prologue of Revelation — verses 1:1-3 say the *"time is near."* The time is now.

Revelation 1:1-3
[1] The Revelation of Jesus Christ, which God gave Him to show to His bond-servants, the things which must soon take place; and He sent and communicated it by His angel to His bond-servant John, [2] who testified to the word of God and to the testimony of Jesus Christ, even to all that he saw. [3] Blessed is he who reads and those who hear the words of the prophecy, and heed the things which are written in it; for the <u>time is near</u>.

The Apostle John received inspiration from Jesus while imprisoned on the Isle of Patmos between 81 and 96 AD. Before imprisonment, John preached about Jesus **Lord and God.** This infuriated Domitian, the Emperor of Rome. He demanded his subjects call him *"Dominus et Deus,"* translated roughly: **Lord and God.** This caused Domitian to have a dilemma with John, and he imprisoned him.

Revelation contains three forms. First, a **letter** talking to the people of his day about what will come in the future. Second, **prophecy** predicting future events for us. This has even greater importance because God makes His will known for us. He expresses issues He expects us to obey. We should not take flippantly or lightly its seriousness. Through prophecy God tells us exactly what He wants us to know. Third, it is **apocalyptic,** enhancing prophecy by using bold, daring, vivid illustrations to drive His points home. God discusses the **Tribulation** in expressive detail. He intentionally tries to make clear points.

I will not go into tremendous detail related to the book of Revelation, but I do desire to share some interesting observations. John, after his Prologue, starts this book with a declaration of Jesus' great love for us:

Revelation 1:4-6
⁴ John to the seven churches that are in Asia: Grace to you and peace, from Him who is and who was and who is to come, and from the seven Spirits who are before His throne, ⁵ and from Jesus Christ, the faithful witness, the firstborn of the dead, and the ruler of the kings of the earth. <u>To Him who loves us</u> and released us from our sins by His blood— ⁶ and <u>He has made us to be a kingdom, priests</u> to His God and Father— to Him be the glory and the dominion forever and ever. Amen.

On a side note: Revelation 1:6—*"He has made us to be a kingdom, priests."* This tells us, in the eyes of Jesus, He considers all of His faithful believers *"priests"* for service to Him. 1 Peter 2:4-5 and 2:9, bolsters this thinking:

1 Peter 2:4-5
⁴ And coming to Him as to a living stone which has been rejected by men, but is choice and precious in the sight of God, ⁵ you also, as living stones, are being built up as a

spiritual house for a holy priesthood, to offer up spiritual sacrifices acceptable to God through Jesus Christ.

<u>*1 Peter 2:9*</u>
⁹ But you are a chosen race, a royal priesthood, a Holy nation, a people for God's own possession, so that you may proclaim the excellencies of Him who has called you out of darkness into His marvelous light;

John wrote the book of Revelation purposefully in symbolic format. John explains some mysterious imagery, along with certain actual literal issues. This includes all of God's planned Tribulation Judgments. But why was Revelation written in such a cryptic format? In John's day the Romans persecuted Christians for their faith in Jesus. John, being in prison on Patmos, needed to deal with Roman censors. The Romans censored anything written that was clearly related to Christianity. If John had written in a literal sense, he would not have gotten his writing past scrutiny. John, with God's help, had to be very shrewd in his approach to writing this book. He essentially wrote this book in code. God both planned and knew we would understand the book of Revelation in its final format. When placed in context along with the other books in both the Old and New Testaments, it fits perfectly in the fully completed Bible.

I believe God had **TWO** defined reasons for the book of Revelation, both of which help current believers and, soon, nonbelievers entering the Tribulation, as well.

FIRST, the subject matter provides a warning to all the people of the world today. Revelation predicts and describes a coming horrendous time. God explains how He will punish sinners and put an end to sin, once and for all. He explains for us, vividly, the defeat of sin during the Tribulation. By God explaining His intended severe Judgments, He motivates us to understand the Bible. By reading the Bible, we learn from God about accepting Jesus, and through the grace of Jesus, we have nothing to fear. He offers a path to safety. The Judgments listed in the book of Revelation are **literal** and not symbolic. They are coming soon. Not one of God's Revelation Tribulation Judgments have occurred yet at any time in world history.

SECOND, the book of Revelation will guide those individuals who will live into the Tribulation. At the exact second after the visual Rapture, for a short period of time, not one Christian will remain on earth—100 percent unbelievers . . . a very dark moment. Right after the visual Rapture, people will begin to realize what happened.

I provide an outline of the terrible Judgments God has in store for those living in this seven-year period. For nonbelievers, I'm hoping this outline will help in the consideration of some options. I know some of you don't take the book of Revelation literally, thinking it is only symbolic. I personally wouldn't want to take the chance against its validity.

No peace of any kind will exist during the entire seven-year Tribulation. As mentioned earlier, some people have the false assumption about a peaceful first half. However, the entire Tribulation will have no semblance of peace.

Twenty-one major judgments occur in this seven-year period . . . three sets of seven judgments. Revelation Chapters 6, 8, 9, and 16 describe these judgments. I am going to list the **seven Seal Judgments** and then the **seven Trumpet Judgments** that happen in the first three and a half years—fourteen Judgments in the first half of the Tribulation. I then list the final **seven Bowl Judgments** that occur in the last three and a half years, so you'll get the total abbreviated seven-year picture.

FIRST HALF OF THE SEVEN-YEAR TRIBULATION

God's master plan includes all of the events, both good and bad, during the Tribulation. He chose the Tribulation as a time of punishment and judgment because the world treated His Son so horribly. God plans to show his ire.

Day one recaps, with some added, educated speculation, all we learned from Scriptural references, in chapter five, regarding the day the visual Rapture occurs and the Tribulation begins.

DAY ONE

- Satan has, by now, brought the overflowing scourge to earth. It will terrify the whole world, particularly Israel.
- God's signs in the heavens, on the earth, and in the seas will happen.
- The visual Rapture occurs just before the signing of a covenant agreement, between the Antichrist and Israel. The whole nonbelieving world will see the visual Rapture and will feel astounded.
- After the visual Rapture has completed, chaos and terror will fill the entire earth. The world continues to see the scourge coming, along with all the other signs God showed us, preceding the visual Rapture.
- The peace covenant is signed between the Antichrist and Israel. This saves Israel from the effects and terror of the scourge — or so they think.
- The signs God placed on the earth to inform us of the visual Rapture will come continue to grow progressively worse into the Tribulation. Peace will no longer exist.
- The loss of possibly one-billion people in the visual Rapture will instantly decimate the world economy.
- The workforce will essentially be crushed. People will quickly determine they can find no way to fix this economic devastation. Hell on earth has arrived.

THE EARLY MONTHS OF TRIBULATION

- God's two witnesses arrive, and they cannot be killed or harmed. They have incredible powers to witness for the Lord for the first half of the Tribulation.

220

- Israel, per previous speculation, may have already reestablished their tribal system identities through Elijah.
- Now, 12,000 Jews, selected by God from each of Jacob's twelve tribes—a total of 144,000—will accept the Lord as their Messiah and will become evangelists for Jesus to the entire world. This 144,000 issue is controversial, and some will say they come on the scene at the mid-point in the Tribulation. But think about this; Earlier we established that one half of all living beings in the world will die in the first half of the Tribulation. So, why would God wait to bring these evangelists into being halfway through His period of punishments and risk losing half of the world before he can minister to them? I strongly believe the 144,000 will arrive quickly, by design, soon after the visual Rapture completion.
- The **seven Seal Judgments** and the **seven Trumpet Judgments** now start to happen.

THE SEVEN SEAL JUDGMENTS

These events happen during the early months of the Tribulation.

SEAL JUDGMENT # 1: (Revelation 6:1-2) The White Horse— with the False Christ (Antichrist) riding it and conquering on it. The Antichrist consolidates power and takes full control right after the start of the Tribulation. We know from earlier in this book he came on the scene before the visual Rapture. This power consolidation may happen easily because of the worldwide chaos that began after Christians were taken in the visual Rapture.

SEAL JUDGMENT # 2: (Revelation 6:3-4) The Red Horse— with the power to take peace from the earth making men desire to kill each other.

SEAL JUDGMENT # 3: (Revelation 6:5-6) The Black Horse—

with the power of famines and to reduce the world's food supply.

SEAL JUDGMENT # 4: (Revelation 6:7-8) The Ashen Horse — with the power of death and given the authority to kill one-fourth of all mankind with the sword, famine, and disease. If after the visual Rapture, six billion people remain on earth, this judgment will kill one and a half billion of them. Therefore, mathematically, four and a half billion will remain.

I doubt the first four Seal Judgments are, literally, horses. They probably fit in categories such as government consolidation, decrees, and accelerated corruption along with famines and plagues. The world will know about all four results in the first four seals. And all four could possibly happen simultaneously.

SEAL JUDGMENT # 5: (Revelation 6:9-11) Martyrs of the Tribulations' early days cry out in mass to the Lord for judgment from God, for the Antichrist. God tells them they still need to wait a bit longer because He has not yet finished with them.

SEAL JUDGMENT # 6: (Revelation 6:12-17) Terror is unleashed, bringing earthquakes, a blacked sun, a bloodlike moon, and the stars will be darkened . . . all much worse than the similar signs seen just prior to the visual Rapture.

We have now reached a brief interlude (Revelation 7:1-17) when God will place His seal of protection on the 144,000 evangelists. He will officially seal and protect them for the balance of the Tribulation.

SEAL JUDGMENT # 7: (Revelation 8:1-5) For one-half hour, only silence will prevail in heaven. This serves as the introduction of the **seven Trumpet Judgments** . . . even more severe than these first seven Seals.

THE SEVEN TRUMPET JUDGMENTS

These events happen after the Seal Judgments.

TRUMPET JUDGMENT # 1: (Revelation 8:7) Hail and fire mixed with blood will come down on earth and will burn up one-third of all the green plants and trees in the entire earth.

TRUMPET JUDGMENT # 2: (Revelation 8:8-9) A burning mountain will fall into the sea; one-third of all the oceans turn to blood, one-third of all ocean life dies, and one-third of all ships are destroyed.

TRUMPET JUDGMENT# 3: (Revelation 8:10-11) A star will fall from the heavens (called Wormwood) and one-third of all the rivers and fresh water turns rotten.

TRUMPET JUDGMENT # 4: (Revelation 8:12-13) One-third of the sun, moon, and stars are smitten (dimmed yet again). The world gets much darker. In Revelation 8:13 we are told *"woe, woe, woe, to those who dwell on the earth, because of the remaining blasts of the trumpet of the three angels who are about to sound!"* Trumpets, five, six, and seven will be severe.

TRUMPET JUDGMENT# 5: (Revelation 9:1-12) Smoke, like the smoke of a great furnace, will come up from a bottomless pit all over the earth, bringing demon scorpion locusts. They will torment and bite those whom God has not sealed and protected. The protected are the people who are still alive and have accepted Jesus inside the Tribulation period. God will not allow unsaved people to die from these bites but they will get horrendous sores all over their bodies. This torture will last for a full five months. People will desire to die, but God will not allow it.

TRUMPET JUDGMENT # 6: (Revelation 9:13-21) A large army from the east (two hundred million actual demons) will be set loose on the world to kill one-third of the remaining people on earth. Remember back in Seal Judgment 4, one quarter of the world was killed, leaving four and a half billion still alive. This Trumpet Judgment will kill one third of the remaining four and a half billion people, or another one and one half billion. There will then be only three billion people left in the world. Some Bible scholars say this army of two hundred million comes from China, based on their great population mass. This is not accurate. Revelation tells us four angels release them. This army is not human, and it is not the scourge; they will be something entirely different.

TRUMPET JUDGMENT # 7: (Revelation 11:15-19) Will announce to the world: Jesus is the ruler of the earth *"He will reign forever and ever."* But the Antichrist has another idea and prepares to make a hideous second half of the Tribulation.

The Bible refers to many false Christ's, and false prophets, and movements that will bring evil at different times, but Jesus also clearly talks about one exceptionally sinister individual that will come on the scene in the end times — the Antichrist. Let's take a look at the Antichrist and their relationship. Some distinctions: the word **anti** has two meanings. In the English language it means **against** someone or something. However, in the **original Greek** text, the word *"anti"* when attached with the title given to Jesus *"Christ,"* or **"Messiah,"** means *"instead of"* or *"in place of."* Therefore, using the original Greek interpretation, the **Antichrist** does not mean **against Christ**, it means **in place of Christ**. This has great significance. The end goal of the Antichrist is not to merely be against Christ, but to **completely replace Jesus,** making Himself God. He will proclaim himself as the only one and true god. Pure unmitigated hubris.

I believe the Antichrist is alive today; he is a man and not Satan at this time. I would even venture to say he does not yet know who he really is. Satan is, however, grooming him now for his coming role on the world stage.

Back in Chapter 4, Ezekiel 28:12 professes that Satan was the most beautiful of all God's angels. After his fall, this did not change. I believe when he arrives, He will use his God-given attributes to his advantage. He will be attractive, charming, cunning, and will prove to be an egomaniac. According to the Bible this man will have certain specific characteristics we should recognize:

- **Daniel 7:8:** he will have *"a mouth uttering great boasts"* against Jesus.
- **Daniel 7:25:** *"he will intend to make alterations in times and in laws,"* which could include changing our calendars away from correlation to Jesus.
- **Psalm 55:21**: *"his speech will be smoother than butter."*
- **2 Corinthians 11:14:** *"Satan disguises himself as an angel of light."*
- **Revelation 12:9:** *"he deceives the whole world."*
- **Daniel 11:37:** *"He will show no regard for the gods of his fathers or for the desire of women, nor will he show regard for any other god; for he will magnify himself above them all."*
- **2 Thessalonians 2:9:** *"he is in accord with the activity of Satan, with all the power and signs and false wonders and with all the deception of wickedness."*
- **Luke 22:3:** As an example of what is yet to come, note: at the time of Jesus' first visit, Satan entered Judas Iscariot and took control of him. Judas was one of the original twelve Disciples of Jesus. He betrayed the Lord with a kiss (Mark 14:44-45) leading to His crucifixion. Judas later committed suicide when he realized what he had done. Satan essentially guided Jesus to the cross, through Judas. Satan will reside within

the Antichrist in a similar fashion at the midpoint of the Tribulation.

- **Daniel 8:23-26:** Finally, paraphrased; he is insolent, skilled in intrigue, powerful but not by his own power; he destroys mighty men and devastates the holy people. Shrewd, a master of deception, he destroys many, and will become arrogant and magnify himself. He will even oppose the *"Prince of princes,"* Jesus, as we see in Daniel 8:25.

The Antichrist will be a wicked individual, and hardly anybody will see it. Satan will pull all the strings within this man. It will appear the Antichrist is killed at the middle of the Tribulation, but he is not dead, only severely wounded. He cannot be dead because Satan has no power over life and death, only God does, so the Deceiver intends to do a **counterfeit resurrection** from supposed death. The Antichrist appears dead for three days. Satan, at this point, enters him with **a miraculous false resurrection**, similar to Jesus. Then he claims to be god, the only god for the balance of the Tribulation. The last half of the Tribulation is referred to as the **Great Tribulation**.

As discussed in an earlier chapter, at the beginning of the Tribulation, ten Kings have power over ten Kingdoms—three of them in strong disagreement with the Antichrist's doings. A battle at the midpoint of the Tribulation appears to kill the Antichrist, and also kills the three Kings who were **restraining him** during the first half of the tribulation.

Now, with the three **restraining kings** dead, the fully Satan-indwelled Antichrist has no restraint or restrictions, and unleashes incredible demonic terror on the whole world for the next three and one half years.

HALFWAY INTO THE TRIBULATION

- Revelation 10:3 tells us those still alive inside the Tribulation have survived 1,260 days in the process.

- At the start of the Tribulation, six-billion people remained on earth after the visual Rapture. At this halfway point, the world population has been reduced to three-billion people. Only half of the world population remains on the earth.
- God allows the death of His two witnesses, and their bodies lay in the street for three and a half days. The people rejoice at their deaths. But after three and a half days, God brings them back to life, and takes them up into heaven in a visual Rapture. This sight terrifies the world. (Revelation 11:11-13).
- As explained above, at this halfway point the Antichrist goes from being an evil man to Satan incarnate. All hell literally has broken loose. The 3 Kings the *"restrainer"* are removed, and Satan has free reign to create terror.
- The Antichrist now enters the Temple, and declares himself the only god. He demands that everyone shall worship him alone. Per Daniel 12:11, this is the *"Abomination of Desolation."*
- Per Revelation 13:17-18, the Antichrist's mark, the number of man, is 666, and all people will now be required to take this mark on their right hand or forehead. Without this mark, you cannot buy or sell things. Without this mark, death is mandatory.
- At this point all Jews flee from Israel for protection. They now know the Antichrist is pure evil, and they run for their very lives.

SECOND HALF OF THE TRIBULATION

THE SEVEN BOWL JUDGMENTS

These events occur during the last half of the Tribulation.

BOWL JUDGMENT # 1: (Revelation 16:2) First Angel will set loose loathsome and malignant sores on those who have taken the mark of the beast 666 on their right hand or foreheads.

Those who worship the beast, the Satan-indwelled, Antichrist.

BOWL JUDGMENT # 2: (Revelation 16:3) Second Angel turns the sea into blood. This is the second time this is done. This time the entire sea turns to blood and everything in it dies. This is much more severe than Trumpet Judgment #2.

BOWL JUDGMENT # 3: (Revelation 16:4-7) Third Angel will turn all the fresh-water lakes and rivers into blood and praises Jesus for His judgments.

BOWL JUDGMENT # 4: (Revelation 16:8-9) Fourth Angel will make the sun hot enough to scorch men fiercely, with fire. The people still do not repent after this and continue to blaspheme His name.

BOWL JUDGMENT # 5: (Revelation 16:10-11) Fifth Angel darkens the planet almost completely. God is terribly angry. He adds pains and sores to the people, also. The people still do not repent after this and continue to blaspheme His name.

BOWL JUDGMENT # 6: (Revelation 16:12-16) Sixth angel will dry up the blood in the Euphrates River in preparation for the army from the east (demons) to come for the final battle of Armageddon.

BOWL JUDGMENT # 7: (Revelation 16:17-21) Seventh Angel will send flashes of lightning, peals of thunder, and a great worldwide earthquake—greater than ever in history. So great an earthquake, that Babylon will split into three parts and the cities of the nations will all fall. All the islands in the world will disappear and no more mountains in the world remain standing. Huge hailstones, one hundred pounds each, will come down from heaven. The remaining people still will not repent and continue to blaspheme God's name.

Satan will be defeated at the end of the Tribulation when Jesus comes back with His great army at the final battle of Armageddon. This army will be made up of all the pre-visual Rapture Christians. **What a glorious day this will be.**

★★★★★★★★★★★★★★★★

When anyone looks at all of this and realizes this *"shall"* happen, would you want to consider going through something like this? I sure wouldn't. The choice and corresponding consequences are purely individual.

When God offers all of us a lifeboat, in the form of Jesus, please consider your decision wisely.

Revelation 1:3

3 Blessed is he who reads and those who hear the words of the prophecy, and heed the things which are written in it; for the time is near.

CHAPTER 7

CLOSING THOUGHTS

It is my hope you have found this fresh concept of the Biblical Rapture interpretation both informative and interesting. Here are some final thoughts for your prayerful consideration.

If any of this interpretation as presented is ultimately wrong and the Rapture happens without warning, then PRAISE THE LORD! We are home with Jesus—end of story.

But what if we do live to see the Ezekiel attack as I've described in this book? And then, shortly after the battle, we begin to see the onset of additional prophecies expounded in the Bible? Our knowledge will help us deal with the events.

We need to fully prepare to evangelize for a short period of time after the Ezekiel attack. Remember after 9-11 how people filled the churches for about a month? The tragedy caused a time of great harvesting for the Lord. The Ezekiel attack will have an even stronger overall impact.

For me, Pascal's Wager comes to mind. Blaise Pascal (1623-1661)—a French philosopher, scientist, mathematician, and probability theorist—created a profound simplistic viewpoint. I have paraphrased his concept:

If there is no God and we believed in Him we have lost nothing.
But if there truly is a God and we do not choose to believe in
Him we have a great deal to lose.

Many people in the world are beginning to say Christians are ignorant, hateful, judgmental, intolerant, and phobic because we love Jesus and accept His written Word, verbatim. Christians will discover that actually, the nonbelievers who discount the Bible and Jesus, and then us by association, will say and do all these things listed in the sentence above to us, not the other way around. This should come as no surprise because Jesus tells us we will be hated on His account.

Matthew 10:22
22 *You will be hated by all because of My name, but it is the one who has endured to the end who will be saved.*

Luke 6:22

22 Blessed are you when men hate you, and ostracize you, and insult you, and scorn your name as evil, for the sake of the Son of Man.

It may actually be a blessing for Christians to live through some adversity. We've learned how Jesus has shown us the right way to deal with the coming travail. He has given us the blessing of knowledge, and time, to help some of our unbelieving friends and family to find and accept Jesus as their personal Savior up until the very day the visual Rapture occurs.

The Ezekiel attack will shake the very roots of faith for millions of Christians who have yet to hear about this version of events. Some people, after this attack, might live in fear because it may appear that Jesus will not come to save us. Doubters might think the Ezekiel attack is actually Armageddon—which, with Biblical understanding, cannot be the case. Others will believe the attack proves the Rapture will happen after all the wars and difficult times in the Tribulation. And no doubt, more will feel the attack begins the Tribulation. But we know otherwise.

I am confident regarding my analysis of end time prophecies as presented. My goal: to share this information with as many people as possible, in order to provide some comfort, truth, and intellectual options should these events begin to soon unfold.

I have made many references to the Catholic Church, specifically, regarding coming events. I choose only to bring attention to what the Deceiver might do to all Christian organizations— particularly Catholics, but Protestants as well. Although no Christians will be safe, I think I have clearly expressed my belief the Deceiver specifically wants to use the Catholic Church to achieve his final plans. When unchristian things start to happen in any church system, I want to have everybody aware and alert with a good feel for what is actually happening.

If Satan is indeed seeping into the Catholic Church, changing **doctrines** in opposition to the Bible, we have a serious problem. Believing and accepting only what our church leaders espouse could result in some serious personal consequences. Blindly accepting bad information humans express, instead of placing our trust in the inerrant Bible, would lead us down a path to destruction.

Jesus uses sheep in the Bible as an example, to represent His flock who have desperate need for a Good Shepherd to guide us. Of all the animals in the world, God could have chosen for this analogy, He selected one with low intelligence. Not mean-spirited, but rather truthful. God knows our weaknesses.

Lack of awareness regarding the actual real truths inside the Bible, independent of all Church doctrines, prevents us from having the ability to protect ourselves from cunning deceptions. Please be careful. I, sincerely — with all my heart — do not want anyone to be fooled, and I give thanks to our loving Lord Jesus for giving us instruction and protection.

God provides us with some added instructions in the book of Jude related to the last days.

Jude 1:17-25

[17] *But you, beloved, ought to remember the words that were spoken beforehand by the apostles of our Lord Jesus Christ,* [18] *that they were saying to you, "In the last time there will be mockers, following after their own un-Godly lusts."* [19] *These are the ones who cause divisions, worldly-minded, devoid of the Spirit.* [20] *But you, beloved, building yourselves up on your most holy faith, praying in the Holy Spirit,* [21] *keep yourselves in the love of God, waiting anxiously for the mercy of our Lord Jesus Christ to eternal life.* [22] *And have mercy on some, who are doubting;* [23] *save others, snatching them out of the fire; and on some have mercy with fear, hating even the garment polluted by the flesh.* [24] *Now to Him who is able to keep you from*

stumbling, and to make you stand in the presence of His glory blameless with great joy, 25 to the only God our Savior, through Jesus Christ our Lord, be glory, majesty, dominion and authority, before all time and now and forever. Amen.

During Christ's crucifixion, one of the two criminals on each side of Him scoffed at Jesus, saying He was not the Christ. He even got to the point of mocking Jesus saying, *"save yourself"* sarcastically, implying **then prove it!**

Luke 23:39-43

39 One of the criminals who were hanged there was hurling abuse at Him, saying, Are You not the Christ? Save Yourself and us! 40 But the other answered, and rebuking him said, Do you not even fear God, since you are under the same sentence of condemnation? 41 And we indeed are suffering justly, for we are receiving what we deserve for our deeds; but this man has done nothing wrong. 42 And he was saying, Jesus, remember me when You come in Your kingdom! 43 And He said to him, Truly I say to you, today you shall be with Me in Paradise.

The second criminal recognized Jesus as his Savior, and although under condemnation, felt the Lord's power to forgive him. He rebukes the first criminal for not recognizing who Jesus really was. The second criminal realized he deserved his own sentence, and recognized Jesus' innocence. In his last minutes of life, he realized he needed and wanted Jesus and humbly asked the Lord to remember him when He gets to His Kingdom. He accepted Jesus at that very moment and what did Jesus then tell him in Luke 23:43? ***"Truly I say to you, today you shall be with Me in paradise."*** This man believed for mere minutes, in our gracious and loving Jesus, and for this *brief faith*, the Lord gave him **a full share of eternity**, with Him, in paradise.

Please remember this: If the majority of the remaining prophecies listed in this book start happening, watch carefully for the final signs. The world appears to look as if achievement of peace and harmony has arrived; strange things happening in the sun, moon, stars, and oceans — the scourge — mankind fearful of what they sense and see. This is the moment in time the Bible tells Christians to literally watch for. The visual Rapture is about to occur.

Please think of this book as an invitation to truly get to know and accept Jesus before His shout to come up (1 Thessalonians 4:16) at the visual Rapture. God has given mankind all the necessary verifiable information to know Him and to accept Him, right up to the absolute last moments, before the Tribulation begins. God shows us how to achieve salvation and escape His punishments that will soon come upon the world (Appendix B).

However, the people who do enter the Tribulation can still be saved by accepting Jesus as their Savior. Heed His Word now and avoid the horrific Tribulation.

In an earlier Chapter, I referred to where the Bible offers five crowns to good and faithful servants. Remember, we can win the **Crown of Righteousness** by **looking up** at the visual Rapture. God has blessed today's population, giving us the chance to win this one particular crown for Jesus, visually, and not simply in our hearts . . . a tremendous honor and gift as long as we understand how to achieve it.

Even though we may have some challenges ahead, we still need to remember to enjoy each day — to stop and take the time to see all the wonderful things God places around us: family, friends, and the natural beauty of the earth the Lord graciously provided. Embrace and appreciate all these gifts for peace of mind as we rapidly move towards our glorious future destiny. Always trust our loving God; He knows everything, and has already perfected all of His plans.

In conclusion, I hope to have helped make the end times a bit more understandable. I wrote this book in anticipation of showing you how to know when to take God's final directed action at the start of the visual Rapture. May you **look up**, as a believer with joyful open arms and welcome our magnificent Lord back in the clouds at the **visual Rapture**.

All praise and glory be given to Jesus Christ our Lord. Amen.

John 16:33
33 These things I have spoken to you, so that in Me you may have peace. In the world you have tribulation, but take courage; "I have overcome the world."

2 Timothy 3:16-17

[16] <u>All Scripture</u> is <u>inspired by God</u> and profitable for teaching, for reproof, for correction, for training in righteousness; [17] so that the man of God may be adequate, equipped for every good work.

APPENDIX A

BIBLE CREDIBILITY

God has provided us <u>evidence</u> in the Bible proving the inerrancy of His Word. This provides validation regarding the visual Rapture.

As Christians we are to accept the credibility of the Bible's passages as the singular, Divine, inspired, inerrant, and infallible Word of the single triune God. This is important because, if the Bible's sacred writings are not reliable and perfect, then the idea of using the Bible to substantiate its own claims creates the problem of **circular logic**. Any Biblical imperfection would doom our whole interpretation, basing our faith on lies. In the following verses Paul addresses what would happen if Jesus is not who he claims to be:

1 Corinthians 15:12-19
12 Now if Christ is preached, that He has been raised from the dead, how do some among you say that there is no resurrection of the dead? 13 But if there is no resurrection of the dead, not even Christ has been raised; 14 and if Christ has not been raised, then our preaching is vain, your faith also is vain. 15 Moreover we are even found to be false witnesses of God, because we testified against God that He raised Christ, whom He did not raise, if in fact the dead are not raised. 16 For if the dead are not raised, not even Christ has been raised; 17 and if Christ has not been raised, your faith is worthless; you are still in your sins. 18 Then those also who have fallen asleep in Christ have perished.19 If we have hoped in Christ in this life only, we are of all men most to be pitied.

In this Appendix, I want to make a case for the validity of the Bible and the accuracy of the prophecies discussed, related to Jesus.

John 1:1-5
1 In the beginning was the Word, and the Word was with God, and the Word was God. 2 He was in the beginning with God. 3 All things came into being through Him, and apart from Him nothing came into being that has come into being. 4 In Him was life, and the life was the Light of

men. ⁵ The Light shines in the darkness, and the darkness did not comprehend it.

The preceding verses explain how God, has known everything from before the beginning and through eternity because time has never bound Him. The words we have in our Bible today **existed from the beginning,** before God created the universe, long before God had men scribe them for use in our Bible today. They were in full force long before God created any physical matter, and long before any possible concept of any proposed evolutionary process.

These truthful words include exactly what will happen in our current-day and in the near future. God is the author.

Up until this century, the Bible has predicted or prophesied over 2,500 events, all of which have come true with 100 percent accuracy. Jesus Himself fulfilled over 300 prophecies at his first coming. Two prophetic examples regarding Jesus, scribed many years prior to His birth:

Isaiah 53:4-6

⁴ Surely our griefs He Himself bore, and our sorrows He carried; Yet we ourselves esteemed Him stricken, smitten of God, and afflicted. ⁵ But He was pierced through for our transgressions, He was crushed for our iniquities; the chastening for our well-being fell upon Him, and by His scourging we are healed. ⁶ All of us like sheep have gone astray, each of us has turned to his own way; but the LORD has caused the iniquity of us all to fall on Him.

Isaiah 9:6-7

⁶ For a child will be born to us, a son will be given to us; and the government will rest on His shoulders; and His name will be called Wonderful Counselor, Mighty God, Eternal Father, Prince of Peace. ⁷ There will be no end to the increase of His government or of peace, On the throne of David and over his kingdom, to establish it and to uphold it with justice and righteousness From then on and forevermore. The zeal of the Lord of hosts will accomplish this.

Both of these Old Testament verses describe Jesus and what He will do for us in the future. The first set of verses talks about the cross and the second set, about His reign. The Prophet Isaiah wrote both verses around 680 BC, and fulfillment occurred in 33 AD at the cross—foretelling future events.

Biblical Scripture predicted the birth, death, and resurrection of Christ numerous times. Many witnessed His death when it occurred in real time and, after His death, historically, at least five-hundred people saw Him alive, 1 Corinthians 15:6.

Acts 1:9-11
⁹ And after He had said these things, He was lifted up while they were looking on, and a cloud received Him out of their sight. ¹⁰ And as they were gazing intently into the sky while He was going, behold, two men in white clothing stood beside them. ¹¹ They also said, Men of Galilee, why do you stand looking into the sky? This Jesus, who has been taken up from you into heaven, will come in just the same way as you have watched Him go into heaven.

He ascended to Heaven per Acts 1:9-11. He *"lifted up"* off the ground, *"while they were looking on"* and *"a cloud received Him."* They literally watched Jesus leave and *"This Jesus, who has been taken up from you into heaven, will come in just the same way as you have watched Him go into heaven."* The witnessing of the ascension in Acts 1:9 and the coming back in the same way in Acts 1:11. One tells of an event actually viewed and the second, a promise of a future viewing.

What about archeology? Numerous archeological finds in the world have related to the Bible. Everything found to correlate with the Bible, or a Bible event, continues to prove the accuracy of God's book. In fact, back in **Road Map** prophecy #17, I explained that Peter's bones may soon be found, in the true City of Babylon (in current-day Iraq) after the Ezekiel attack. From an archeological standpoint, this discovery will shake the religious world.

God, in His Scriptures, presented certain aspects of the true configuration of the universe a long time before mankind could actually prove or anticipate these things:

Isaiah 40:22
22 *It is He who sits above the <u>circle of the earth</u>, and its inhabitants are like grasshoppers, Who stretches out the heavens like a curtain and spreads them out like a tent to dwell in.*

God talks about the fact that *"He sits above the (circle) of the earth"* which says the earth is round. Some people refer to Christians as flat-earthers because the Bible refers in some places to the *"four corners of the earth."* The Bible made it clear that the earth was not flat, long before Columbus discovered this.

Ecclesiastes 1:7
7 *All the <u>rivers flow into the sea, yet the sea is not full</u>. To the place where the rivers flow, there they flow again.*

God describes how rivers work in a cycle. They *"flow into the sea,"* and *"yet the sea is not full,"* and then *"there they flow again."* A mystery related to where this continuous water supply is coming from. A mystery that God understood, but man could not contemplate, written in 935 BC.

Jeremiah 33:22
22 *As the host of heaven cannot be counted and the sand of the sea cannot be measured, so I will multiply the descendants of David My servant and the Levites who minister to Me.'*

Here Jeremiah relates to an infinite number of stars in the heavens. Man could see stars, but had no idea of the infinite number because mankind at that time had no concept about deep space. God compared the number of stars to the number of grains of sand on a beach, a totally incomprehensible yet accurate number.

Job 26:7
7 He stretches out the north over empty space and hangs the earth on nothing.

Job states that the earth exists in *"empty space"* and God *"hangs the earth on nothing"* in 1800 BC. How could these men, at the verifiable times these Scriptures were written, know all this? They didn't, but God did . . . more proof that a higher power inspired Bible Scripture.

The Bible is a compilation of sixty-six Canonical (Canon) Books (Catholics seventy-three) written by forty authors over 2,000 years, with all books completed by around 95 AD. Many of the Old Testament writers did not know each other or live at the same time, yet their writings were collected into one book, through God's inspired direction. The Scriptures flow in perfect unity and consistency with remarkable structure and symmetry. Everything works together in perfect mathematical harmony. In no way could this be chance, but rather: Divine authorship. Obviously, our Lord perfectly planned and spread the Word out over time, and as a result we can read His Divinely inspired document today.

In the New Testament, when we look at the **Gospels, (Matthew, Mark, Luke, and John),** we know these four authors knew each other. They lived with Jesus and witnessed, personally, almost everything He did during His earthly ministry. These disciples wrote the gospel books between 55 AD/CE and 95 AD/CE. Note: The suffix CE (Common Era) has replaced AD, (Anno Domini = day of our Lord). I will stay with AD; I like it better. Also interesting: BC (Before Christ), used for the time periods prior to Jesus, has also been changed to BCE (Before Common Era). All this gamesmanship by the Deceiver adds to apostasy, continually taking God out of the equation.

Our calendar years today totally revolve around the birth of Jesus because of His importance.

At the time the four apostles scribed the Gospels, many other people who witnessed Jesus, personally, also could have easily disputed anything they wrote through God's inspiration. But, this did not occur. People, at that time, knew of Jesus, and accepted the interpretations of these four men, without dispute, because of the accuracy of their written accounts. This adds yet another level of credibility to the foundations of the New Testament.

Why do we have so many translations of the Bible? The original writings of the books of the Bible were in Hebrew, Aramaic, and Greek. The Pentateuch – the first five books of the Old Testament (Genesis, Exodus, Leviticus, Numbers, and Deuteronomy), written by Moses – were transcribed from clay tablets. From the time of Adam until the time of Moses, tablets provided preservation for their accurate content and genealogies. During the time of Moses, these earlier table document writings were rewritten onto parchments, the current best technology of his time.

For 1,400 years from the time Christ lived on the earth, only the clergy had copies of the Bible. They informed the masses about God and did a less-than-accurate job with their interpretations. Then around 1440 AD, Johannes Guttenberg invented the first printing press and things would soon change. The printing press now made it possible to make quality copies of the Bible for royalty and the wealthy. In 1455, using this new technology, Guttenberg printed two-hundred Bibles.

As time went on, other people wanted Bibles in their languages and needed translators. These translators made every effort to keep consistent to the actual written meaning or intent of the original written languages (Hebrew, Aramaic, and

Greek). They converted the original text into different languages using the current words and phrases customary to each new language group.

The reason we even needed to translate the Bible at all, results in the consequence of the Tower of Babel, which is discussed in Genesis 11:1-10. Mankind built the tower to reach God, which showed arrogance. As a result of this Tower (built in Babylon), God confused languages and this has resulted in our current-day translation problems—a curse we need to deal with due to man's earlier sins. This makes our understanding of God's word today more challenging than it ever should have. All sin has lasting consequences.

In 1384, John Wycliffe created the first English Bible translation. In the English language today we have two major widely accepted versions of the Bible. The King James (1611) Bible contains sixty-six books. This is made up of thirty-nine total books in the Old Testament. Judaism combines these thirty-nine books into twenty-four books . . . an arrangement issue. The Old Testament in both the Protestant and Hebrew Bibles are virtually identical. The Catholic Bible differs a bit. There are twenty-seven books in New Testament. All Christian versions have twenty-seven books in the New Testament; Protestant faiths consider the sixty-six book version (39+27=66) as the true complete official canon. The canon is the accepted God-inspired collection of books that make up our current Bibles.

The Catholic Church uses the Douay-Rheims Bible. This contains the original sixty-six books translated from the Latin Vulgate version completed around 400 AD. Today this Bible version has seventy-three books which include the sixty-six mentioned above, and seven main additional sections: Deuterocanonical books, also referred to as Apocryphal books. Today the Catholic Church has forty-six books in their Old Testament and twenty-seven in their New Testament (46+27=73).

The Apocryphal books written before and during Christ's time here on earth have some controversial writings. As discussed earlier, these seven books were added into the Catholic Bible, by the Catholic hierarchy at the Council of Trent in 1,546 A.D., **Road Map** prophecy #17. These books all intertwine within their Old Testament. They include: the books of Tobit, Judith, Wisdom, Sirach, Baruch, 1 Maccabees, and 2 Maccabees. Protestants do not accept these extra seven books, because they believe the content contains some concepts contradicting the mutually accepted sixty-six Canonical Books. Due to contradictions, their authenticity as God-inspired writings is open to suspicion. Additionally, at some point within its text, the New Testament references the majority of the thirty-nine universally accepted Old Testament books. The New Testament never refers to the specific seven additional Catholic books.

In Luke 24:44 Jesus indicates He, as a Rabbi, used the **twenty-four** book **Tanach** during His earthly ministry. The Tanach is, to this day, the Holy Scriptures of Judaism. The Tanach includes *"the Law of Moses and the Prophets and the Psalms,"* from the book of Genesis through the book of Malachi:

Luke 24:44
44 Now He said to them, "These are My words which I spoke to you while I was still with you, that all things which are written about Me in the <u>Law of Moses and the Prophets and the Psalms must be fulfilled</u>."

Malachi, written by the prophet Malachi, is the youngest of the books in the Tanach, completed around 420 BC. The seven Apocryphal books were written between 350 BC and 50 AD. Jesus, per Luke 24:44 gave them no mention, and therefore, no credibility. He states clearly that He recognizes *"the law of Moses and the Prophets and the Psalm."* The Apocryphal books do not fit within these specific defined categories.

As you may recall, there were only handwritten copies of all the Biblical verses up until the time of the printing press; only the clergy had actual copies. Moses wrote the first books in about 1450 BC (3,460+ years ago). The onset of the printing press made Bibles attainable in quantity a mere 550 years ago, but plentiful and affordable to masses for only the last 150 years. God wanted to warn, prepare, and protect His family for what will soon come. More importantly, He has chosen to provide us all with peace regarding His coming wrath against nonbelievers. God desires for everybody, in our current time, to have availability to a personal Bible—a tool and guide to warn us, prepare us, and comfort us in these last days.

Some history: the Old Testament contains some of the oldest known books in the world—between 2,450 and 3,500 years old. Throughout history, over time, archeologists have discovered over 5,800 copies or portions of the Old Testament, and many more original and partial-manuscript copies of the New Testament. Our current Bible today is identical to the original manuscripts scribed up to between 50 to 95 years after the birth of Christ.

The greatest archeological find of Bible parchments was the Dead Sea Scrolls, first discovered in 1947, one year before Israel's rebirth. They date back to between 200 BC and approximately 68 AD. After the initial find in one cave, they found ten additional caves in the area that contained additional scrolls. Collectively, these scrolls contained multiple copies of the entire Old Testament. However, the book of Esther is missing. Also, interestingly, many of the seven Apocryphal books the Catholic Church added to their Old Testament in 1546 AD are missing. They found other items explaining a link to the new faith, Christianity, which came out of Judaism. God has protected His Word perfectly for our accurate use today. We have everything absolutely correct as originally written—this in itself, another miracle.

Of interest to note: the major attacks on the Bible's credibility have occurred now for only about two hundred years. These attacks have grown in intensity with the purpose of completely discrediting God's word—also part of the Divine plan. Mankind has become extremely arrogant.

2 Timothy 4:1-5

[1] I solemnly charge you in the presence of God and of Christ Jesus, who is to judge the living and the dead, and by His appearing and His kingdom: [2] preach the word; be ready in season and out of season; reprove, rebuke, exhort, with great patience and instruction. [3] For the time will come when they will not endure <u>sound doctrine</u>; but wanting to have their ears tickled, they will accumulate for themselves teachers in accordance to their own desires, [4] and will turn away their ears from the truth and will <u>turn aside to myths</u>. [5] But you, <u>be sober in all things</u>, endure hardship, do the work of an evangelist, fulfill your ministry.

Titus 1:8-9

[8] be hospitable, loving what is good, sensible, just, devout, self-controlled, [9]holding fast the faithful word which is in accordance with the teaching, so that he will be able both to exhort in <u>sound doctrine</u> and to refute those who contradict.

God tells us to preach the Word using *"sound doctrine."* This refers to the literal Bible itself. The complete text tells us everything we need to know. I am not a perfect man: however, both Jesus and His Word are perfect. Therefore, when anybody has beliefs or theories they attach to God, they need to back them up using actual Scripture as their sole proof for any alternate points of view. This is called being *"sober in all things"* per 2 Timothy 4:5. God says not to ascribe to **beliefs** without heeding verification found in Scriptures. He tells us not to stray away from truth by listening or *"turning aside to myths."* We need to take care not to speculate about anything that differentiates from His stated Word. We are not allowed to read between the lines. We have to provide and share the solid Word of God as He has given it to us.

In the near future, many will accept the sweet talk by evil leaders promising the nearness of achieving final peace on earth. This mistake will lead to ultimate peril for the unbelieving masses. Deception will persuade the majority, and we need to help share the truth with as many people as possible by introducing them to Jesus and what will soon come. God will do the rest.

John 1:1-5
¹ In the beginning was the Word, and the Word was with God, and the Word was God. ² He was in the beginning with God. ³ All things came into being through Him, and apart from Him nothing came into being that has come into being. ⁴ In Him was life, and the life was the Light of men. ⁵ The Light shines in the darkness, and the darkness did not comprehend it.

Genesis 1:26
²⁶ Then God said, Let Us make man in <u>Our image</u>, according to Our likeness;

As explained earlier, God has told us His Word existed, and was in place, and perfect from before creation. God knew when He created man, that Adam and Eve would choose the sin option. Fortunately, He had everything prepared in advance to fix sin through His Son. Jesus existed from the beginning. Note the words *"Our image."* God pre-designated Jesus to become the perfect God/Man to save us at the correct moments in history. He came once and will soon return a second time, forever.

Hebrews 6:18
¹⁸ so that by two unchangeable things in which <u>it is</u>

impossible for God to lie, we who have taken refuge would have strong encouragement to take hold of the hope set before us.

As previously mentioned, the Scriptures tell us *"it is impossible for God to lie."* We should expect this of a perfect God. We can feel confident that what He shares with us will actually occur.

Ephesians 5:13-17

13 But all things become visible when they are exposed by the light, for everything that becomes visible is light. 14 For this reason it says, awake, sleeper, and arise from the dead, and Christ will shine on you. 15 Therefore be careful how you walk, not as unwise men but as wise, 16 making the most of your time, because the days are evil. 17 So then do not be foolish, but understand what the will of the Lord is.

As Christians, we are to walk in *"wisdom,"* because *"the days are evil."* We cannot merely coast through life, especially at this late hour. We are His army. He expects us to be good soldiers for Him fighting the evil in the world. Through Christ and with Christ, we represent the introduction of His hope for many.

1 Timothy 4:11-16

11Prescribe and teach these things. 12 Let no one look down on your youthfulness, but rather in speech, conduct, love, faith and purity, show yourself an example of those who believe. 13 Until I come, give attention to the public reading of Scripture, to exhortation and teaching.14 Do not neglect the spiritual gift within you, which was bestowed on you through prophetic utterance with the laying on of hands by the presbytery. 15 Take pains with these things; be absorbed in them, so that your progress will be evident to all. 16 Pay close attention to yourself and to your teaching; persevere in these things, for as you do this you will ensure salvation both for yourself and for those who hear you.

I desire to live as a good and faithful servant for Jesus. I feel strongly that the story I have shared with you is what God intends for us to know in these last days. I encourage you, again, to research my comments for yourselves to determine if they are right for you. Can I answer all possible questions regarding God's plans? No. That would be impossible and also not my job. Everybody has a responsibility to discover their own path with God and to do research on their own. Test everything for yourself against the Bible provided to you from our Lord for your benefit. My intention has been to open a thought process and contribute a viable option of coming events. Hopefully, this information has enhanced your levels of joy, peace, understanding and personal relationship with the Lord for His ultimate glory.

2 Timothy 3:16-17
[16] All Scripture is inspired by God and profitable for teaching, for reproof, for correction, for training in righteousness; [17] so that the man of God may be adequate, equipped for every good work.

2 Peter 1:20-21
[20] But know this first of all, that no prophecy of Scripture is a matter of one's own interpretation, [21] for no prophecy was ever made by an act of human will, but men moved by the Holy Spirit spoke from God.

Man did not create the Bible. They scribed the books through the inspiration of God and the Holy Spirit, and it is therefore 100 percent reliable.

James 1:22-25
[22] But prove yourselves doers of the word, and not merely

hearers who delude themselves. [23] For if anyone is a hearer of the word and not a doer, he is like a man who looks at his natural face in a mirror; [24] for once he has looked at himself and gone away, he has immediately forgotten what kind of person he was. [25] But one who looks intently at the perfect law, the law of liberty, and abides by it, not having become a forgetful hearer but an effectual doer, this man will be blessed in what he does.

Christians are not to simply listen to the Word; we are to do what it says.

Psalm 33:4
[4] For the word of the Lord is upright and all His work is done in faithfulness.

The Lord is faithful in all He does.

Psalm 119:97-104
*[97] Oh, how I love your law! I meditate on it all day long.
[98] Your commands are always with me and make me wiser than my enemies.
[99] I have more insight than all my teachers, for Your testimonies are my meditation.
[100] I understand more than the aged, because I have observed your precepts
[101] I have restrained my feet from every evil way that I may keep Your word.
[102] I have not turned aside from Your ordinances, for You Yourself have taught me.
[103] How sweet are Your words to my taste, yes, sweeter than honey to my mouth!
[104] From Your precepts I get understanding; Therefore I hate every false way.*

These Old Testament Psalm verses refer to the *"law."* The law represents over six-hundred moral commandments contained in the first five books of the Old Testament (the Penta-teuch) and, specifically, Leviticus. God required mankind to ad-here to them.

Because God knew we could never follow the *law* perfectly within the New Testament, He provided us with a pardon through the sacrifice of His Son Jesus on the cross. This gave us grace for all our sins, no longer subject to the *law.* Christians may substitute *law* in these verses with the word **gospel**. The first four books of the New Testament contain the four Gospels. By meditating on the **Gospels**, God provides joy, peace, wis-dom, understanding, protection, perseverance, and apprecia-tion. The **Gospels** teach us about the full forgiveness and grace of God.

Hebrews 4:12-13
12 For the word of God is living and active and sharper than any two-edged sword, and piercing as far as the division of soul and spirit, of both joints and marrow, and able to judge the thoughts and intentions of the heart. 13 And there is no creature hidden from His sight, but all things are open and laid bare to the eyes of Him with whom we have to do.

These verses tell us how the Bible is alive, precise, and pow-erful.

Remember; all through the Bible Jesus tell us stories. He talks about history — the present, and the future. He tells of His desires and explains how to live and act in life. His instruction and oratory often reveals something specific about His person-ality, makeup, abilities and overall character. Even though He uses these characteristics in designated verses in a particular context, they also have deeper overall meanings. In Matthew 10, Jesus provides instructions to His Disciples on how to serve. They yield a couple of clear examples:

Matthew 10:26-31
²⁶ *"Therefore do not fear them, <u>for there is nothing</u>*
<u>*concealed that will not be revealed, or hidden that will*</u>
<u>*not be known.*</u>   ²⁷ *What I tell you in the darkness, speak*
in the light; and what you hear whispered in your ear,
proclaim upon the housetops. ²⁸ *Do not fear those who kill*
the body but are unable to kill the soul; but rather fear
Him who is able to destroy both soul and body in hell.
²⁹*Are not two sparrows sold for a cent? And yet not one of*
them will fall to the ground apart from your Father. ³⁰ <u>*But*</u>
<u>*the very hairs of your head are all numbered.*</u> ³¹ *So do not*
fear; you are more valuable than many sparrows.

In verse 26 Jesus says *"for there is nothing concealed that will not be revealed, or hidden that will not be known."* In verse 30 *"But the very hairs of your head are all numbered."*

Even though in context He is talking to His disciples, we can derive comfort from these two representations of His nature. Example 1: Jesus tells us God does *"nothing in secret that will not be revealed."* This is why we have the Bible. God has no plans in the last days to be secretive about telling us what is happening. God's full disclosure is evident in His Scriptures. Example 2: *"But the very hairs on our heads are numbered."* God is precise and has everything well planned out. Both examples 1 and 2 yield intentions and attributes of Jesus. They build upon themselves through the entire text to create a full picture of His grandeur for us.

Revelation 1:3
³ *Blessed is he who reads and those who hear the words of*
the prophecy, and heed the things which are written in it;
for the time is near

Please remember, all the individual books of the Bible were completed over 1,900 years ago and then combined into the official Canonical Bible, by Divine intervention. The Bible has predicted things that are actually happening today right before our eyes. The mathematical odds that this could be happening in an expressed sequence for us to see at this time, as predicted almost 2,000 years ago, are astronomical.

As an architect, when I design buildings, I draw detailed plans showing how to construct them—right down to the multiple different types and sizes of nails to use to put them together. Of course God is a whole lot smarter than I. From my perspective, His New Testament writings, scribed shortly after His Son lived on this earth, provide us with an incredibly detailed set of blueprints for our current time in history—flawlessly designed and extremely precise—and absolutely in no way, random chance.

The Bible **credibly** shows us we are truly in the end times. The world has hit the iceberg and now spirals down. The only question remaining: how many people will be able, or even willing, to get into the lifeboats? I thought this an appropriate analogy as this book went to print in 2015, after the 102nd anniversary of the sinking of the Titanic. It's sinking makes a fitting metaphor. The only difference: God has provided enough lifeboats for everybody on this earth, but individuals need to enter of their own free will. Sadly, few will choose to enter a boat.

John 3:3

³ *Jesus answered and said to him, truly, truly, I say to you, unless one is born again he cannot see the kingdom of God.*

APPENDIX B

WHO ARE CHRISTIANS?

By God's Biblical standards, how can we know with
certainty that we are truly Christians?

What is God's simple process for nonbelievers to
become Christians?

Who are Christians? The Bible gives us answers. God provides a great deal of information so we can make a decision either to accept His son Jesus as our Savior, or not accept Him. Choosing Jesus will allow someone eternal life in paradise with God. Not accepting Him will send someone somewhere else, a place that is extremely horrible, a real location. All human souls will live forever, so a right choice in this life is critical.

C.S. Lewis (1898-1963), a noted author, scholar and Christian apologist, wrote about Jesus:

"I am trying here to prevent anyone saying the really foolish thing that people often say about Him: 'I'm ready to accept Jesus as a great moral teacher, but I don't accept His claim to be God. That is the one thing we must not say.' A man who was merely a man and said the sort of things Jesus said would not be a great moral teacher. He would either be a lunatic — on the level with the man who says he is a poached egg — or else he would be the Devil of Hell. You must make your choice. Either this man was, and is, the Son of God, or else a madman or something worse. You can shut him up for a fool, you can spit at him and kill him as a demon or you can fall at His feet and call Him Lord and God, but let us not come with any patronizing nonsense about His being a great human teacher. He has not left that open to us. He did not intend to."

Many people think of Jesus as simply a good and kind man, and acknowledging Him as a **great moral teacher** classifies them as **Christians.** They find no need to accept Christ as God. A grave error in thinking.

Others think of the title **Christian** as generic, referring to a good person who believes in any god . . . a totally inaccurate assessment. To become a true Christian, per the Bible, Jesus requires specific acknowledgements and concessions. And Jesus requires some simple actions from us to become a true *"born again"* believer. To be a saved Christian, a person must be spiritually *"born again."*

Apostasy has marginalized and demeaned the term *"born again."* Some Christians have told me the term *"born again"* bothers them. If you feel this way, please consider what **Jesus Himself** says regarding being *"born again."*

John 3:3
³ Jesus answered and said to him, truly, truly, I say to you, unless one is <u>*born again*</u> *he cannot see the kingdom of God.*

John 3:7
⁷ Do not be amazed that I said to you, 'you must be born again.'

1 Peter 1:3
³ Blessed be the God and Father of our Lord Jesus Christ, who according to His great mercy has caused us to be <u>*born again*</u> *to a living hope through the resurrection of Jesus Christ from the dead.*

1 Peter 1:23
²³ for you have been <u>*born again*</u> *not of seed which is perishable but imperishable, that is, through the living and enduring word of God.*

Being *"born again"* has a specific spiritual meaning and significance. But first, we need to fully understand who Jesus is and His great importance related to our ultimate salvation. The Bible is all about Jesus, so let's look at a sampling from the Scriptures, describing who Jesus is:

Matthew 1:21
²¹ She will bear a Son; and you shall call His name Jesus, for He will save His people from their sins.

John 3:35-36

35 The Father loves the Son and has given all things into His hand. 36 He who believes in the Son has eternal life; but he who does not obey the Son will not see life, but the wrath of God abides on him.

John 8:23-24

23 And He was saying to them, you are from below, I am from above; you are of this world, I am not of this world. 24 Therefore I said to you that you will die in your sins; for unless you believe that I am He, you will die in your sins.

John 10:25-30

25 Jesus answered them, I told you, and you do not believe; the works that I do in My Father's name, these testify of Me. 26 But you do not believe because you are not of My sheep. 27 My sheep hear My voice, and I know them, and they follow Me; 28 and I give eternal life to them, and they will never perish; and no one will snatch them out of My hand. 29 My Father, who has given them to Me, is greater than all; and no one is able to snatch them out of the Father's hand. 30 I and the Father are one.

John 11:25-27

25 Jesus said to her, "I am the resurrection and the life; he who believes in Me will live even if he dies, 26 and everyone who lives and believes in Me will never die. Do you believe this?" 27 She said to Him, "Yes, Lord; I have believed that You are the Christ, the Son of God, even He who comes into the world."

John 14:6

6 Jesus said to him, I am the way, and the truth, and the life; no one comes to the Father but through Me.

John 20:29

29 Jesus said to him, because you have seen Me, have you believed? Blessed are they who did not see, and yet believed.

Acts 4:12

¹² And <u>there is salvation in no one else</u>; for there is no other name under heaven that has been given among men by which we must be saved.

1 Corinthians 12:3

³ Therefore I make known to you that no one speaking by the Spirit of God says, Jesus is accursed; and no one can say, Jesus is Lord, except by the Holy Spirit.

1 John 5:9-12

⁹ If we receive the testimony of men, the testimony of God is greater; for the testimony of God is this, that He has testified concerning His Son. ¹⁰ The one who believes in the Son of God has the testimony in Himself; the one who does not believe God has made Him a liar, because he has not believed in the testimony that God has given concerning His Son. ¹¹ And the testimony is this, that God has given us eternal life, and this life is in His Son. ¹² He who has the Son has the life; he who does not have the Son of God does not have the life.

1 Timothy 2:3-6

³ This is good and acceptable in the sight of God our Savior, ⁴ who desires all men to be saved and to come to the knowledge of the truth. ⁵ <u>For there is one God, and one mediator also between God and men, the man Christ Jesus</u>, ⁶ who gave Himself as a ransom for all, the testimony given at the proper time.

John 3:16

¹⁶ For God so loved the world, that He gave His only begotten Son, that whoever believes in Him shall not perish, but have eternal life.

These verses speak for themselves. Let's, however, review a couple of repeated categorical statements. 1 Timothy 2:5 says *"there is one God, and one mediator also between God and men, the man Christ Jesus,"* His Son. Acts 4:12, tells us *"there is salvation in no one else,"* Jesus is the only way. The majority of the verses also make it clear that judgment will come to those who do not accept Jesus. The good news: grace, salvation, and forgiveness await all those who truly accept Him. To get to know Jesus a bit better, I recommend reading the four Gospels: the first four books of the New Testament . . . Matthew, Mark, Luke, and John.

Why do we need a Savior, a mediator, somebody to intercede for our sins with the Father in the form of Jesus? Due to sin, we need grace, forgiveness, and salvation leading to eternal life, only attainable through Jesus. This sin problem goes back to the original discretion by Adam and Eve, prompted by Satan in the Garden of Eden. The process of atonement for sins in the Old Testament is quite detailed, so I will try to simply explain the overall concept of why Jesus now holds such great importance.

Because of sin, God provided the Law for all people to obey. Per the Old Testament — specifically the first seven Chapters of Leviticus — when somebody sinned, God required a blood sacrifice to atone for each specific sin activity. God required sacrifice to make things **right and whole** again . . . usually the sacrifice of a **pure unblemished lamb**.

After shedding the lamb's blood, this act of obedience washed away the sin committed and made things right again with God. He never intended sin for mankind. When Adam and Eve sinned in the garden, they essentially let the genie out of the bottle. Both sin and death entered the world. This necessitated sacrifice due to sin being set loose on the world. God would have preferred not to go the sacrifice route, but man — His creation — gave Him no choice.

But, why did God require such a severe atonement for sin? The killing of an animal and the shedding of its blood, the taking of its life for correcting sin, seems so Draconian . . . exceedingly drastic and purposefully so. God is perfect—sinless; to Him sin of any size is a serious thing. So serious, in fact, that He cannot even look upon it. What better way to show His creation the seriousness of sin than by requiring a blood sacrifice as the only way to atone for it . . . a highly visual way to show us all how severe all sin actually is, in the eyes of God. Sin is death. God knew all along, from the beginning of time, man would choose the sin option. But He requires perfection. He knew the very minute when Adam and Eve opened sin's door that no created human could cure this disease. So out of pure love, God intervened. He gave mankind a feasible remedy for the entire sin problem through His Old Testament sacrificial system explained in Leviticus. But it turned out futile. Mankind had no way to put the genie back in the bottle. Again, fortunately, for us, God had, from the beginning, designed a way to fix this problem once and for all. The solution came through His only begotten Son, Jesus the Christ, the Lamb of God.

God sent His one and only **perfect** Son Jesus into the world to die on the cross, and to become the **final perfect unblemished sacrifice** for us all. Jesus is the only human who lived a **perfect** life on earth, ever. By the shedding of His blood on the cross for us, Jesus fulfilled the Law (Scriptural prophecy) and became the final pure sacrifice. Jesus did it once, and for all time, through the shedding of His own blood, and His death. Then God resurrected Him, and today He sits at the right hand of the Father in Heaven.

By accepting Jesus as our personal Savior, we have essentially fulfilled the Law through His blood sacrifice for us. By accepting Jesus as our Savior, we are indeed saved by His perfect grace. God forgives us for all our sins and we have obtained salvation and eternal life through Him. **Through the faith of Jesus**, and **our placing our faith on Him**, God sees us as perfect—washed by the blood of the Lamb. **We have been purified through the love of Jesus**. God always desires to make things right . . . precisely why Jesus holds so much importance for us all individually.

When the Bible talks about sin, it specifically points out actions that God considers unacceptable. However, the only unforgivable sin today comes with non-acceptance of Jesus as our Savior. Even after salvation we will all still sin, but **through the love of Jesus** God forgives all transgressions. He requires us to acknowledge and confess to Him when we sin and always faithfully forgives us through grace . . . free unmerited favor.

All sins, regardless—big or small—are all the same to God with no distinction. God gives both heavenly and worldly consequences for sins. Some sins have a much larger range of human consequences, but God sees only black or white, right or wrong. Sin, of any size, is sin—period . . . the reason we need grace.

1 Corinthians 6:9-11
*9 Or do you not know that the unrighteous will not inherit the kingdom of God? Do not be deceived; neither fornicators, nor idolaters, nor adulterers, nor effeminate, nor homosexuals, 10 nor thieves, nor the covetous, nor drunkards, nor revilers, nor swindlers, will inherit the kingdom of God.
11 Such were some of you; but you were washed, but you were sanctified, but you were justified in the name of the Lord Jesus Christ and in the Spirit of our God.*

God does not condone any sin. In the verses above there is quite a list of activities that, without Jesus, will keep people from inheriting the Kingdom of God. Note something profound mentioned here: *"Such were some of you."* If we accept the Lord as our Savior God gives grace and full forgiveness for all our transgressions. None of the sin activities listed in 1 Corinthians 6:9-11 are more hideous to God than any of the others. All are hideous and vile. He cannot even look upon them. To God, sin is sin—period. Also, when we accept Jesus, we instantly change from spiritual death into spiritual life through Christ. This is becoming *"born again"* as explained earlier. In this earthly life, and in our worldly bodies, we will all struggle with sin, yes, even after salvation. We do, however, all need to work out our sinful imperfections individually, at personal levels with God, through prayer.

How does God tell Christians to relate to people in this life? He tells us how He judges, and what He requires of us regarding judgment and association with others. We also learn about different ways to relate and to associate with believers and non-believers:

Matthew 7:1-5

1 Do not judge so that you will not be judged. 2 For in the way you judge, you will be judged; and by your standard of measure, it will be measured to you. 3 Why do you look at the speck that is in your brother's eye, but do not notice the log that is in your own eye? 4 Or how can you say to your brother, 'Let me take the speck out of your eye,' and behold, the log is in your own eye? 5 You hypocrite, first take the log out of your own eye, and then you will see clearly to take the speck out of your brother's eye.

1 Corinthians 5:9-13

9 I wrote you in my letter not to associate with immoral people; 10 I did not at all mean with the immoral people of this world, or with the covetous and swindlers, or with idolaters, for then you would have to go out of the world. 11 But actually, I wrote to you not to associate with any so-called brother if he is an immoral person, or covetous, or an idolater, or a reviler, or a drunkard, or a swindler - not even to eat with such a one. 12 For what have I to do with judging outsiders? Do you not judge those who are within the church? 13 But those who are outside, God judges. Remove the wicked man from among yourselves.

In Matthew 7:1-5, God tells us how not to judge others, because we also will receive judgment. These verses also tell us how we should look at fellow believers or *"brothers."*

In 1 Corinthians 5:12, the Lord asks a question *"Do you not judge those who are within the church?"* Yes, we are to judge only those inside the church; those outside the church God will deal with. This is not a judgment of condemnation and guilt, but one of compassion and guidance. God wants us to lovingly reprove wayward professed Christians *"within the church,"* to compassionately help our friends when they are possibly walking down a dangerous path. God wants us to help and support each other. But we must never be dogmatic.

In 1 Corinthians 5:9-12, the Lord explains how we are to deal with *"immoral people."* He talks here about only *"brothers"* — people who proclaim to be Christians — believers not following what God expects of us in His Word. The Bible even tells us *"not even to eat with such a one."* This refers to so-called believers who justify certain activities in their lives — issues God considers sinful. These believers wholeheartedly feel that a loving God accepts alternate ways of looking at things, even when in full contradiction to the Bible. They consider those who believe in God's written word, literally, as intolerant, unloving, and ungodly — for not accepting their flawed, alternate views, attached to God, in error. Worse yet, when disagreements escalate into confrontation, they willfully take their family, fellow Christians who disagree with their flawed Biblical interpretations, into the **secular** court system. A court system that, by honest analytical review of case outcomes over the last fifty years, has attacked and sided almost totally against all true Biblical standards.

The government, as a whole, has taken God out of schools, public parks, government buildings and institutions. We have blatantly endured a flawed version of **separation of church and state,** against God . . . in His face. The original concept of the founding fathers was to keep the **government** out of the **church,** but today we live under the corrupted opposite viewpoint. In the last days rebellious **quasi-Christians** may obtain shallow human court victories against the true Bible. God is not happy when this occurs. All of this happens today, as God has told us it would. One cannot truly love God and blatantly deny what He says in His own word. This is utter folly and self-serving rebellion.

If, after accepting Jesus, a Christian sins, does this mean he will lose his salvation? May it never be. But God asks us not to associate with *"brothers"* who persistently sin; otherwise others will see us as validating inappropriate behaviors. As believers, God wants us to represent Him accurately, by His expressed Biblical standards.

Now, on the other hand, if we have non-Christian friends, our allowable relationships with them are entirely different. By their own validation, they do not accept Jesus, and per 1 Corinthians 5:10, we are allowed to freely associate with them. We do not need to try to address their life's sinful activities in any way. God will do this, personally, per 1 Corinthians 5:13. We are not to join in any inappropriate sin activities with them, but God wants us near them so we can be ambassadors for the Lord, 2 Corinthians 5:20. Hopefully, they will see something about us, the light of Jesus within our spirit, and we may gain the opportunity, by their own invitation, to share about Jesus. When given this opportunity, our sharing must be done with patience, love, and kindness.

In 1 Corinthians 5:13, God tells us to *"Remove the wicked man from among yourselves."* So, who is the wicked man? . . . again, a practicing Christian who wholeheartedly embraces any sin nature. And also the unbeliever, so far lost he could impose a threat to a Christian spiritually or physically.

Matthew 7:21-23, and 1 John 2:18-19 teach us that God tells us not everyone who professes to be a Christian truly qualifies.

Some are in the church today and do not realize *"they were not really of us."* Just because some people think of themselves as Christians and talk the talk, doesn't guarantee salvation. Jesus tells us many people who profess His name openly will not receive salvation—specifically, because they have taken His words in the Bible and from a human perspective have changed them into something He never intended. When anyone departs from or **modifies** God's specific *"laws"* in His Bible, this is *"lawlessness"* also described in Matthew 7:21-23.

Matthew 7:21-23
²¹ Not everyone who says to Me, 'Lord, Lord,' will enter the kingdom of heaven, but he who does the will of My Father who is in heaven will enter. ²² Many will say to Me on that day, 'Lord, Lord, did we not prophecy in Your name, and in Your name cast out demons, and in Your name perform many miracles?' ²³And then I will declare to them, 'I never knew you: depart from Me, you who practice lawlessness.'

1 John 2:18-19
¹⁸ Children, it is the last hour; and just as you heard that Antichrist is coming, even now many Antichrists have appeared; from this we know that it is the last hour. They went out from us, but they were not really of us; for if they had been of us, they would have remained with us; but they went out, so that it would be shown that they all are not of us.

Every individual needs to assess for themselves if they do truly abide in God's Word. We need to be wise, not foolish.

Ecclesiastes 10:2
² A wise man's heart directs him toward the right, but the foolish man's heart directs him toward the left.

Matthew 25:31-34
[The Judgment] ³¹ "But when the Son of Man comes in His glory, and all the angels with Him, then He will sit on His

glorious throne. [32] *All the nations will be gathered before Him; and He will <u>separate them</u> from one another, as the shepherd separates the sheep from the goats;* [33] *and He will put the <u>sheep on His right</u>, and the <u>goats on the left</u>.* [34] *"Then the King will say to <u>those on His right</u>, 'Come, you who are blessed of My Father, inherit the kingdom prepared for you from the foundation of the world.*

<u>Matthew 25:41 and 46</u>

[41] *"Then He will also say to <u>those on His left</u>, 'Depart from Me, accursed ones, into the eternal fire which has been prepared for the devil and his angels;...* [46] *These will go away into eternal punishment, but the righteous into eternal life."*

God defines wisdom and foolishness from His perspective. Note, God defines wisdom in Ecclesiastes 10:2. Then, in His final Judgment period, Matthew 25:31-33, 41, and 46, He tells us about blessings and punishments based on which direction we guide our hearts and, finally, tells us of consequences we will endure based on our decisions.

Because of Adams and Eve's original sin in the Garden of Eden, we now come into the world as sinners at birth. Due to original sin, we are currently spiritual beings inside an earthly imperfect body. God has set all souls (our spirits) to live on forever into eternity. <u>The question</u>: which eternity will we choose?

In John 14:2-3, God tells us about heaven, a place in the presence of God. He also tells us vividly in Matthew 13:49-50 and 2 Thessalonians 1:6-9 about a place of darkness . . . eternal separation from God. For Christians, eternal separation from God would be Hell, so let's call it that. We get to choose our own eternal destiny by the choice of free will. This means the only person in this world who can place us into Hell is ourselves.

Jesus talks a great deal in the Bible about **Hell** as **a real and horrible place**. Hell has many pseudonyms. In the Old Testament: Sheol, the grave, death and destruction, and the pit. In the

New Testament: Hell, Hades, eternal fire, furnace of fire, lake of fire, the second death and, most horrible of all, separation from God. God tells us Hell is both eternal and torments *"forever and ever"* in the following verse:

Matthew 25:41
[41] *"Then He will also say to those on His left, 'Depart from Me, accursed ones, into the eternal fire which has been prepared for the devil and his angels;*

Revelation 20:9-11
[9] *And they came up on the broad plain of the earth and surrounded the camp of the saints and the beloved city, and fire came down from heaven and devoured them.* [10] *And the devil who deceived them was thrown into the lake of fire and brimstone, where the beast and the false prophet are also; and they will be tormented day and night* forever and ever.

Here are some additional verses for consideration:
- Psalm 30:30
- Psalm 49:13-14
- Job 24:19
- Proverbs 15:24
- Matthew 5:22
- Matthew 10:28
- Mark 9:42-48
- Revelation 14:9-11

In all of these verses, Jesus tells us about **a literal Hell**.

To expand on an earlier point, the Lord presented the *"born again"* concept as a way to explain accepting personal spiritual rebirth. When individuals realize what sin really does within their souls they desire a pardon—offered to mankind only through Jesus.

Appendix B: Who are Christians?

Romans 10:9-13 provides us with the steps an individual must complete to become *"born again."* These issues are personal between one individual and God, one-on-one.

Romans 10:9-13
⁹ *that if you confess with your mouth Jesus as Lord, and* *believe in your heart that God raised Him from the dead, you* *will be saved;* ¹⁰ *for with the heart a person believes, resulting in righteousness, and with the mouth he confesses, resulting in salvation.* ¹¹ *For the Scripture says, whoever believes in Him will not be disappointed.* ¹² *For there is no distinction between Jew and Greek; for the same Lord is Lord of all, abounding in riches for all who call on Him;* ¹³ *for Whoever will call on the name of the Lord will be saved.*

To become a true *"born again"* Christian, people must accept and understand some Godly characteristics of Jesus and some humbling truths about themselves:
1. Acknowledge they are a sinner.
2. Understand they need a pardon . . . only possible through accepting Jesus as their Savior.
3. Believe Jesus died on the cross for their sins.
4. Accept by faith Jesus' resurrection on the 3rd day.
5. Accept by faith that God raised Him from the dead.
6. Accept by faith that Jesus sits at the right hand of God today.
7. Believe that Jesus is the King of kings and Lord of lords.

Then, one must do the following two easy steps listed in Romans 10:9 — if you:

1. *"confess with your mouth Jesus as Lord"*
2. *"believe in your heart that God raised Him from the dead, you will be saved."*

After completing these two simple steps, I suggest offering up a verbal prayer to God similar to this:

Dear Jesus,
I am a sinner and I am thankful for Your forgiveness. I accept
You Jesus as my personal Savior. Thank you for taking my sins
upon Yourself, on the cross, shedding Your blood for me and for
saving me through Your loving grace. I know You live today,
and are sitting at the right hand of the Father. Thank you Jesus,
for saving my life.
I love you Lord.

Once people complete these simple steps, they have entered into a new perfect spiritual relationship with Jesus, thusly **born again.** At this point new Christians obtain a full pardon, perfect eternal Grace, and full forgiveness through Jesus, from God the Father. They can never lose it.

The Bible lists no other earthly actions or rituals that anyone must follow from this point forward, to keep or maintain salvation. Jesus completed everything on the cross. If any church system requires anyone to do any kind of **works** or **actions** to maintain salvation, then grace has no true meaning. Proclaiming that God requires **works** or **actions** to maintain salvation is false doctrine.

New **born again** Christians can now freely work out their personal life issues directly with the Lord. This requires no third party; we only need to read the Bible, and pray within a new special loving relationship with Jesus. **Born again** Christians receive a strong veil of protection from God:

Romans 8:38-39
38 For I am convinced that neither death, nor life, nor
angels, nor principalities, nor things present, nor things to
come, nor powers, 39 nor height, nor depth, nor any other

created thing, will be able to separate us from the love of God, which is in Christ Jesus our Lord.

Christianity is like a marriage proposal by Jesus to our souls . . . a very intimate thing. We can accept His proposal only prior to our physical death in this world. We have the ability to accept Jesus, only until our last breath. Because unexpected events might occur in our lives each day and with longevity unknown, this decision should not be taken lightly. At risk: eternal life with God, or eternal separation from Him (Hell).

1 Thessalonians 5:3-6

3 *While they are saying, Peace and safety! Then destruction will come upon them suddenly like labor pains upon a woman with child, and they will not escape. 4 But you, brethren, are not in darkness, that the day would overtake you like a thief; 5 for you are all sons of light and sons of day. We are not of night nor of darkness; 6 so then let us not sleep as others do, but let us be alert and sober.*

APPENDIX C

IMMINENCE?

The Bible clearly tells us that the visual Rapture should not come as a surprise to Christians. We are to literally expect its arrival and be prepared to actually see Jesus coming in the clouds.

The **imminence doctrine** defines the Rapture as non-visual and in secret and can happen at any time, without any warning—without any prophecies preceding this event. Some Bible teachers justify this inaccurate doctrine by using Bible verses that include the phrases *"at hand"* or *"quickly"* in their texts. These teachers seem to imply the phrases *"at hand"* or *"quickly"* both mean imminent . . . a weak interpretation of the original Biblical text. In all of these verses, when we see the phrases *"at hand"* or *"quickly,"* they actually mean **it is certain to happen** . . . a large and very significant distinction.

Some believe the *"last days"* started at Pentecost (the day the Holy Spirit came upon the disciples) and, therefore, the Rapture could happen at any time with no *"signs"* needed beforehand (imminence). A detailed study of Joel 2 completely dispels this concept.

I propose a couple of questions about imminence for those who still feel strongly in favor of this weak, secret Rapture concept. What Biblical text literally describes this theory? Might it possibly be the Scriptures telling us the Rapture happens in the *"twinkling of an eye"* or *"at a day and hour when we least expect it?"* What about *"nobody, not even Jesus, knows the day or time but only the Father?"* These proclamations from the Bible—when originally spoken by **Jesus, as a man**, during His earthly life here—were, at that moment in History, true:

Philippians 2:5-9

5 Have this attitude in yourselves which was also in Christ Jesus, 6 who, although He existed in the form of God, did not regard equality with God a thing to be grasped, 7 but emptied Himself, taking the form of a bondservant, and being made in the likeness of men. 8 Being found in appearance as a man, He humbled Himself by becoming obedient to the point of death, even death on a cross. 9 For this reason also, God highly exalted Him, and bestowed on Him the name which is above every name,

When Jesus became a man he *"emptied Himself"* temporarily of some of the attributes of God and took on the *"likeness of man."* He needed to be a real man to be able to die on the cross.

John 17:1-5
¹ Jesus spoke these things; and lifting up His eyes to heaven, He said, "Father, the hour has come; glorify Your Son, that the Son may glorify You, ² even as You gave Him authority over all flesh, that to all whom You have given Him, He may give eternal life.³ This is eternal life, that they may know You, the only true God, and Jesus Christ whom You have sent. ⁴ I glorified You on the earth, having accomplished the work which You have given Me to do ⁵Now, Father, <u>glorify Me together with Yourself</u>, with the glory which I had with You before the world was.

After Jesus completed His work on the cross, after His resurrection, in John 17:1-5, He asked God to *"glorify Himself back together with the father,"* essentially asking the Father to give Him back all the authority He had in heaven *"before the world was."* Today Jesus has no limited knowledge. **He is a full equal part of our triune God** and knows all—including when the Rapture will happen.

What really happens in the *"twinkling of an eye"*? It is not the Rapture, but all our bodies changing at the final trumpet. A group of people here on earth at the start of the visual Rapture event will get *"caught by surprise."* But not Christians; it is the secular nonbelievers, as explained earlier.

God never planned for the Rapture to be a surprise event; it is Satan who wants us to think this. If we do not follow God's explicit teachings, we may experience some unwarranted fear, and will not get our crown. Please do not be deceived.

Luke 12:35-37
³⁵ Be dressed in readiness, and keep your lamps lit. ³⁶ Be like men who are waiting for their master when he returns from the

wedding feast, so that they may immediately <u>open the door to him</u> when he comes and knocks. ³⁷ Blessed are those slaves whom the master will find <u>on the alert</u> when he comes;

God wants us to keep our lamps on and to know what the Bible tells us about the visual Rapture event, so we can stay alert in readiness to open the door for Him, so-to-speak, upon His return. But how can we know the process necessary to stay *"alert"* and ready to *"open the door for him?"* If God meant to hide the Rapture from us or not to expect it, He wouldn't have told us to prepare. Why would He have us stay alert, if the Rapture were a hidden surprise event? Those of us in the light must understand about the visual Rapture and its arrival. Putting our lamps on the lampstands means God is asking us to share this light with others. This includes telling our Christian friends to understand what will soon come upon the world.

Luke 21:34-36
³⁴ <u>Be on guard</u>, so that your hearts will not be weighted down with dissipation and drunkenness and the worries of life, and that day will not come on you suddenly like a trap; ³⁵ for it will come upon all those who dwell on the face of all the earth. ³⁶ But <u>keep on the alert</u> at all times, praying that you may have strength to escape all these things that are about to take place, and to stand before the Son of Man.

"Be on guard." Do not let our earthly problems allow us to keep our eyes off the ball. Stay alert and stand strong because God has given us all the information we need to know exactly when He will return. The Bible lights our way. God also wants us to pray for the strength to escape the horrors of the Tribulation.

1 Thessalonians 5:1-4
¹ Now as to the times and the epochs, brethren, you have no need of anything to be written to you. ² For you

yourselves know full well that the day of the Lord will come just like a <u>thief in the night</u>. ³ While they are saying, Peace and safety! Then destruction will come upon them suddenly like labor pains upon a woman with child, and they will not escape. ⁴ <u>But you, brethren, are not in darkness, that the day would overtake you like a thief;</u>

<u>1 Thessalonians 5:6-11</u>

⁶ *so then let us not sleep as others do, but let us be alert and sober. ⁷ For those who sleep do their sleeping at night, and those who get drunk get drunk at night. ⁸ But since we are of the day, let us be sober, having put on the <u>breastplate of faith</u> and <u>love</u>, and as a <u>helmet</u>, the <u>hope of salvation</u>. ⁹ For God has not destined us for wrath, but for obtaining salvation through our Lord Jesus Christ,¹⁰ who died for us, so that whether we are awake or asleep, we will live together with Him. ¹¹ Therefore encourage one another and build up one another, just as you also are doing.*

The *"thief in the night"* does not refer to the Rapture, but rather, specifically, to the start of the Tribulation. Again, God is going to *"steal away"* the secular world's supposed peace, not steal Christians away secretly in His rapture event.

God specifically asks all living believers not to sleep, which means staying aware, per Thessalonians 5:7-8. We are to stay alert and be ready.

God does not intend for the Rapture to be a secret event. It will be fully visual on a grand scale.

John 4:25-26

25 The woman said to Him, I know that Messiah is coming, He who is called Christ; when that One comes, He will declare all things to us. 26 Jesus said to her, I who speak to you am He.

APPENDIX D

IS JESUS THE MESSIAH?

Is Jesus truly the prophesied Jewish Messiah?

I am a Christian because of a young Jewish Rabbi, who along with twelve bold Jewish young men of His choosing, changed the world. This Rabbi explained how He was the Son of God, the Promised One, not always recognized although all the Biblical evidence pointed to Him as actually who He said He was, the Messiah.

As Christians we have a New Testament covenant with Jesus. We are saved by accepting Him as our Savior, our Messiah. Some Christian churches falsely teach that the Jews of today live under a different Old Testament covenant. These churches say the Jews may have a separate path to God because Jesus never revealed His true identity to the Jewish leaders of His day. These churches maintain that, because Jesus **supposedly** never claimed to be the Messiah, Christians today do not need to try to share with the Jews regarding Him. This view is not Biblically correct. Jesus did, in fact, tell the Jewish people and their leaders that He was the Christ.

I take the Scriptures literally and believe throughout the Bible, God makes it clear who the Messiah was, and still is, today. He is Jesus. Some Scriptures from Mark and John:

Mark 14:60-63
⁶⁰ The high priest stood up and came forward and questioned Jesus, saying, do You not answer? What is it that these men are testifying against You? ⁶¹ But He kept silent and did not answer. Again the high priest was questioning Him, and saying to Him, Are You the Christ, the Son of the Blessed One? ⁶² And Jesus said, I am; and you shall see the Son of Man sitting at the right hand of power, and coming with the clouds of heaven. ⁶³ Tearing his clothes, the high priest said, What further need do we have of witnesses?

John 4:25-26
²⁵ The woman said to Him, I know that the Messiah is coming He who is called Christ; when that One

*comes, He will declare all things to us. [26] Jesus said
to her, I who speak to you am He.*

Jesus admitted to the Jewish High Priest and the Sanhedrin that He was indeed the Messiah. They should have known Jesus spoke the truth, because they were Biblical experts and the scholars of their day. Clearly, Jesus fulfilled all the Old Testament prophecies confirming His identity. The Jewish rulers of the day did not accept Him as the Christ because Jesus did not fit within their limited earthly expectations. They thought (intellectually) God would make the Messiah a human King like David (not an **eternal everlasting** God/Man). They considered it blasphemous that Jesus declared Himself the Messiah. These experts did not follow their own Scriptures and entirely dismissed Jesus at His first visit. The Jewish leaders did not recognize Him, due to a serious misunderstanding of what the Messiah should represent . . . the main reason Jesus will come back soon for His second coming. This time they will not miss Him, to their ultimate Glory.

Romans 1:16-17

[16] For I am not ashamed of the gospel, for it is the power of God for salvation to everyone who believes, to the Jew first and also to the Greek. [17] For in it the righteousness of God is revealed from faith to faith; as it is written, but the righteous man shall live by faith.

If God intended different paths for the Jews and the Greeks (gentiles) for salvation, why did He tell us here in Romans 1:16 the *"gospel"* is the *"power of God for salvation"* (Jesus) for *"everyone?"* He even went so far as saying specifically *"to the Jew first."* Christians are required to witness Jesus to our Jewish family as God calls us to do. We all need Christ as our Savior. God has but one covenant given to us in the personhood and resurrection of Jesus, for all mankind, including our brothers, the Jews. In fact, in the book of Acts, God sent Paul to minister about Jesus the Messiah *"to the Jews first"* and then the gentiles. **Paul always went to the Jews first** to proclaim Jesus. A couple of examples regarding Paul's Jewish ministry in sharing about the Messiah to the Jews of his day:

Acts 13:46

⁴⁶ *Paul and Barnabas spoke out boldly and said, "It was necessary that the word of God be spoken to you first; since you repudiate it and judge yourselves unworthy of eternal life, behold, we are turning to the Gentiles.*

Acts 14:1-7

¹ *And it came about in Iconium they entered the synagogue of the Jews together, and spoke in such a manner that a large number of people believed, both of Jews and of Greeks. ² But the Jews who disbelieved stirred up the minds of the Gentiles and embittered them against the brethren. ³ Therefore they spent a long time there speaking boldly with reliance upon the Lord, who was testifying to the word of His grace, granting that signs and wonders be done by their hands. ⁴ But the people of the city were divided; and some sided with the Jews, and some with the apostles. ⁵ And when an attempt was made by both the Gentiles and the Jews with their rulers, to mistreat and to stone them, ⁶ they became aware of it and fled to the cities of Lycaonia, Lystra and Derbe, and the surrounding region; ⁷ and there they continued to preach the gospel.*

As mentioned in Acts 14:1, Paul went into the Synagogue first. We also can see he did the same thing in Acts 13:5, 13:13, 13:42 14:1, 17:1, 17;17, 18:4-11, 19:8, 28:17, and 28:28. This indicates how the concept of going to the Jews first is important to God. As an adopted member of the Jewish family, grafted in by

God Himself, I accept and trust in my Jewish Rabbi, my Messiah. Jesus.

If any of our current Jewish family chooses to dislike this news or even feels hate for Jesus or Christians by association for sharing about Him, please take the following information into serious consideration. Because of atrocities committed on the Jewish people in the **supposed name of Jesus** throughout history, please remember this: **misguided human beings** perpetrated all past atrocities on the Jewish people . . . **in severe contradiction to the Holy Scriptures**. As one gigantic example, <u>**Hitler was not a Christian!**</u> Although he claimed to be, when looking at his writings on the subject, they are evil, misguided non-Biblical garbage. Everything he did to the Jewish people during WWII was Satanic and had nothing to do with any valid interpretation of the true Biblical New Testament. He was a vile individual. Please do not let the actions of severely misguided, flawed, and obviously Satanically indwelled human beings cause any reason for any kind of justifiable separation from the one man who came to save us all—the Jewish man/God, Jesus the Christ.

For clarification, in reference to the Lord, Jesus Christ, these are not His first and last names. Jesus is **His name** and Christ is **His Title. Christ translates to Messiah.** Actually, saying **Jesus the Christ** or Jesus the Messiah is more accurate.

Another interesting thought regarding the Messiah: The Jewish faith that currently does not recognize Jesus as the Messiah waits for some future leader, yet to come, through the bloodline of King David—the prophesied Messiah. This pertains to the Davidic Covenant, to my understanding, as referred to in 2 Samuel 7:

2 Samuel 7:8-13
[8] *"Now therefore, thus you shall say to My servant David, 'Thus says the Lord of hosts, "I took you from the pasture,*

from following the sheep, to be ruler over My people
Israel. [9] I have been with you wherever you have gone and
have cut off all your enemies from before you; and I will
make you a great name, like the names of the great men
who are on the earth. [10] I will also appoint a place for My
people Israel and will plant them, that they may live in
their own place and not be disturbed again, nor will the
wicked afflict them any more as formerly, [11] even from the
day that I commanded judges to be over My people Israel;
and I will give you rest from all your enemies. The Lord
also declares to you that the Lord will make a house for
you. [12] When your days are complete and you lie down
with your fathers, I will raise up your descendant after
you, who will come forth from you, and I will establish
his kingdom. [13] He shall build a house for My name, and I
will establish the throne of his kingdom forever.

2 Samuel 7:16-17
[16] Your house and your kingdom shall endure before Me
forever; your throne shall be established forever. [17] In
accordance with all these words and all this vision, so
Nathan spoke to David.

I have read about the importance of the Jewish Messiah coming through the bloodline of David. Jesus, by the way, did fulfill this requirement completely. The entire Bible documents His precise lineage. As detailed earlier, in the Old Testament, God gives the significant genealogies of mankind and their ancestral relationships, in complete detail, from Adam to Abraham and Isaac in Genesis 5:1-32, 11:10-32, and 21:1-3. Interestingly, they all point to the lineage of Jesus. Is this all chance? No.

In the first book of the New Testament, Matthew 1:1-17, God completes the entire proven bloodline of Jesus by showing all accurate verifiable genealogies from Abraham and Isaac to Joseph the husband of Mary, the mother of Jesus. Joseph, the earthly father (custodian) of Jesus, raised Him under his family's bloodline which goes back through David. David appears within these genealogies—verification that Jesus was and is, to this very day, the Jewish Messiah prophesied in the Old Testament.

This now brings up some interesting questions. From the birth of Jesus by Mary, Joseph's wife, until today, have we any complete records of all the genealogies of all the twelve tribes of Israel? No. How would a possible future Messiah, someone other than Jesus, prove his heritage today as a direct descendent back through the bloodline of David? He couldn't. I can see no current way to prove the lineage of a future Messiah directly to David (even through DNA) unless our Jewish family will accept a possible bloodline relationship to David by pure faith alone. Jesus is the Biblical prophesied Messiah. He came once, and He will soon come again and prove His true identity, once and for all, to His beloved family, Israel. God never abandons His family.

Did you know the world today has approximately 2.2 billion Christians and 1.6 billion Islamic believers? Do you know how many Jews live on the earth today? Only **14 million,** in a **7.2 billion** total population in 2014 . . . quite a minority. Yet, God Himself says the **Jews are His chosen . . . His Glory,** and He wants them to acknowledge **the special Son** He sent **for their eternal blessing**.

Something unfortunate is happening today in Judaism and it breaks my heart. Some Rabbis today say the **Tenach,** when interpreted correctly, tells us that Mary, the mother of Jesus, was a prostitute, and thusly, Jesus was a bastard child. Please, do not accept this pure dreck.

The Prophet Isaiah wrote one of the greatest books in the Bible. In Chapter 48, God talks about how He promises liberation for Israel. What God promises, He delivers. In Isaiah 48:16, God has foretold Israel about His Son. In fact it is actually Jesus Himself talking to the Jewish people in this verse.

Isaiah 48:16

[16] *"Come near to Me, listen to this: from the first I have not spoken in secret from the time it took place, I was there. And now the Lord GOD has sent Me, and His Spirit."*

Notice in the verse above *"And now the Lord GOD has sent Me, and His Spirit."* All through the Old Testament *"the Lord God"* (the Father) talks about a sent second person *"Me"* (Jesus) and a third entity *"His Spirit,"* the Holy Spirit. The Old Testament **acknowledges the Trinity**. God tells Israel today in the **Tanach** who Jesus is and who He was from the beginning. God — as always, truthful and non-secretive with His people, Israel. I hope today's Jews are indeed *"Coming near to God"* and *"listening"* regarding who God is as required in Isaiah 48:16, **God is the Trinity.**

One more highly profound verse from the Prophet Isaiah, offering the House of David a *"sign"* of who the Messiah will be:

Isaiah 7:13-14

[13] *Then he said, "Listen now, O house of David! Is it too slight a thing for you to try the patience of men, that you will try the patience of my God as well?* [14] *Therefore the Lord Himself will give you a sign: Behold, a virgin will be with child and bear a son, and she will call His name Immanuel.*

The only person who has ever lived that fulfilled this prophetic sign scribed by the Prophet Isaiah was **Jesus the Christ.** God has told Israel all along who Jesus is.

In all truthfulness, in the eternal order of God's kingdom, I am but a humble beggar in this lifetime. God blessed me by bringing me to recognize Jesus as my Messiah. Through placing my faith in Him, I have found sustenance, comfort, rest, and — I believe — eternal life though this wonderful kind and gracious, young, Jewish Rabbi who died on the cross and rose again to save my life. I find true value in my life by offering the loving gift of an introduction of Jesus to others in my same lowly position. It is with humility, that I ask any Jewish reader to please take a serious look at this wonderful individual. I believe He holds you in high regard and wants you to believe in Him through your free-will choice.

For more on this subject, the Old Testament offers greater detail and support to learn how Jesus truly is the promised Jewish Messiah. There is a section at the end of the book called (**The 144,000 Project)** and it tells about a powerful booklet on this entire subject: *The Messiah of the Tanach, Targums, Talmuds.*

MY WRITING JOURNEY

During my study of the visual Rapture, I recalled some verses in Psalm 119, which gave me a great deal of added comfort and inspiration:

Psalm 119:97-100

⁹⁷ Oh, how I love your law! I meditate on it all day long.⁹⁸ Your commands are always with me and make me wiser than my enemies. ⁹⁹ I have more insight than all my teachers, for Your testimonies are my meditation. ¹⁰⁰ I understand more than the aged, because I have observed your precepts.

Do I personally have *"more insight than all my teachers"* or do I *"understand more than the aged?"* No. But these verses remind us all to remember that God tells us something profound: any one of His children who *"loves"* the Bible (the law) can gain wisdom and offer valid teaching and information to others for Jesus, through Jesus. God works through ordinary people. If we will take a risk and walk with the Lord outside our comfort zones, God will walk with us and guide us lovingly in His correct path when we do work for His kingdom. All of the Apostles of Jesus were average men. God used these average men to change the world. Never underestimate what God can do—in and through our lives.

About nine years back, I attended my first in-depth weekly Bible study with a sagacious Bible teacher. At eight years of age, in 1934, he decided he wanted to become a minister and now holds five doctorate degrees. Over eighty years he has studied, researched and taught the Bible with a special emphasis on end times prophecy. I took some time off over the nine years but, for the past three years, have attended regularly. Through him, at each precise moment in my walk with the Lord, God seemed to fill in specific holes in my thinking process. I felt astounded at how timely each specific study appeared for me in my learning path . . . too often for coincidence. God graciously, through this insightful man, provided me with the missing pieces. They have solidified my current personal understanding of this positive version of the end times prophecy story along with the glue needed to put it all together.

I prayed a great deal about doing this book and daily asked God if He really wanted me to do it. The result of my prayers turned into an unbelievable desire to write. Words and ideas constantly flowed. Historic issues I learned about years ago came right to the forefront of my mind. I even woke up at midnight and wrote until breakfast on more nights than I can count, and I did it all with incredible joy and passion. Often, I woke up from a dead sleep with something I felt God compelled me to add. I took this all as God's answer to my prayers.

All of us take various paths in our life's journey and will encounter different people in our lives. After we read Scriptures and gain our own understanding, God then asks us to share similar points of view from different perspectives to help as many different Christians understand what He does and why. I do not want to get to heaven and find out from God that any friend I had in my life missed out on joy, and the understanding of what Jesus does for our Christian family in these last days, because I took no action.

Did I get everything right? Only God knows, I am human. With general ideas thoughtfully and reasonably outlined, using the Bible as the foundation, I would hope the following might happen: the light shining within God's **Road Map** might ignite a candle in some people who had not yet learned the Lord's plans for our last days and also, this candle might help some discover the peace that comes from knowing what will happen and why.

THE 144,000 PROJECT

The Messiah of the *Tanach, Targums, Talmuds*

Because Israel did not recognize the Messiah, Jesus the Christ, at His first visit, Jesus tells us a Tribulation period must take place prior to His physical second coming. At the end of the Tribulation, Israel will finally accept that Jesus was and is indeed the living prophesied Messiah of the Old Testament as explained in the booklet called *The Messiah of the Tanach, Targums, Talmuds.* This 48-page booklet (cover illustration above) explains how Jesus was and is today the Messiah that our Jewish family still awaits.

Additionally this booklet takes the Old Testament prophecies about the Messiah and correlates them with the New Testament, explaining—in detail—how Jesus fulfilled prophecy related to the Messiah's identity. Jesus fits perfectly in all prophecy. Unfortunately, our current-day Jewish family adamantly disagrees with this.

In the following verses, God, through the Apostle Paul, explains how He granted gentiles the greatest gift possible, due solely to the Jews rejecting Jesus as the Messiah at His first visit:

Romans 11:11-16

[11] I say then, they did not stumble so as to fall, did they? May it never be! But by their transgression salvation has come to the Gentiles, to make them jealous. [12] Now if their transgression is riches for the world and their failure is riches for the Gentiles, how much more will their fulfillment be! [13] But I am speaking to you who are Gentiles. Inasmuch then as I am an apostle of Gentiles, I magnify my ministry, [14] if somehow I might move to jealousy <u>my fellow countrymen</u> and save some of them. [15] For if their rejection is the reconciliation of the world, what will their acceptance be but life from the dead? [16] If the first piece of dough is holy, the lump is also; and if the root is holy, the branches are too.

The Apostle Paul was a Jew. He never relinquished his religion or heritage. He even calls the Jewish people *"my fellow countrymen"* in Romans 11:14. The difference; He recognized Jesus to be the promised Messiah, per the Old Testament.

Just as with Paul, God required Christians to share about Jesus with our Jewish family. Soon the world will witness the visual Rapture. So, how might we plant some seeds today, to help in the harvest of our Jewish family towards faith in Jesus, after we have departed?

At the conclusion of the visual Rapture no Christians will remain in the world to help explain about Jesus. Revelation 7:4-8 stipulates: at the beginning of the Tribulation, 144,000 Jewish evangelists will come to know Jesus as their promised Messiah. Twelve thousand members from each of the Twelve Tribes of Israel make up this group. God's 144,000 will receive a seal of protection and no harm will come to them. They will minister about the Messiah, Jesus, to the whole world for the majority of the Tribulation period. They will turn into 144,000 indestructible evangelists, vastly surpassing all contemporary counterparts — magnificent to behold.

But how might these 144,000 gain the knowledge about Jesus the Messiah if, in fact, all the Christians have departed? Earlier I mentioned God telling us to love Israel for their ultimate future glory. Well, my teacher has taken this command to an exciting next level.

He has decided to mail copies of this 48-page booklet to every Jewish family in the United States. This will require about 2,000,000 copies in total. 165,000 have gone out to date. But why has he undertaken this mission? Because, once we have departed in the visual Rapture, the literature could play a vital role in providing our Jewish family with the tools needed to figure out who Jesus really is. I understand our Jewish family, for the most part, will think of this as arrogant, but the Lord has told us to share information about who He is with them, regardless. If you are Jewish, I would ask only if you get one of these booklets, please read it for familiarity. If you don't believe in the contents, keep it and place it somewhere for possible future reference. Then later, if you should see the happening of events listed in this book, you may appreciate having this information for later study.

Many Christians ask what the role the United States might ultimately play in Biblical prophecy. I have seen no mention of direct involvement but note: Per the Biblical **Road Map** explained in this book, no country as defined today will have their original identities when God allows the formation of the One World Government. The United States will have some new name in one of the new ten Kingdoms. So, the fact that the United States has no direct mention in the Bible lends more credence to the concept about the One World Government happening before the Tribulation begins. As a general point of reference in our current lexicon, the West includes the Americas, so this point has some relevance in Scripture.

In the book of Isaiah, chapter 24, God talks about the set of judgments that will come to the earth in the distant future. He talks about the judgments that will happen inside the coming Biblical Tribulation. In Isaiah 24:14-15, He explains something interesting and joyful within the midst of all the terrible troubles happening inside the Tribulation description:

Isaiah 24:14-15

14 They raise their voices, they shout for joy; they cry out from the west concerning the majesty of the Lord.
15Therefore glorify the Lord in the east, the name of the Lord, the God of Israel, in the coastlands of the sea.

Possibly, our Jewish brothers in one of the ten Kingdoms — the one formally known as the United States — may read these booklets the Christians will have left on earth. And, the provided information might then play a pivotal role in helping the 144,000 come to know the Lord for their glorious mission inside the Tribulation. Feasibly, by sending out these booklets, Christians could provide our Jewish family with the tools needed to help them individually find Jesus for the ultimate future glory of Israel. Is God possibly telling us all this in Isaiah 24:14? Highly likely. Our country, even in its new form and although weakened, will stand for true faith in Jesus. We will probably provide the last dim light for Jesus right up until the visual Rapture. This leaves us in the West with some large responsibilities for the Lord in these last days.

If 2,000,000 copies of this booklet circulate within our Jewish family, many will figure out the happenings and who Jesus really is . . . similar to helping plant some seeds for the beginning of the greatest harvest revival in all of human history. Did you know that during the Tribulation, billions of people living under the severe adversity of this very horrible time will come to a loving knowledge of Jesus? More people will come to the Lord inside the Tribulation period than came to Him in all of history up to the Rapture.

Isaiah 26:9
⁹ At night my soul longs for you, indeed, my spirit within me seeks You diligently; For when the earth experiences Your judgments the inhabitants of the world learn righteousness.

I hope, God willing, to do as much as I can for the balance of my life to help all who cross my path, to find a loving relationship with our wonderful loving Lord, Jesus the Christ.

ACKNOWLEGEMENTS

I am so thankful for our Lord Jesus, who died on the cross, took away our sins and provides grace, forgiveness, and salvation.

I am thankful for my beautiful, devoted, godly wife Jana—the light of my life for twenty-five years. Without her love, support, and incredible patience, this book could not have happened.

I thank my parents (now deceased) for the introduction to Jesus and planting solid roots early-on.

Many thanks, to my friend Burr, a bold, rugged, and graciously wise Arizonian. He gave me wonderful generosity, moral support, suggestions, recommendations, and ebullient encouragement which were vital factors in the creation of this book.

My friend Mark (once a Catholic seminarian) was instrumental also, as we attend Bible studies and talk about current events and how they connect with prophecies. I gained insight from his sharing intellect, wisdom, and knowledge.

Also Bob and Carol—kind friends for over twenty-five years—for their generous moral and financial support to this endeavor through their Christian Charitable Organization.

Thank you Sandy for your tenacity, continually considering my initial writings as a book. You finally got me to believe, that a book, is actually what they needed to be. I am eternally grateful.

God has everything perfectly planned, and I have yet another confirmation of this in my editor, Shirl. She has been incredibly patient and wise, and without her help and guidance, I could not have honed and refined my story.

MY BIBLE TEACHER

What a wonderful Godly man. My teacher has studied diligently and knows the Bible in incredible detail. He has been a brightly shining spiritual searchlight who has ignited a candle within me. In my life, I know God directed me to this wise man whose knowledge of Jesus has changed my life in unimaginably profound, positive ways.

My teacher is Dr. F. Kenton Beshore Sr. (Doc), President of the World Bible Society, based in Costa Mesa, California.

In addition to his **144,000 Project**, he also has additional published **books** and **booklet** resources that he offers on end times prophecy explaining highly detailed information.

His books provide well-documented viewpoints regarding Biblical end time prophecies. In this book, I have included my personalized student's perspective. In his books, he includes much more than the brief story I related. His publications are marvelous textbooks.

Amazingly, at eighty-eight years of age, Doc has almost total recall of the entire Bible when he teaches. Sometimes it seems his brain is on-line with a full Wi-Fi connection with the Lord . . . incredible to comprehend. I can handle a great deal of information at one time, as a detailed person, but it is almost impossible to keep up with him. He is amazing to watch. Every week it seems as if we get a month's worth of Bible studies in each one-hour session. What an awesome blessing.

In 1954, Doc started a radio ministry called the **Bible Institute of the Air,** which airs five days a week. He has produced over 15,700 weekly broadcasts. He has also printed Bibles for distribution to multiple countries in over forty languages (ten million Bibles for Russia alone, since 1989). Additionally, Doc broadcasts God's word inside Israel. His preaching about Jesus, the Messiah, is broadcast, on a daily basis, across the radio airwaves, to our Jewish family.

I encourage you to get Doc's publications from the World Bible Society. They would be a welcomed addition to any Bible prophecy library.

ADDITIONAL RESOURCE

This 406-page book provides a tremendous amount of support and in-depth research related to fulfilled prophecies and those that are yet to come before the Rapture. It also explains in detail, with great documentation, about the events that will happen leading to the Rapture, the Tribulation, the final battle of Armageddon, and the 1000 Millennium. Dr. Beshore also lists many different views of the end times, pointing out past and present Biblical scholars, and documented shortcomings.

To order copies of the 144,000 Project, (A.K.A. The Jewish Scriptures) books, booklets, DVDs and CDs by Dr. Beshore, contact the:

WORLD BIBLE SOCIETY
P.O. BOX 5000
COSTA MESA, CA 92648

714-258-3012 or 800-866-WORD

www.worldBible.com
www.worldBible.org

18327000R00172

Made in the USA
San Bernardino, CA
09 January 2015